FIRST NORTH AMERICAN EDITION

Kindly Corpses © 2016 by Zoran Penevski and Ivica Stevanović
Cover and interior artwork © 2016 by Ivica Stevanović
Additional typesetting © 2016 by Samantha Beiko

Distributed in Canada by
Publishers Group Canada
76 Stafford Street, Unit 300
Toronto, Ontario, M6J 2S1
Toll Free: 800-747-8147
e-mail: info@pgcbooks.ca

Distributed in the U.S. by
Consortium Book Sales & Distribution
34 Thirteenth Avenue, NE, Suite 101
Minneapolis, MN 55413
Phone: (612) 746-2600
e-mail: sales.orders@cbsd.com

Library and Archives Canada Cataloguing in Publication

Penevski, Zoran, 1967-, author

    Kindly corpses / written by Zoran Penevski ; art by Ivica Stevanović.

Previously published in 2004.

Issued in print and electronic formats.

ISBN 978-1-77148-379-7 (paperback).--ISBN 978-1-77148-380-3(pdf)

    1. Graphic novels. I. Stevanović, Ivica, illustrator II. Title.

PN6790.S43P46 2016   741.5'94971   C2016-901700-1

                                      C2016-901701-X

CHIGRAPHIC
An imprint of ChiZine Publications
Peterborough, Canada
www.chizinepub.com
info@chizinepub.com

Edited by Samantha Beiko
Proofread by Brett Savory

Shelfie

A **free** eBook edition is available
with the purchase of this print book.

CLEARLY PRINT YOUR NAME ABOVE IN UPPER CASE

Instructions to claim your free eBook edition:
1. Download the Shelfie app for Android or iOS
2. Write your name in **UPPER CASE** above
3. Use the Shelfie app to submit a photo
4. Download your eBook to any device

Canada Council   Conseil des arts
for the Arts   du Canada

We acknowledge the support of the Canada Council for the Arts which last year invested $20.1 million in writing and publishing throughout Canada.

ONTARIO ARTS COUNCIL
CONSEIL DES ARTS DE L'ONTARIO

an Ontario government agency
un organisme du gouvernement de l'Ontario

Published with the generous assistance of the Ontario Arts Council.

Printed in Canada

When death was a little girl
She wanted eternity as a gift
And with her faceless smile
She took my calendar.

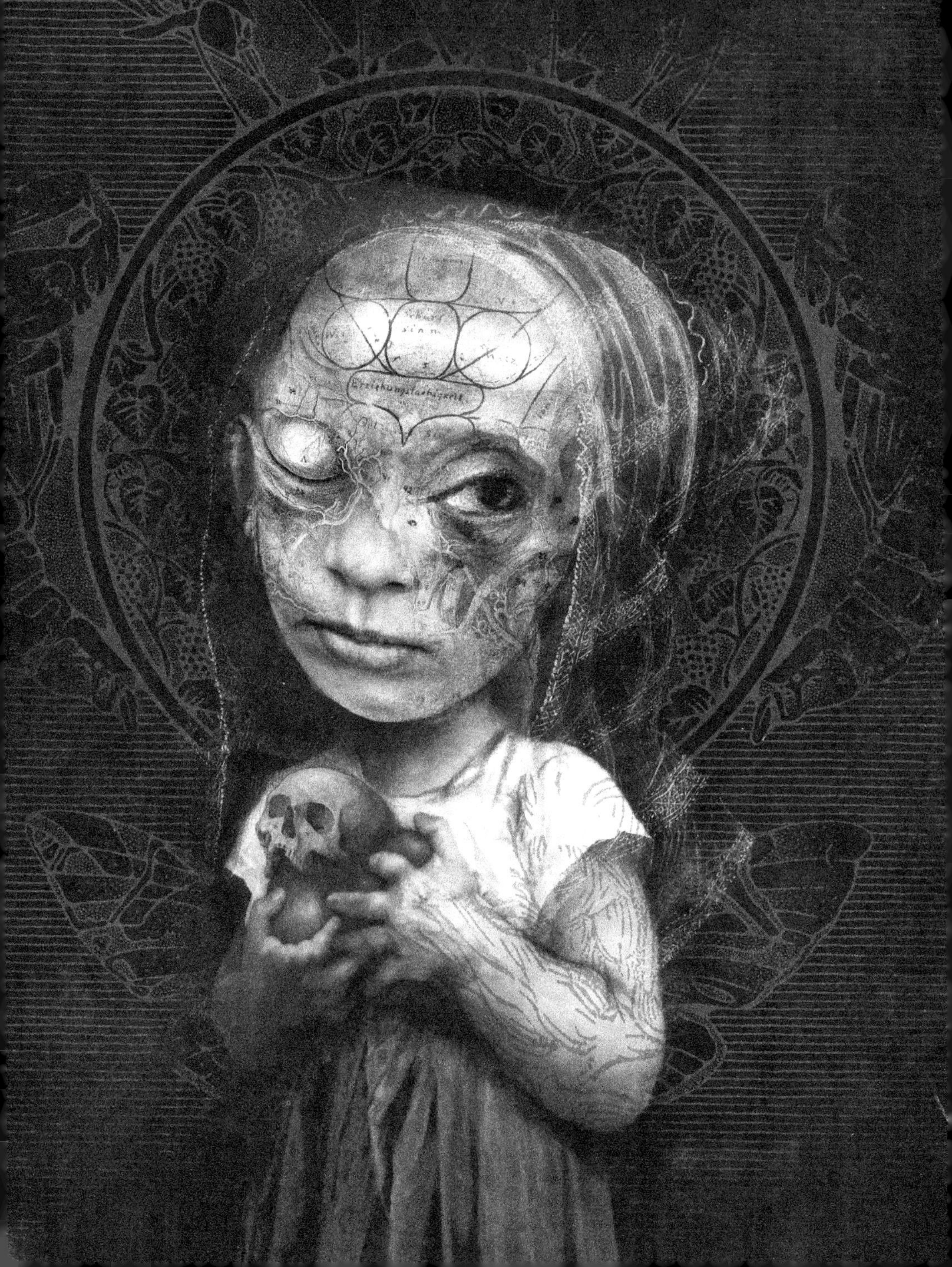

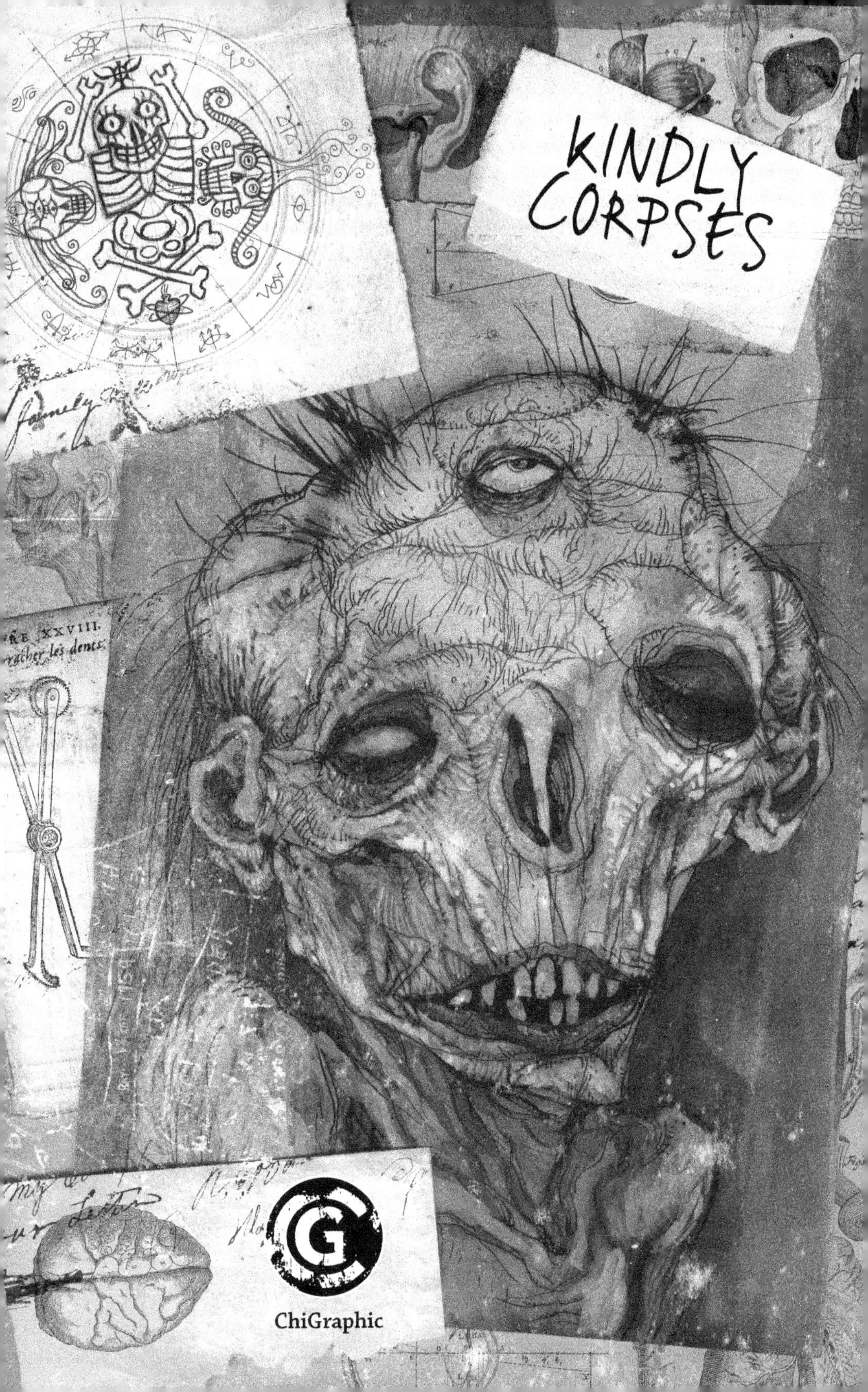
KINDLY CORPSES
ChiGraphic

I felt a scream rise up inside me
Like a child's terror unexplained
My body is an abyss that hunts me again.

And whose eyes could bring me back
When only the vagaries of words know of me?
I scream through the morning hours
Until someone hears me.

The world stales like a barren field.
The sky falls like a brown leaf
Perhaps weakly, perhaps willingly
In the dawn of longing.
The arrow is a paintbrush
But the scream is better
Because its touch is soft, vulnerable,
and clean.

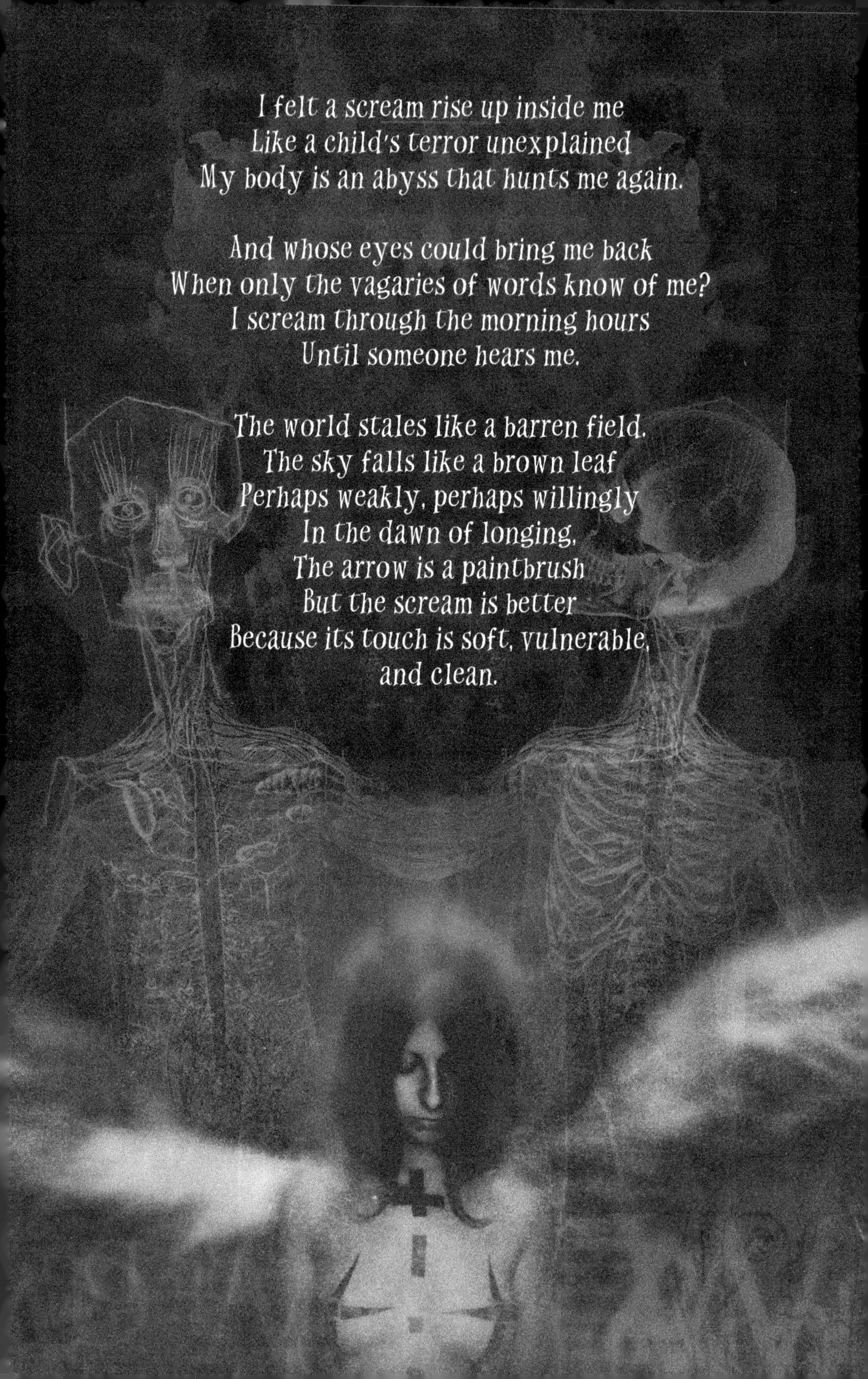

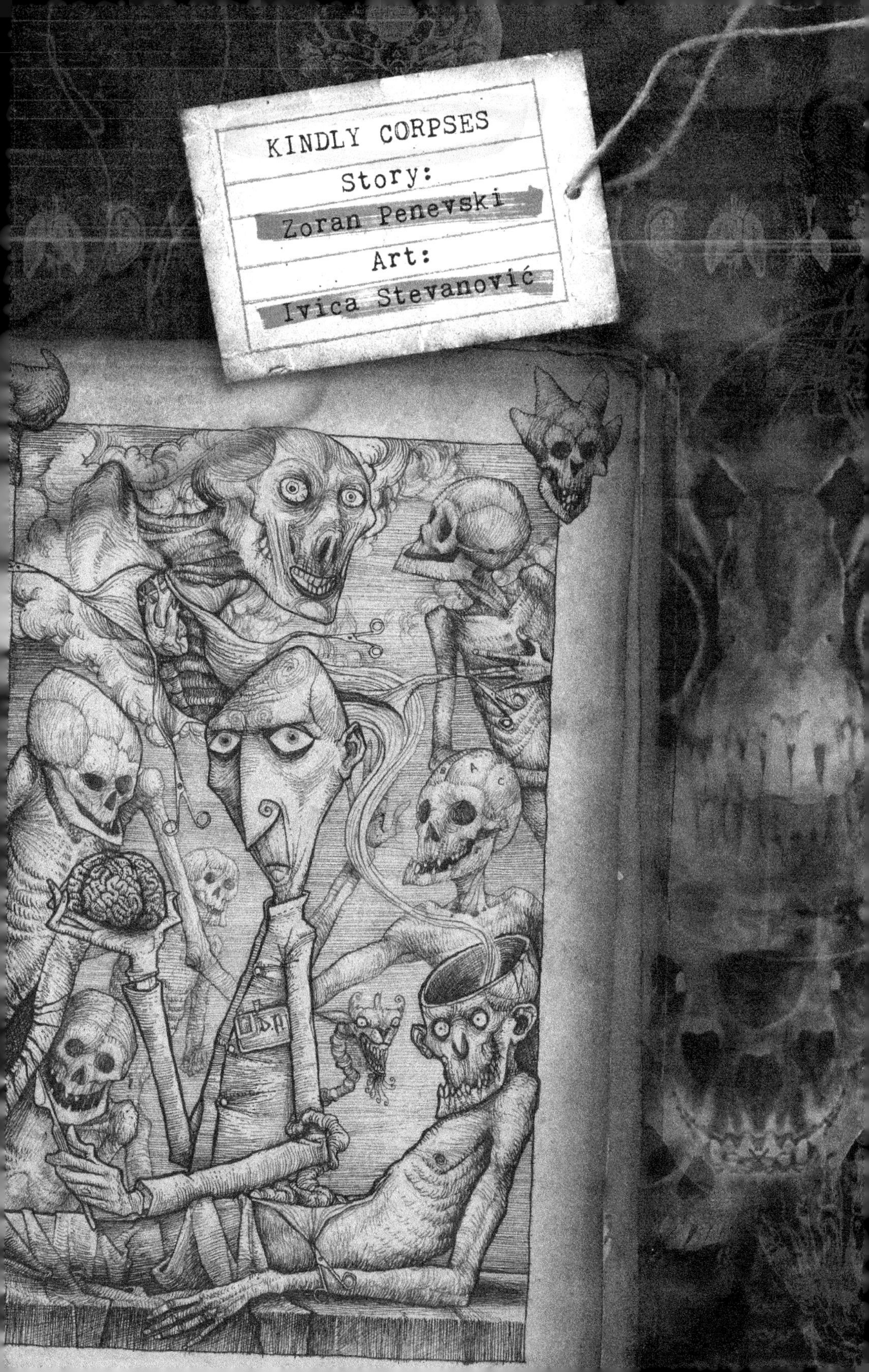
KINDLY CORPSES
Story:
Zoran Penevski
Art:
Ivica Stevanović

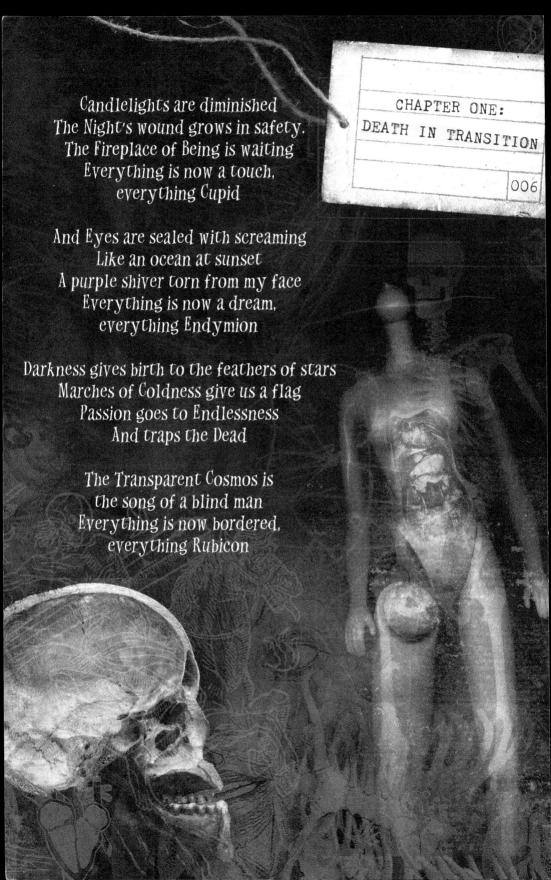

Candlelights are diminished
The Night's wound grows in safety.
The Fireplace of Being is waiting
Everything is now a touch,
everything Cupid

And Eyes are sealed with screaming
Like an ocean at sunset
A purple shiver torn from my face
Everything is now a dream,
everything Endymion

Darkness gives birth to the feathers of stars
Marches of Coldness give us a flag
Passion goes to Endlessness
And traps the Dead

The Transparent Cosmos is
the song of a blind man
Everything is now bordered,
everything Rubicon

CHAPTER ONE:
DEATH IN TRANSITION

006

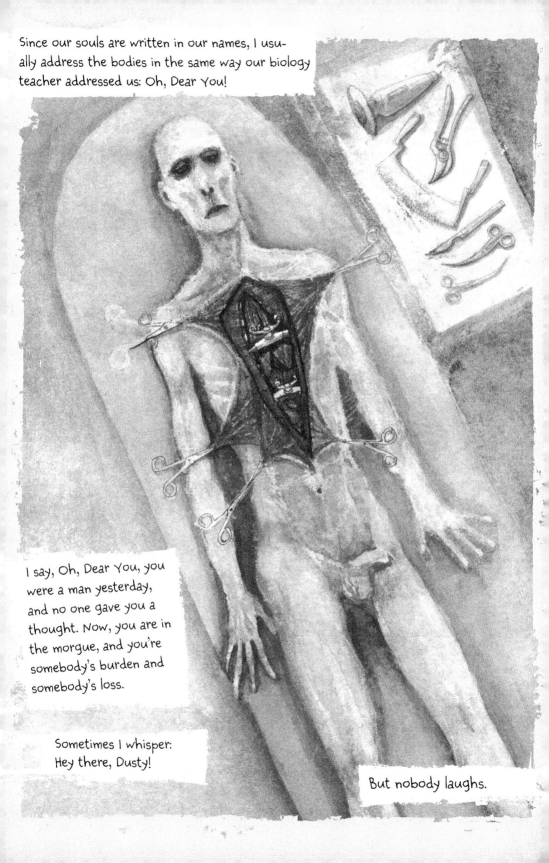

Since our souls are written in our names, I usually address the bodies in the same way our biology teacher addressed us: Oh, Dear You!

I say, Oh, Dear You, you were a man yesterday, and no one gave you a thought. Now, you are in the morgue, and you're somebody's burden and somebody's loss.

Sometimes I whisper: Hey there, Dusty!

But nobody laughs.

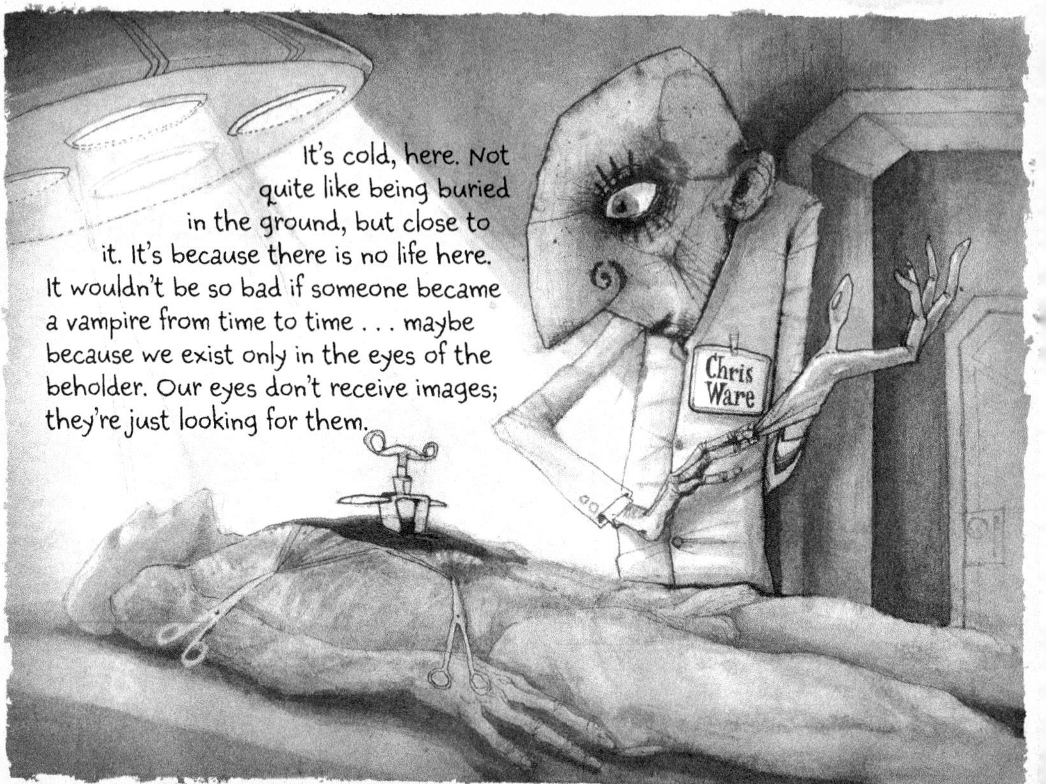
It's cold, here. Not quite like being buried in the ground, but close to it. It's because there is no life here. It wouldn't be so bad if someone became a vampire from time to time . . . maybe because we exist only in the eyes of the beholder. Our eyes don't receive images; they're just looking for them.
Chris Ware

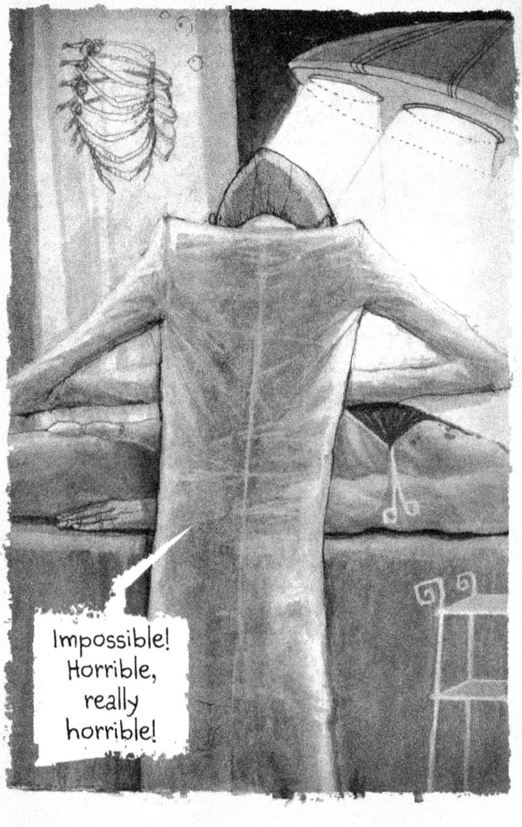
Impossible! Horrible, really horrible!

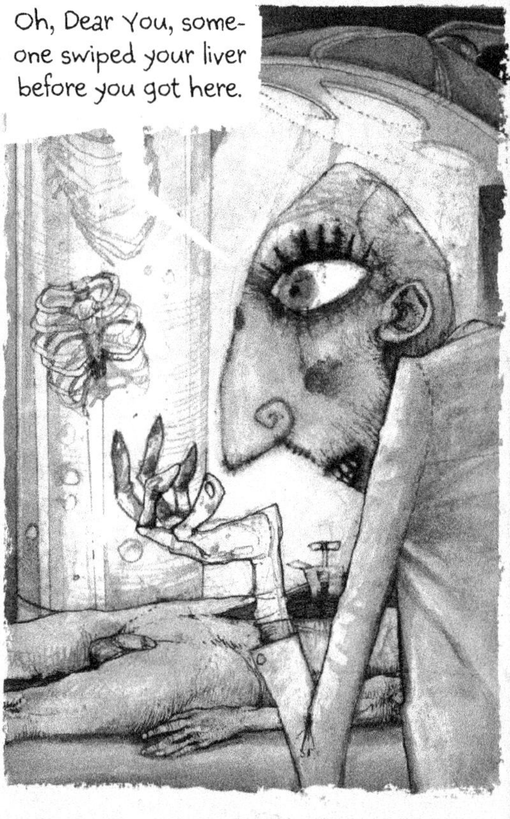
Oh, Dear You, someone swiped your liver before you got here.

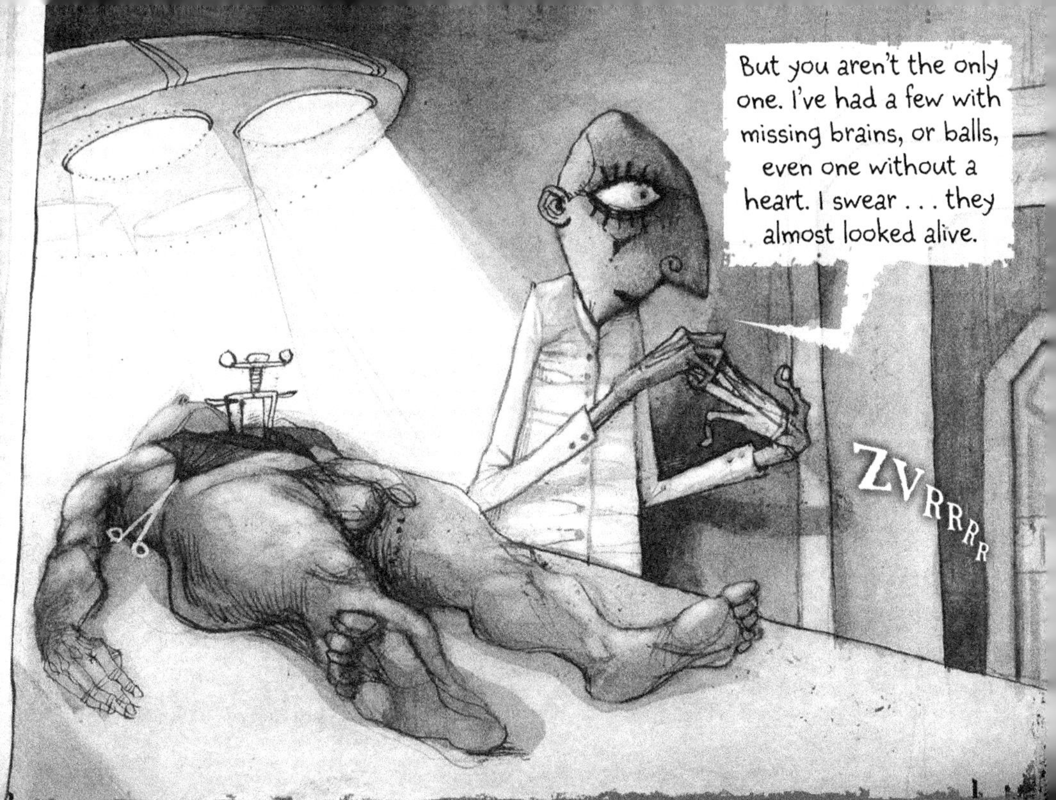
But you aren't the only one. I've had a few with missing brains, or balls, even one without a heart. I swear . . . they almost looked alive.
ZVRRRRR

It was Marc Hempel at the door. He usually brings letters, reports and such. He always asks the same thing:

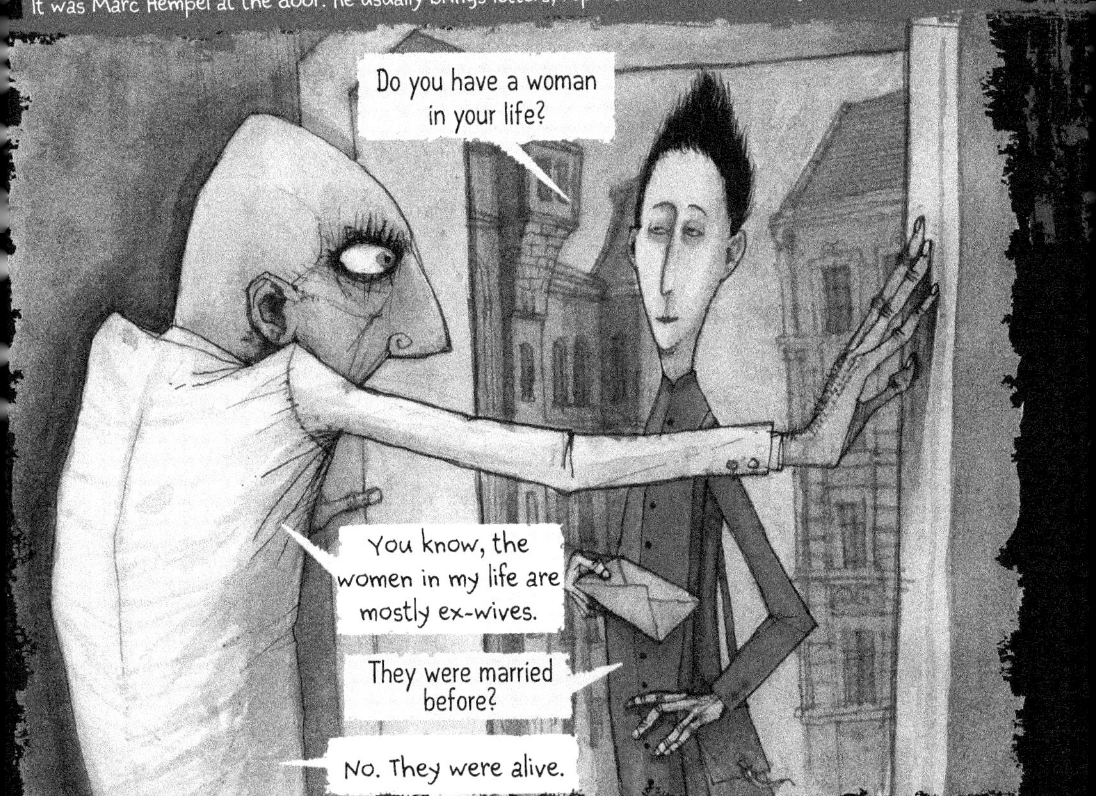
Do you have a woman in your life?
You know, the women in my life are mostly ex-wives.
They were married before?
No. They were alive.

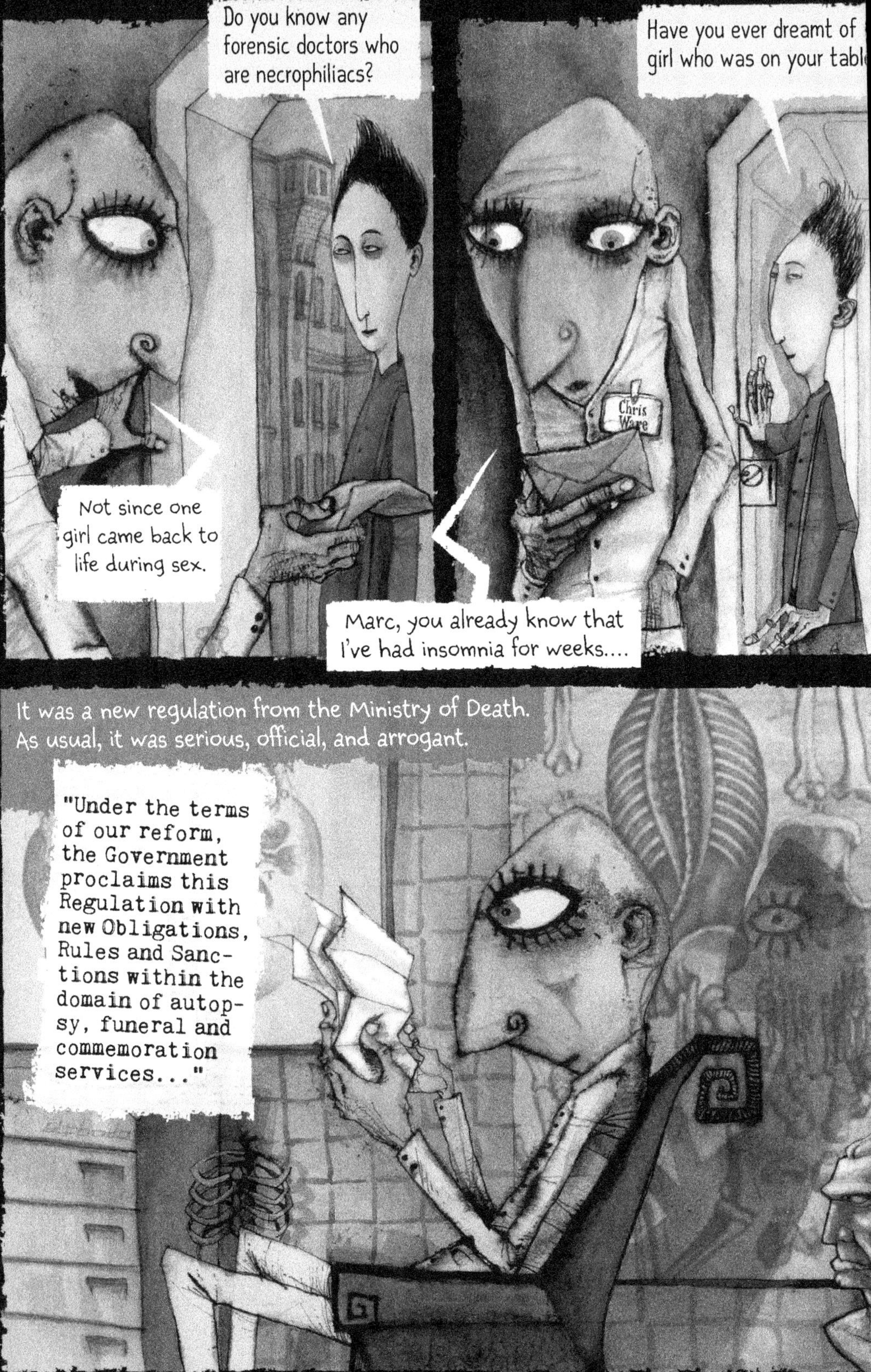
Do you know any forensic doctors who are necrophiliacs?
Not since one girl came back to life during sex.
Have you ever dreamt of
girl who was on your tabl
Chris Ware
Marc, you already know that I've had insomnia for weeks....
It was a new regulation from the Ministry of Death. As usual, it was serious, official, and arrogant.
"Under the terms of our reform, the Government proclaims this Regulation with new Obligations, Rules and Sanctions within the domain of autopsy, funeral and commemoration services..."

Fig. 01/PRESCRIBED LOOK OF A CORPSE / ANFAS

If you discover a corpse possessing this new anatomy, do not cremate it. Perform the autopsy and forward your results to us.

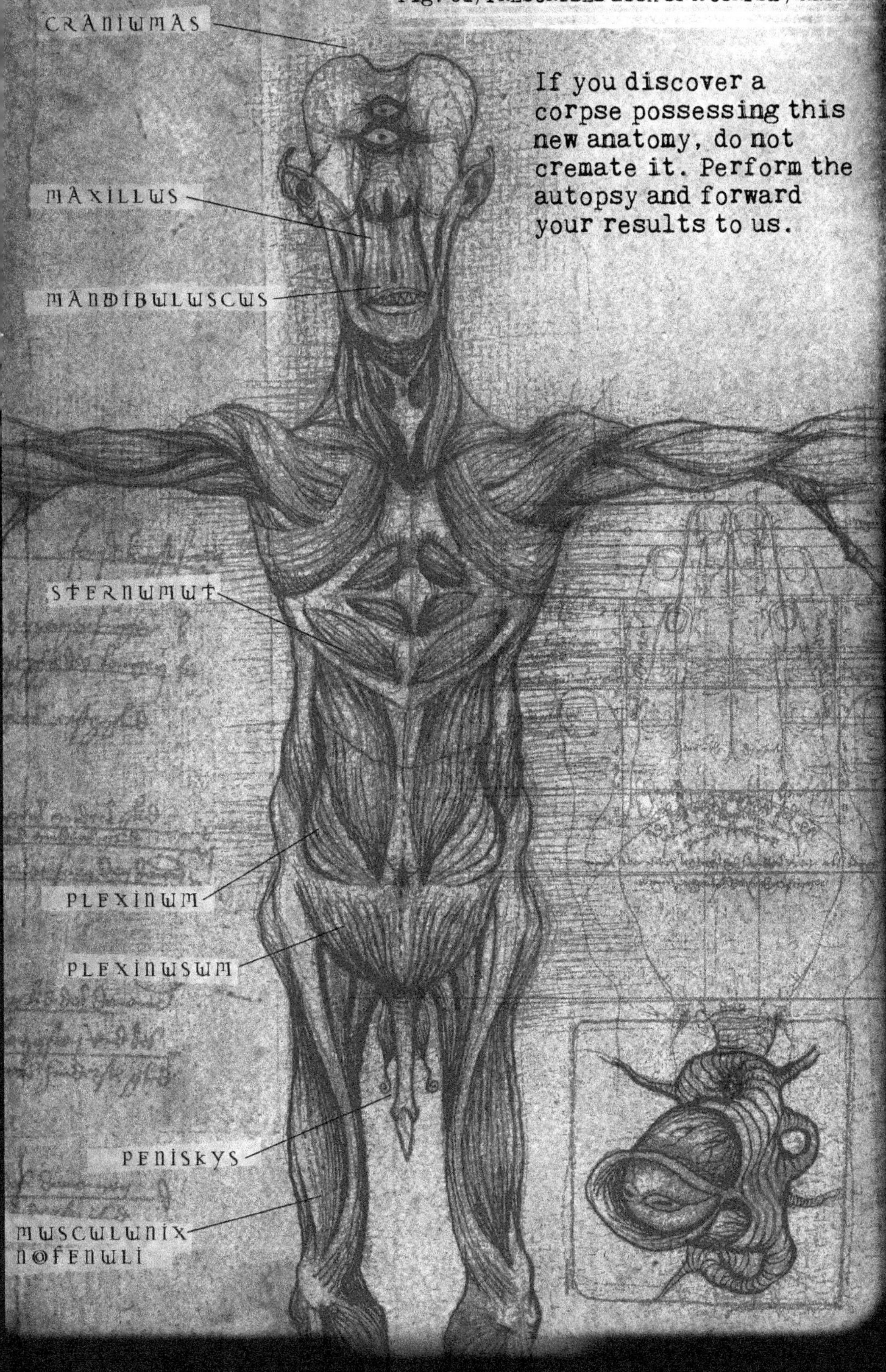

CRANIUMAS
MAXILLUS
MANDIBULUSCUS
STERNUMUT
PLEXINUM
PLEXINUSUM
PENISKYS
MUSCULUNIX
NOFENULI

Fig. 02/PRESCRIBED LOOK OF A CORPSE / PROFILE

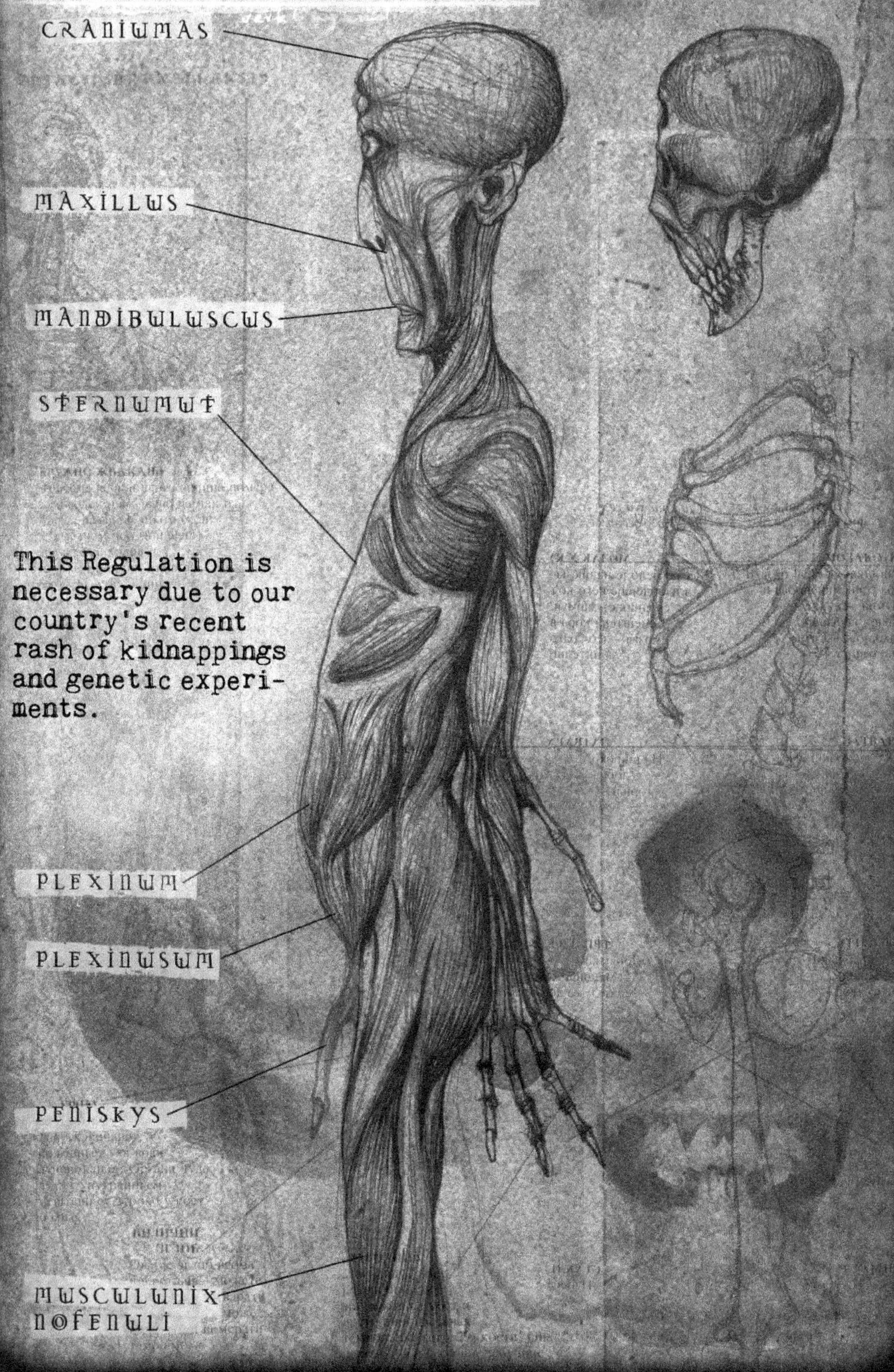

CRANIUMAS
MAXILLUS
MANDIBULUSCUS
STERNUMUT
PLEXINUM
PLEXINUSUM
PENISKYS
MUSCULUNIX NOFENULI

This Regulation is necessary due to our country's recent rash of kidnappings and genetic experiments.

Also, obituaries must now exhibit a higher standard of beauty than before...

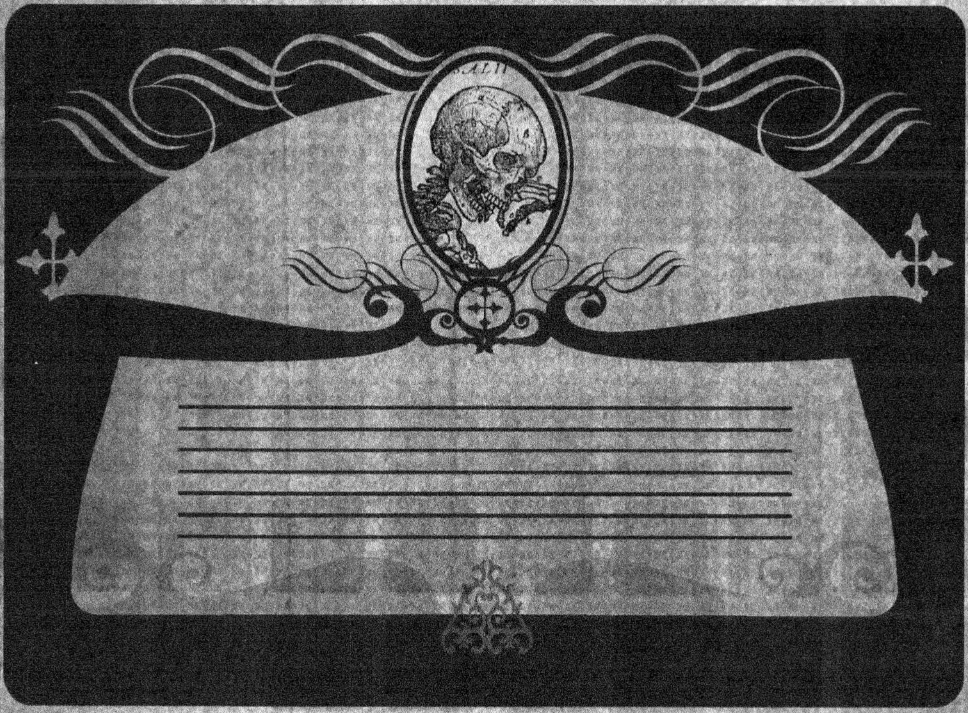

And to further reform Death, we require new coffins as well as new concepts for mourning, if, and only if, they do not contradict religious beliefs . . .

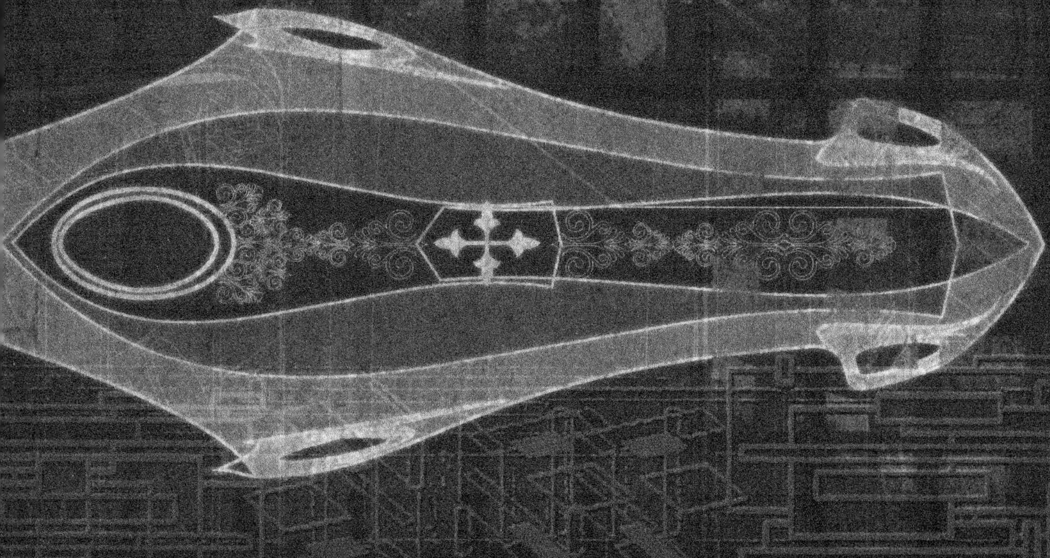

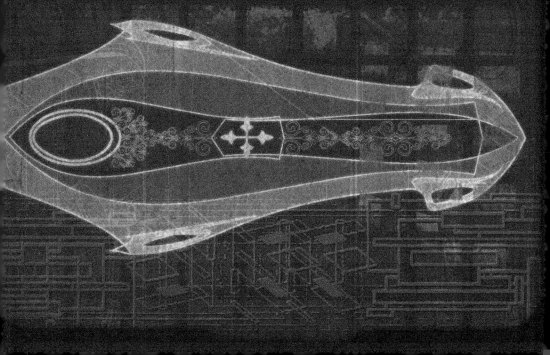

It was quite strange.

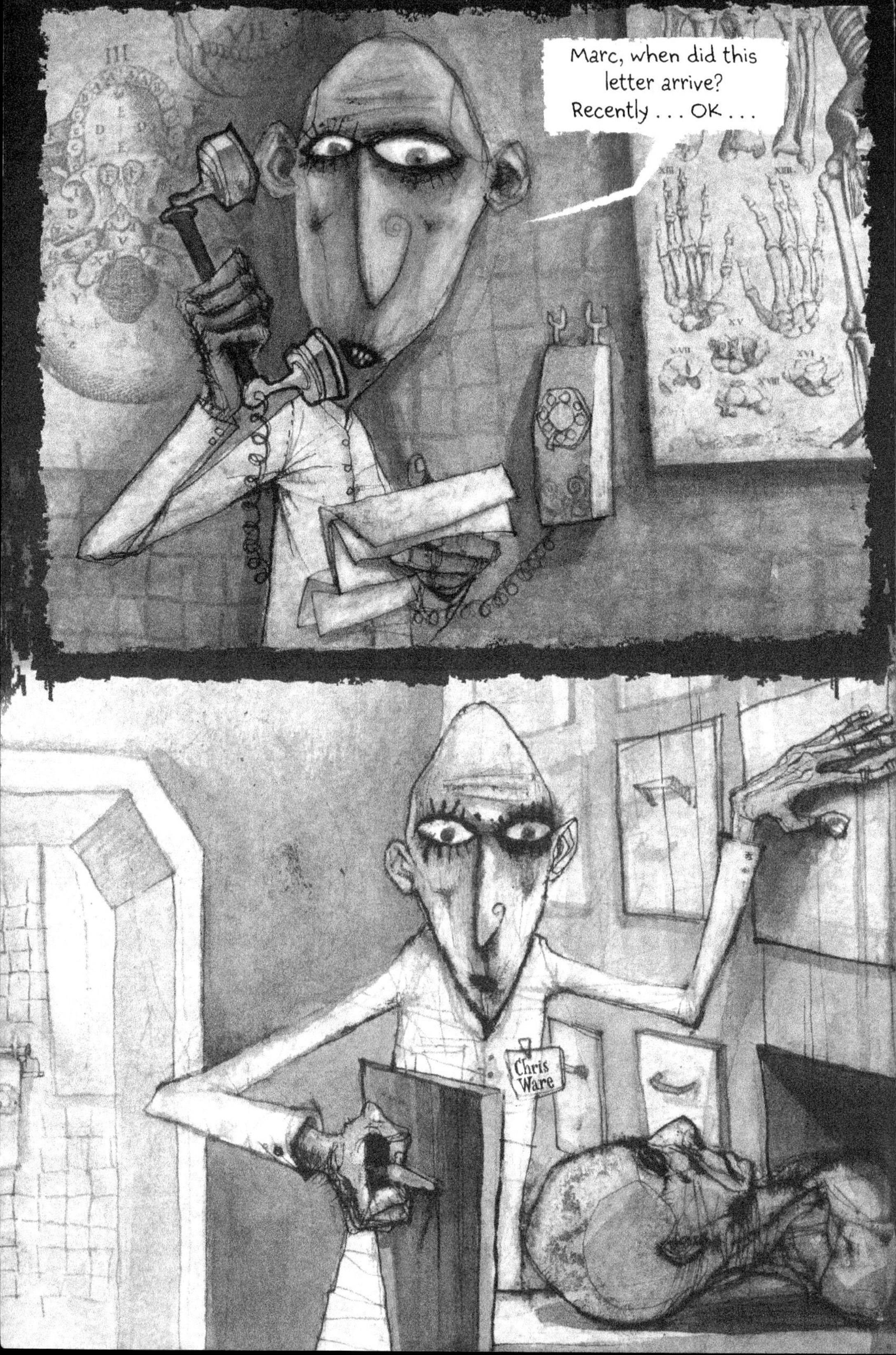
Marc, when did this letter arrive? Recently . . . OK . . .
Chris Ware

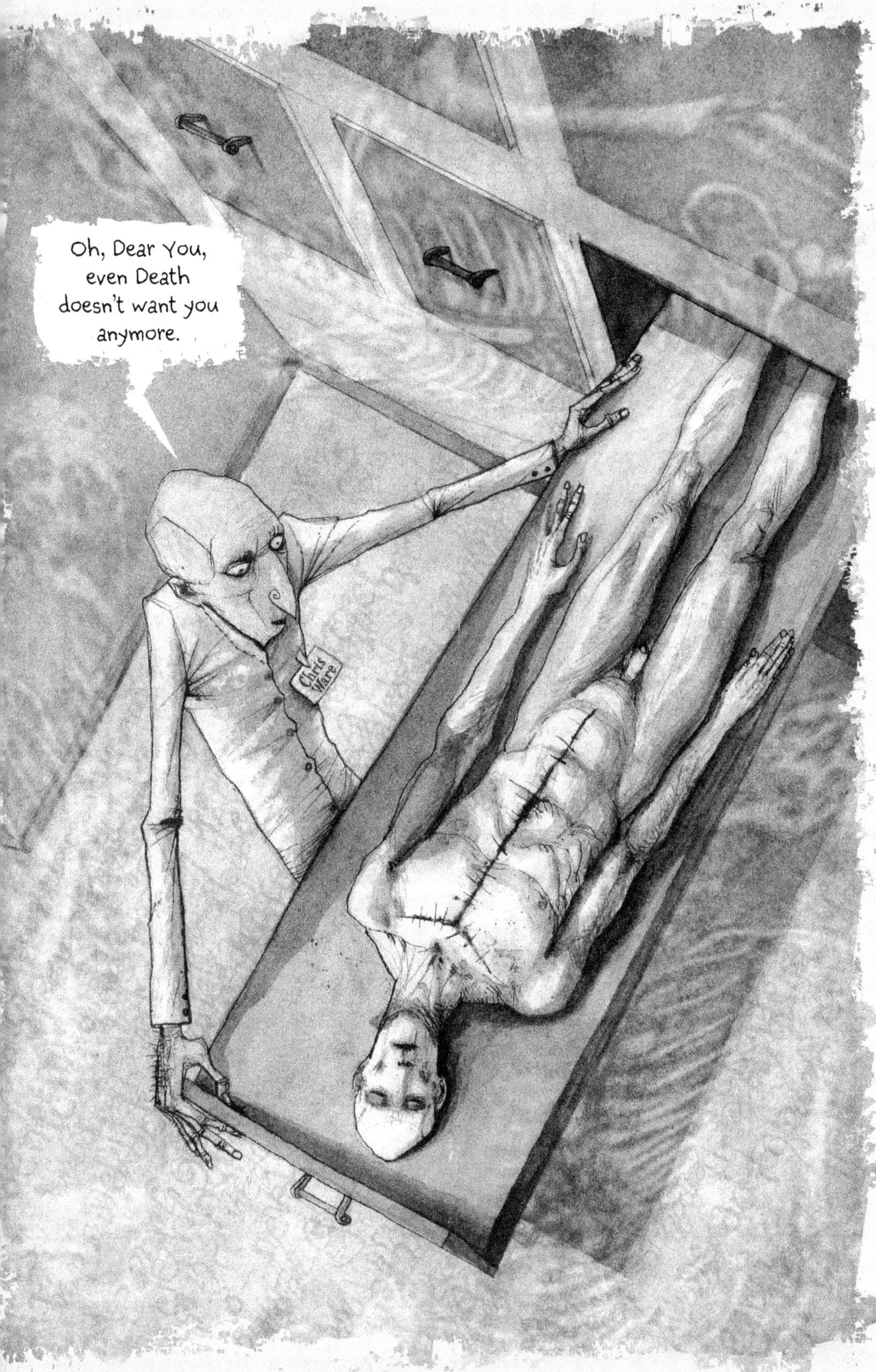
Oh, Dear You, even Death doesn't want you anymore.
Chris Ware

CHAPTER TWO: PROTOCOL OF DEFORMATIONS

I sink into the endless night
and dream
Wordless ashes create my destiny
Dusk is sorrow, I am
hypnotized by pain
I write my unchosen grave

Where are my leisure and fireflies,
Whose life destroys my rising?
The visions are shattered screams
And somebody else's intestines
sleep in me

My crown is made of
fossils and rocks
Miracles are written on the body
The sun reiterates itself like a siren
I am the being who links everything

Desire is hidden in returning
And it sings a requiem for me

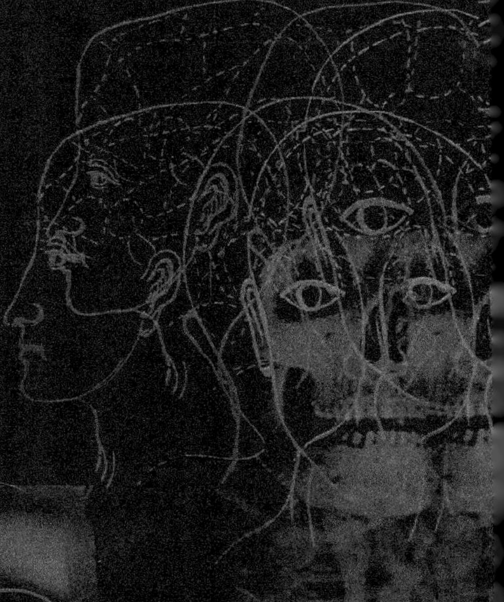

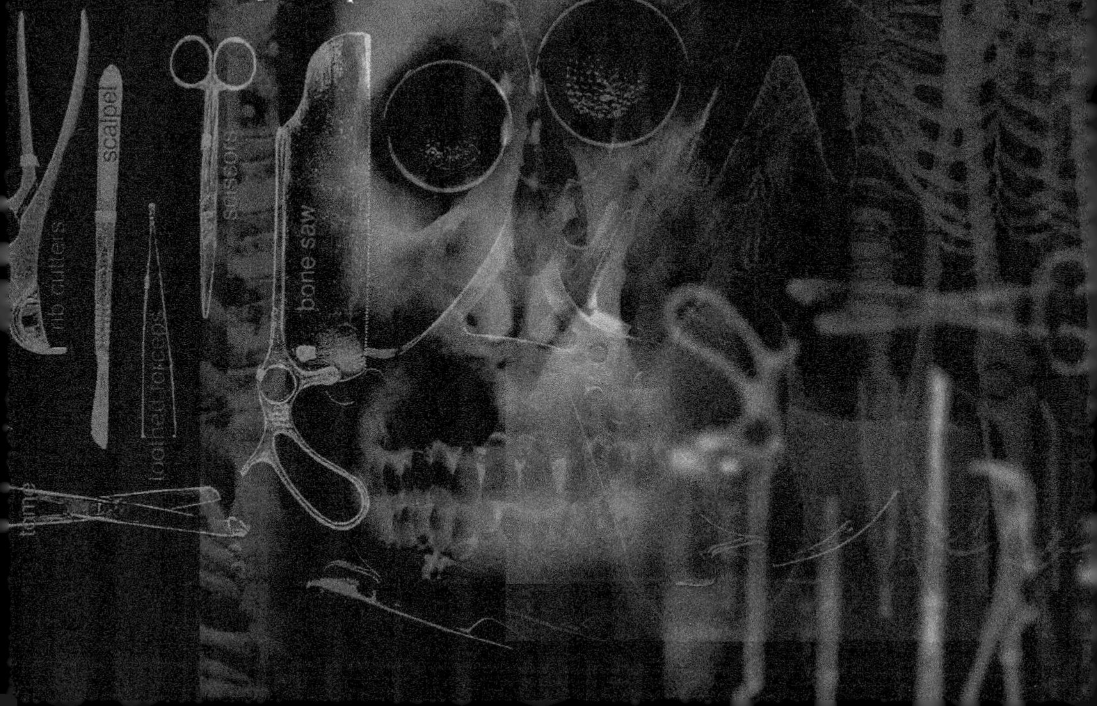
rib cutters
scalpel
scissors
bone saw
toothed forceps

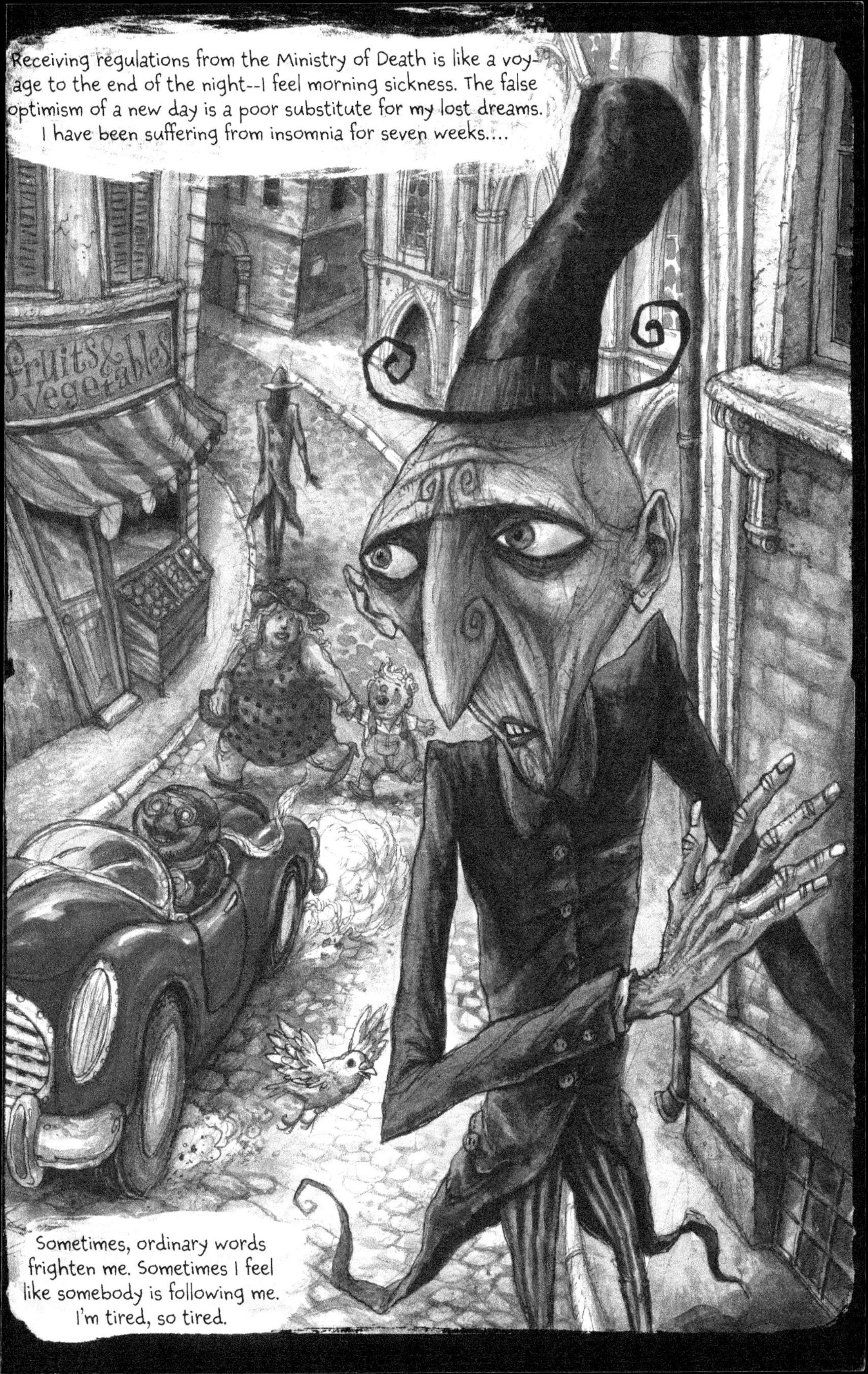
Receiving regulations from the Ministry of Death is like a voyage to the end of the night--I feel morning sickness. The false optimism of a new day is a poor substitute for my lost dreams. I have been suffering from insomnia for seven weeks....
fruits & vegetables
Sometimes, ordinary words frighten me. Sometimes I feel like somebody is following me. I'm tired, so tired.

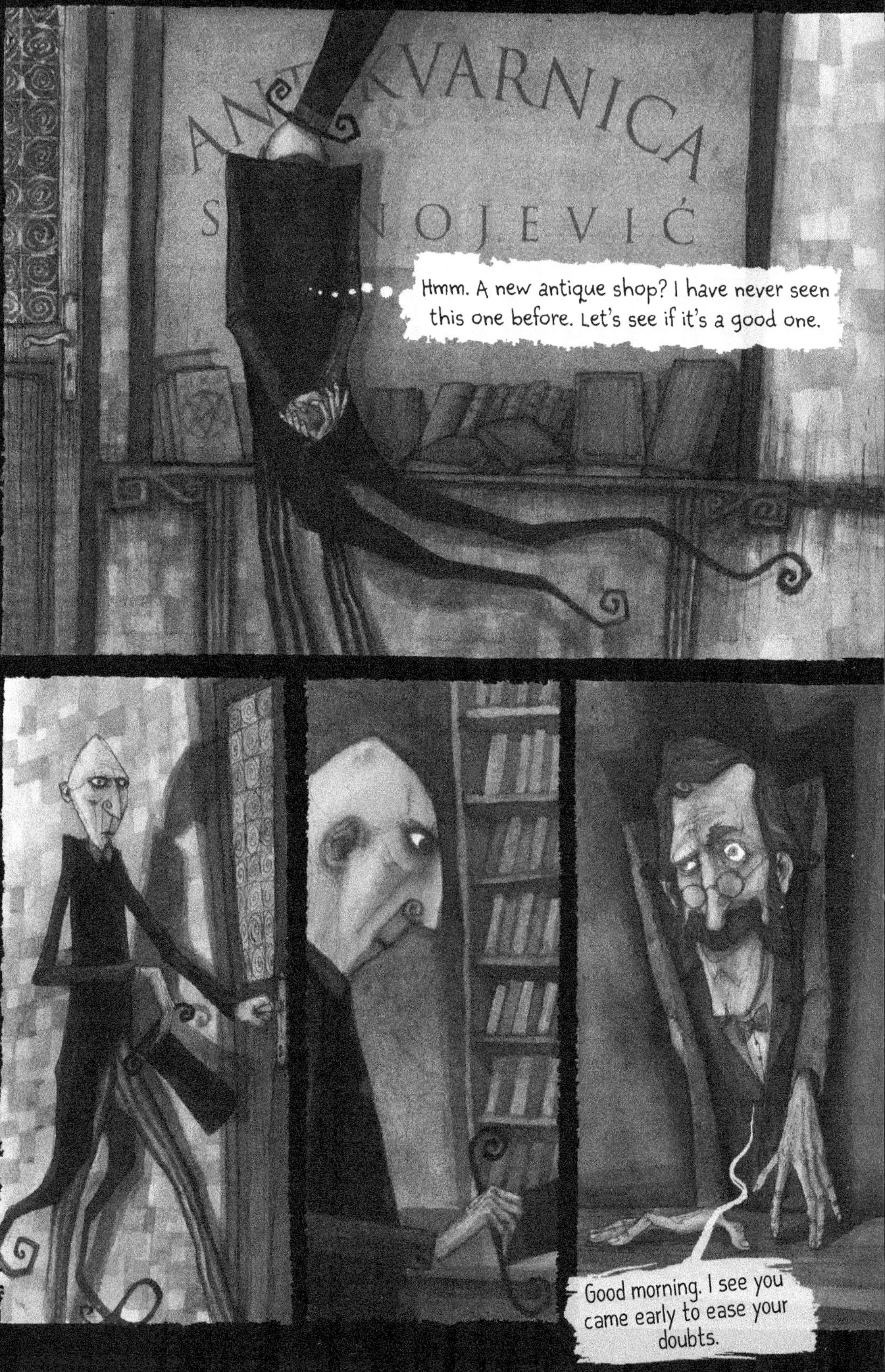
Hmm. A new antique shop? I have never seen this one before. Let's see if it's a good one.
Good morning. I see you came early to ease your doubts.

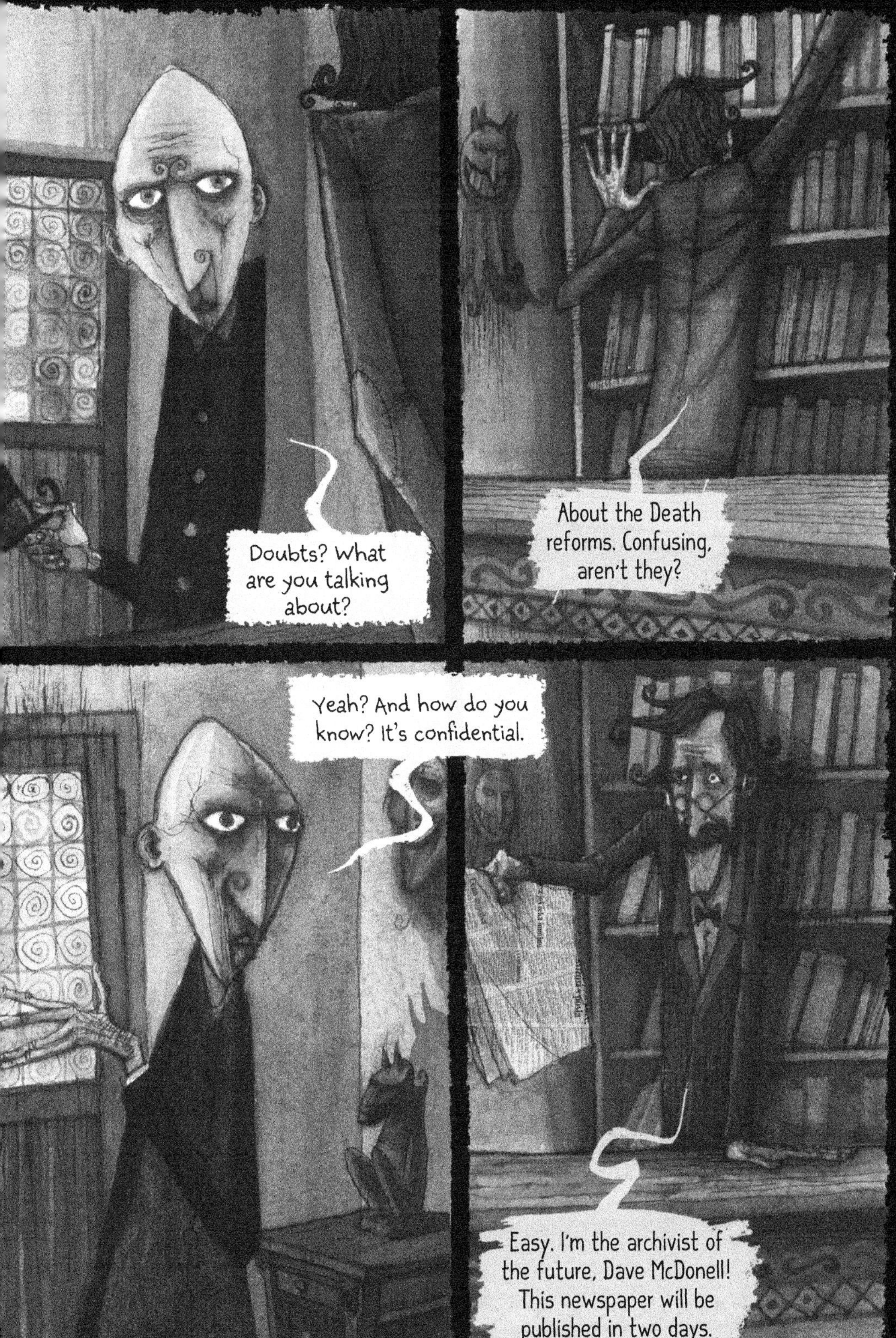
Doubts? What are you talking about?
About the Death reforms. Confusing, aren't they?
Yeah? And how do you know? It's confidential.
Easy. I'm the archivist of the future, Dave McDonell! This newspaper will be published in two days.

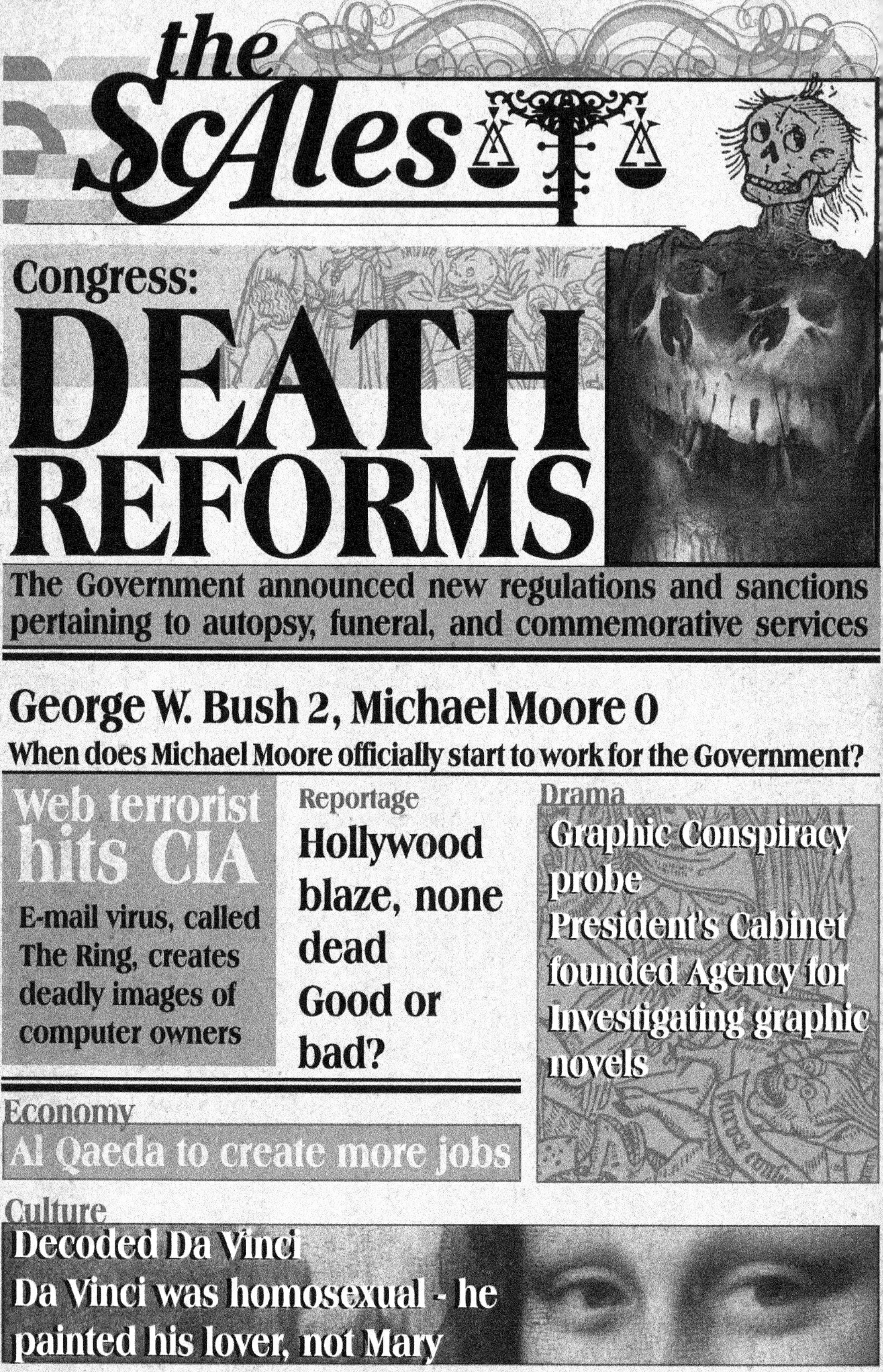

the Scales

Congress:

DEATH REFORMS

The Government announced new regulations and sanctions pertaining to autopsy, funeral, and commemorative services

George W. Bush 2, Michael Moore 0

When does Michael Moore officially start to work for the Government?

Web terrorist hits CIA

E-mail virus, called The Ring, creates deadly images of computer owners

Reportage

Hollywood blaze, none dead

Good or bad?

Drama

Graphic Conspiracy probe

President's Cabinet founded Agency for Investigating graphic novels

Economy

Al Qaeda to create more jobs

Culture

Decoded Da Vinci

Da Vinci was homosexual - he painted his lover, not Mary

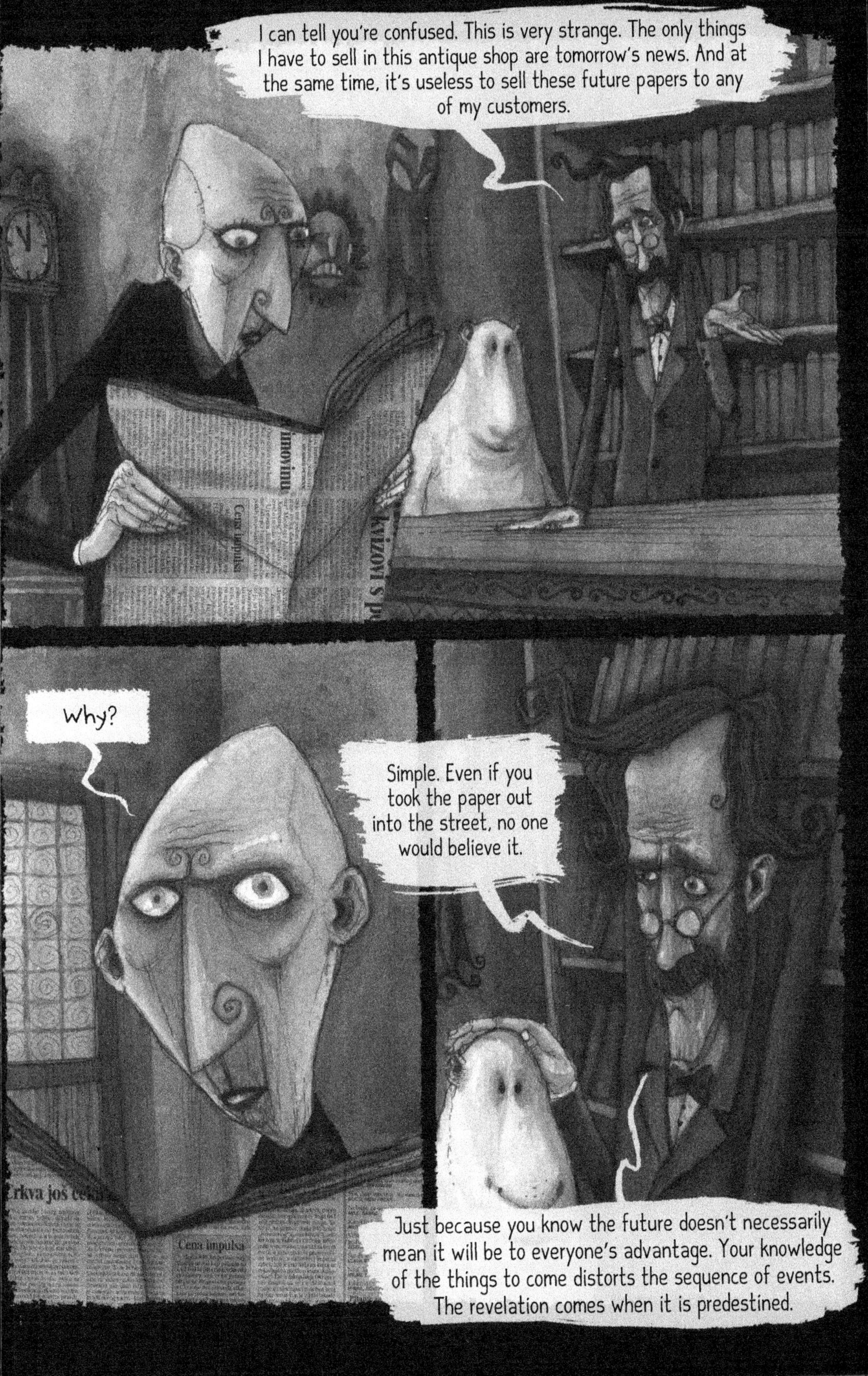
I can tell you're confused. This is very strange. The only things I have to sell in this antique shop are tomorrow's news. And at the same time, it's useless to sell these future papers to any of my customers.
Why?
Simple. Even if you took the paper out into the street, no one would believe it.
Just because you know the future doesn't necessarily mean it will be to everyone's advantage. Your knowledge of the things to come distorts the sequence of events. The revelation comes when it is predestined.

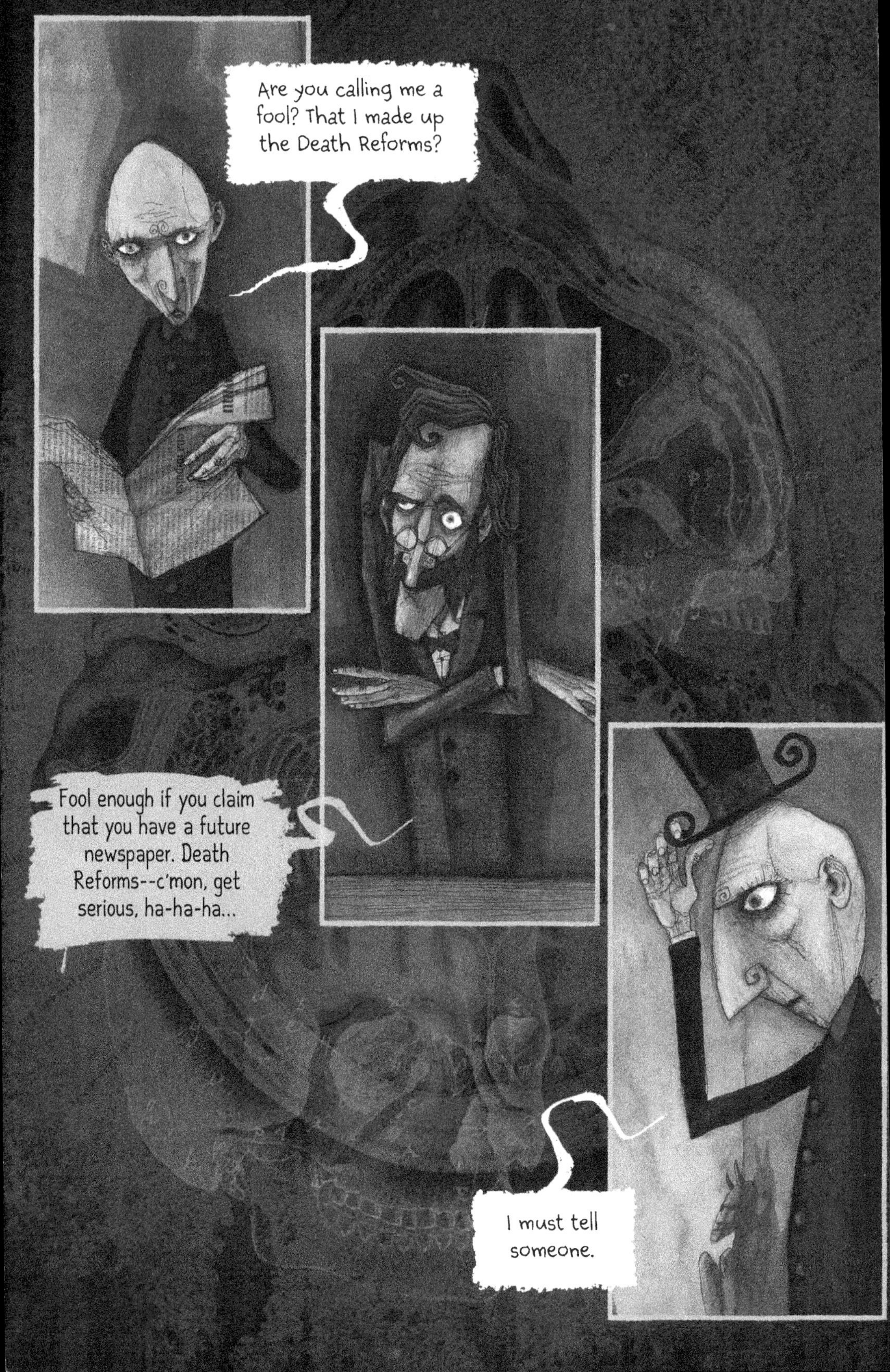
Are you calling me a fool? That I made up the Death Reforms?
Fool enough if you claim that you have a future newspaper. Death Reforms--c'mon, get serious, ha-ha-ha...
I must tell someone.

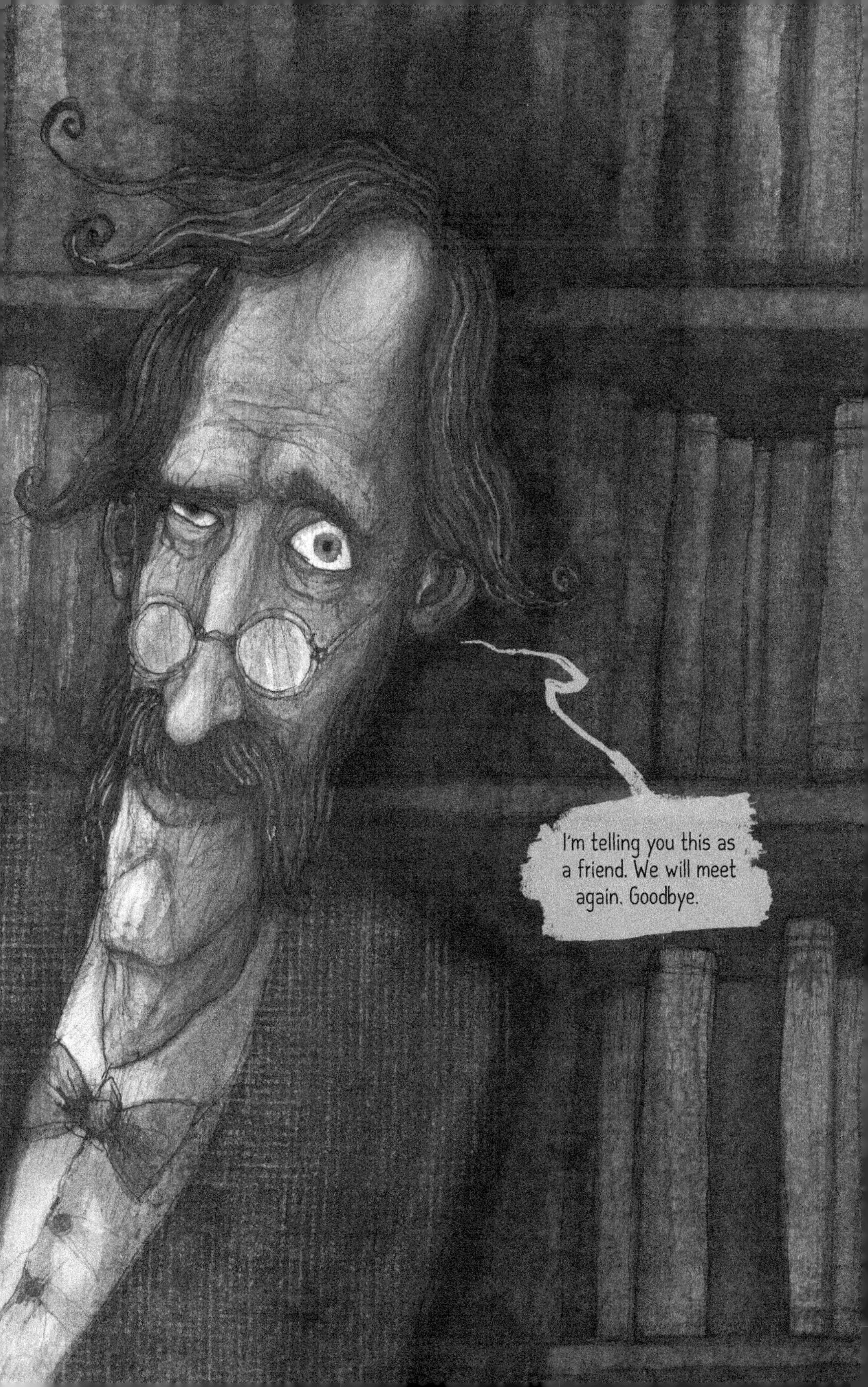
I'm telling you this as a friend. We will meet again. Goodbye.

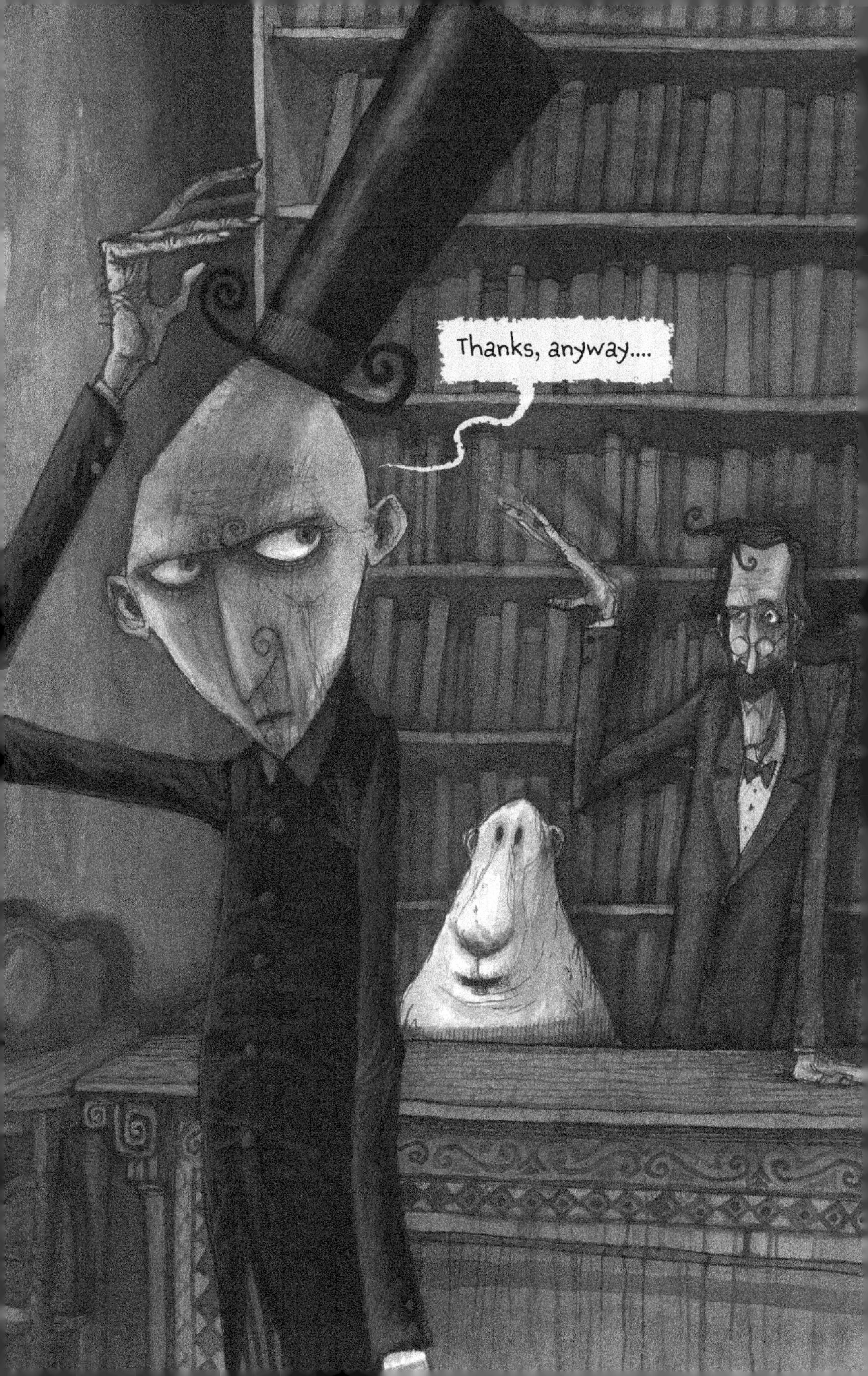
Thanks, anyway....

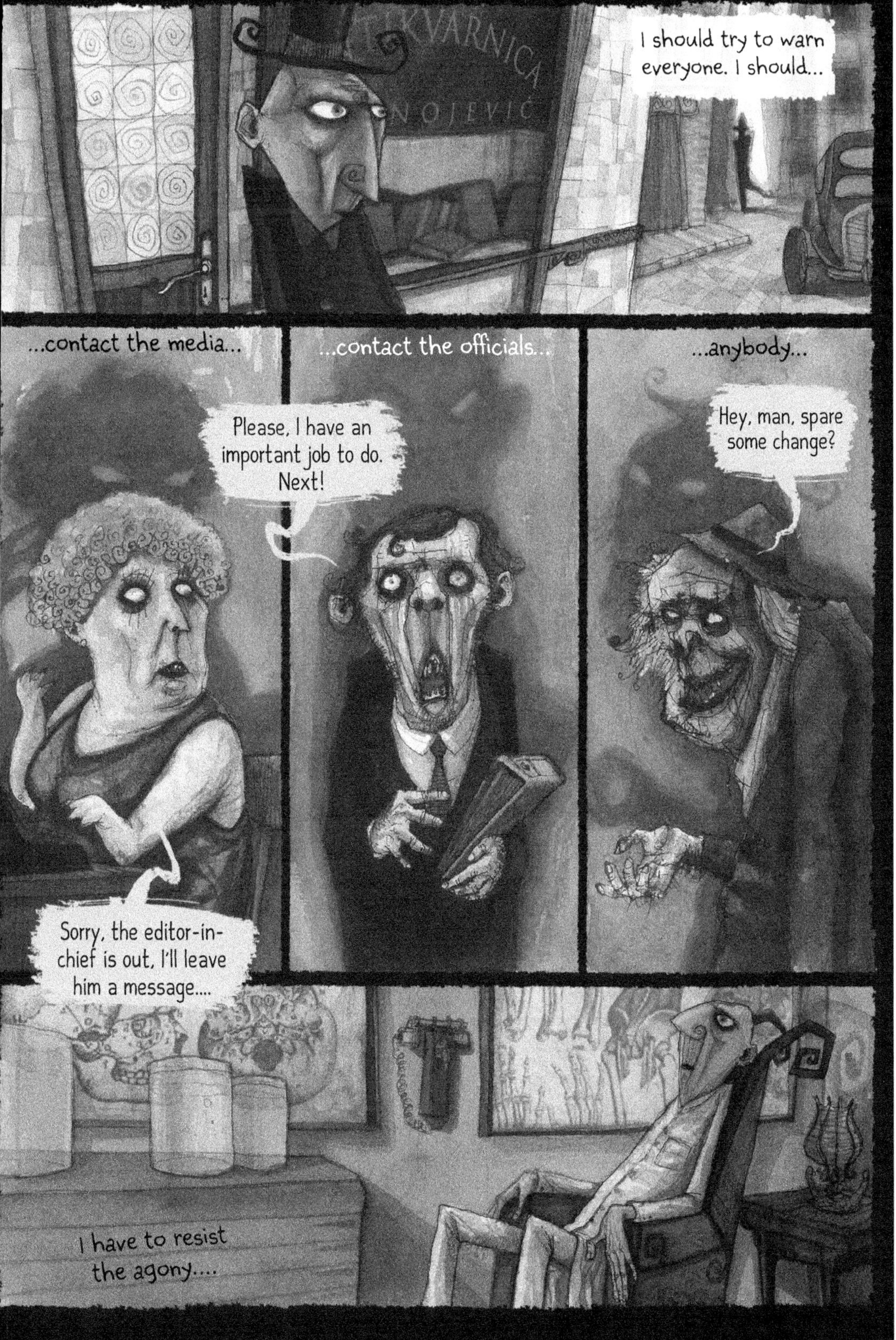
ANTIKVARNICA
NOJEVIĆ
I should try to warn everyone. I should...
...contact the media...
Sorry, the editor-in-chief is out, I'll leave him a message....
...contact the officials...
Please, I have an important job to do. Next!
...anybody...
Hey, man, spare some change?
I have to resist the agony....

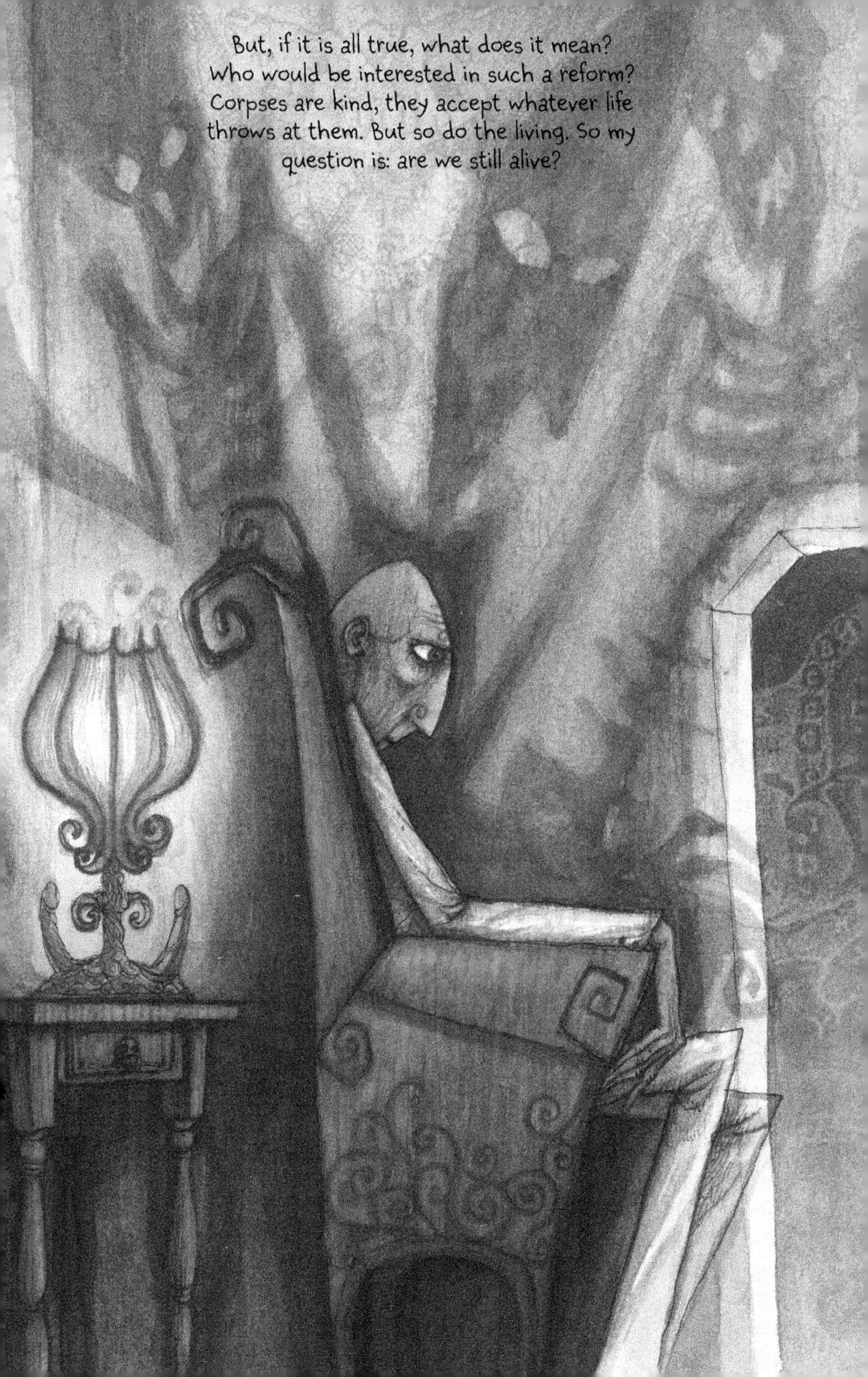
But, if it is all true, what does it mean? Who would be interested in such a reform? Corpses are kind, they accept whatever life throws at them. But so do the living. So my question is: are we still alive?

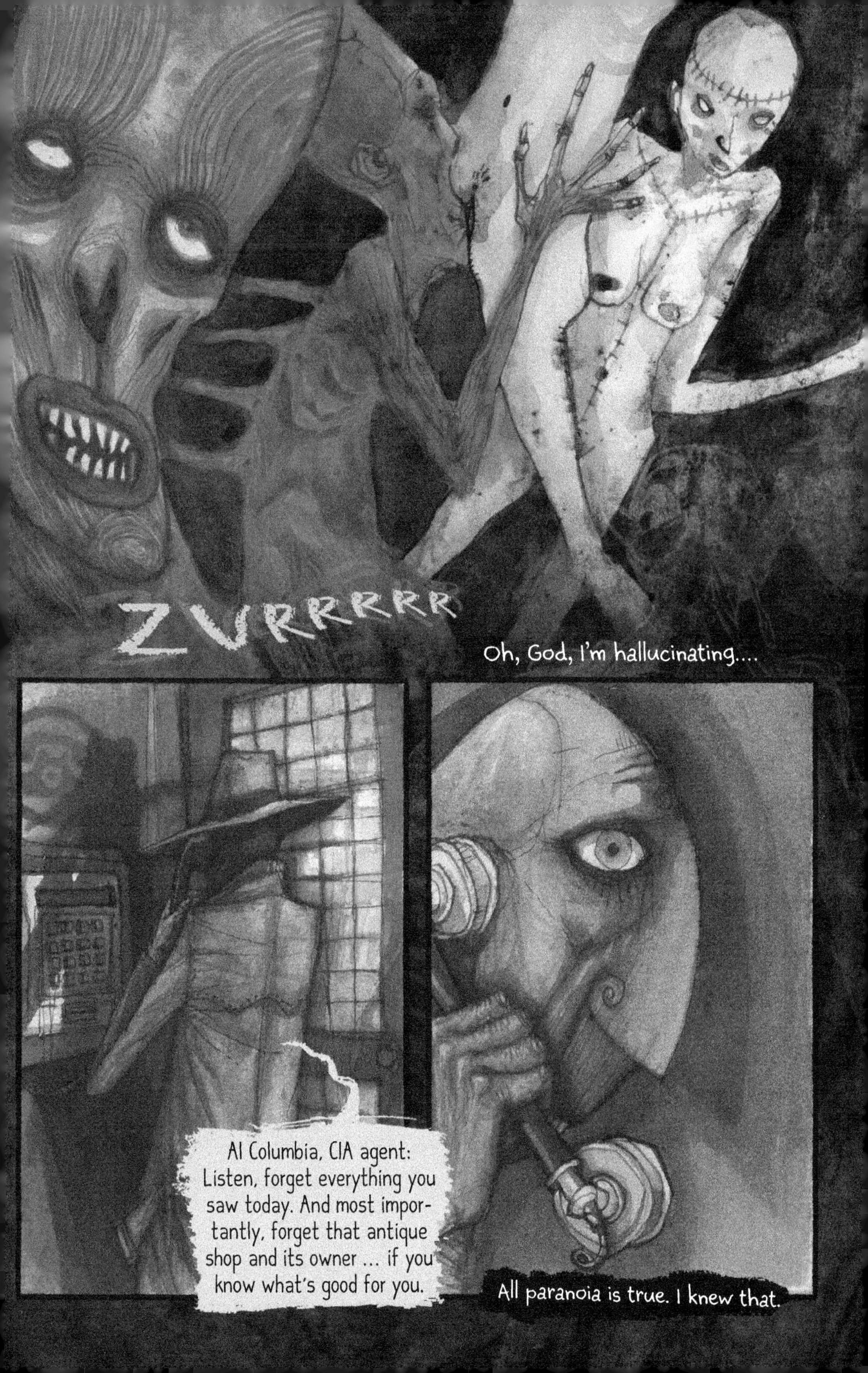
ZVRRRRR
Oh, God, I'm hallucinating....
Al Columbia, CIA agent: Listen, forget everything you saw today. And most importantly, forget that antique shop and its owner ... if you know what's good for you.
All paranoia is true. I knew that.

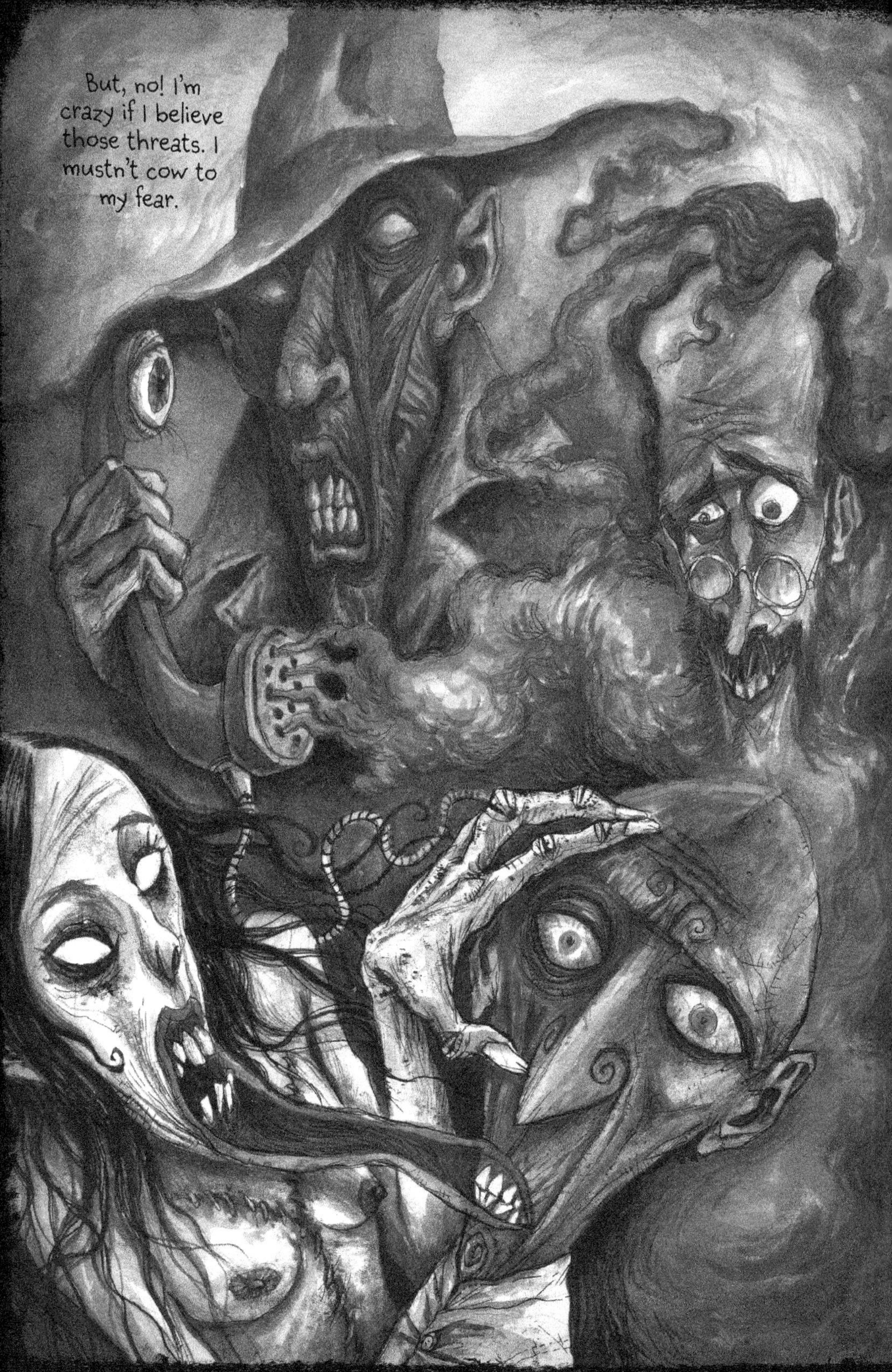
But, no! I'm crazy if I believe those threats. I mustn't cow to my fear.

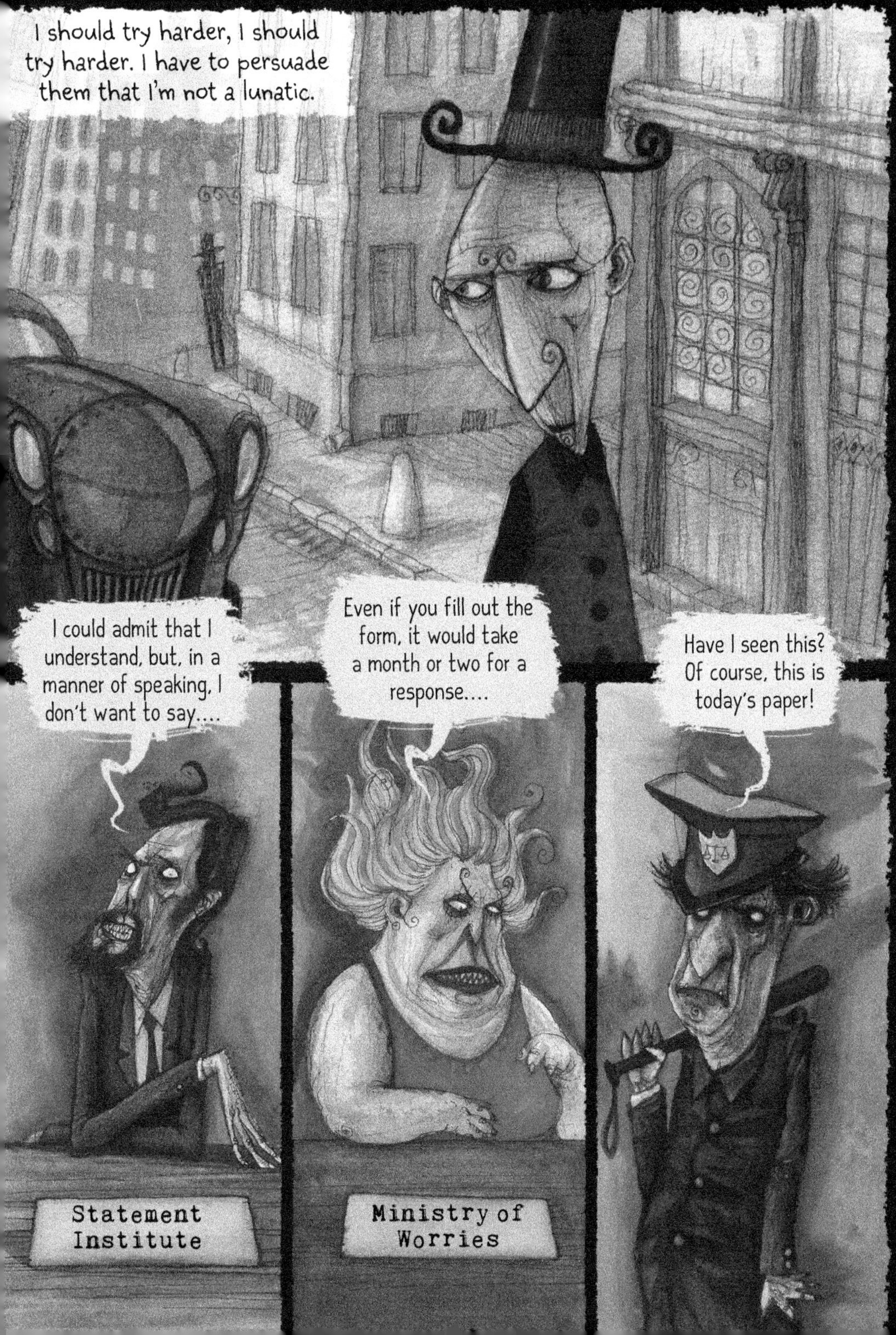
I should try harder, I should try harder. I have to persuade them that I'm not a lunatic.
I could admit that I understand, but, in a manner of speaking, I don't want to say....
Statement Institute
Even if you fill out the form, it would take a month or two for a response....
Ministry of Worries
Have I seen this? Of course, this is today's paper!

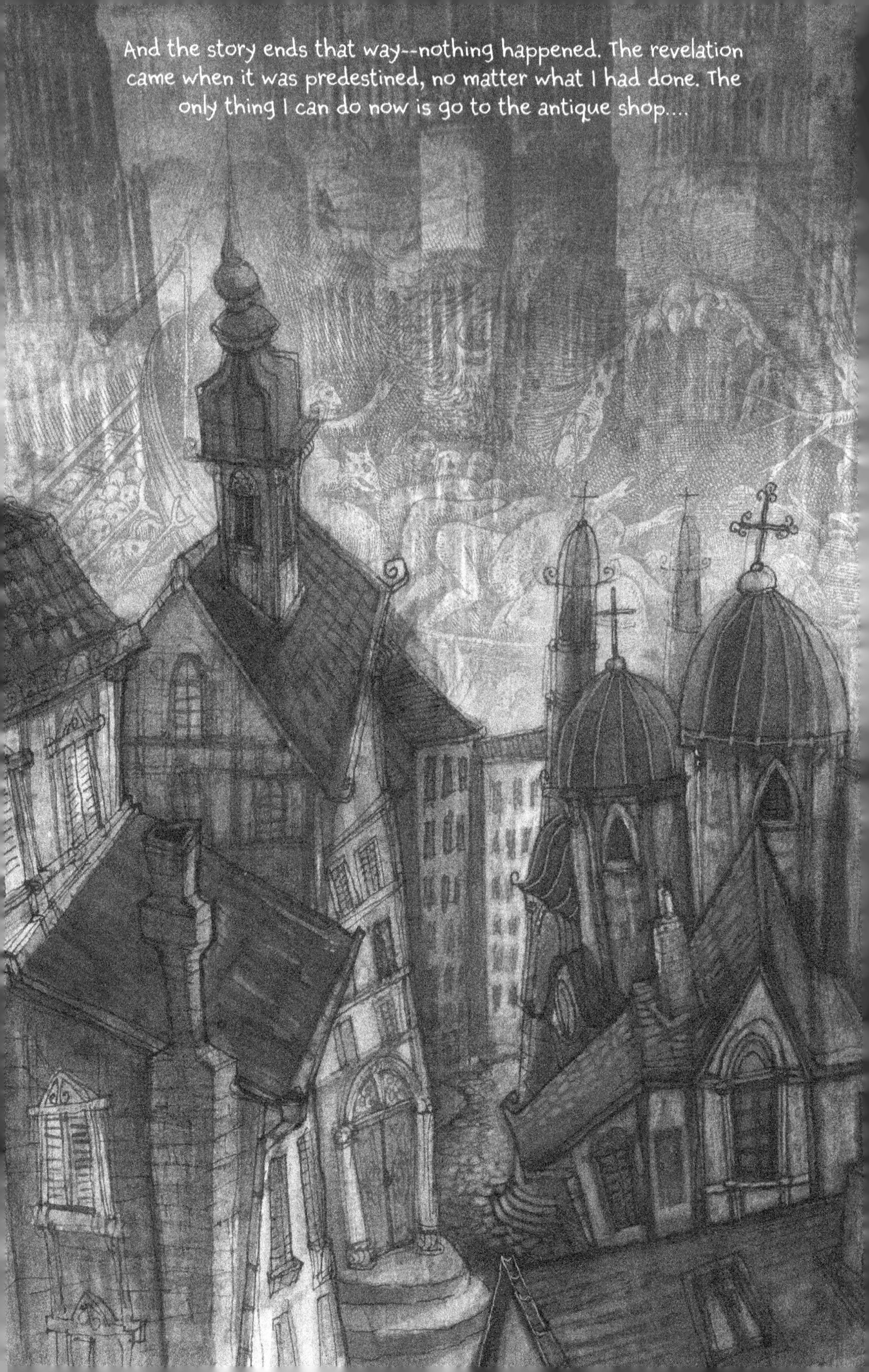
And the story ends that way--nothing happened. The revelation came when it was predestined, no matter what I had done. The only thing I can do now is go to the antique shop....

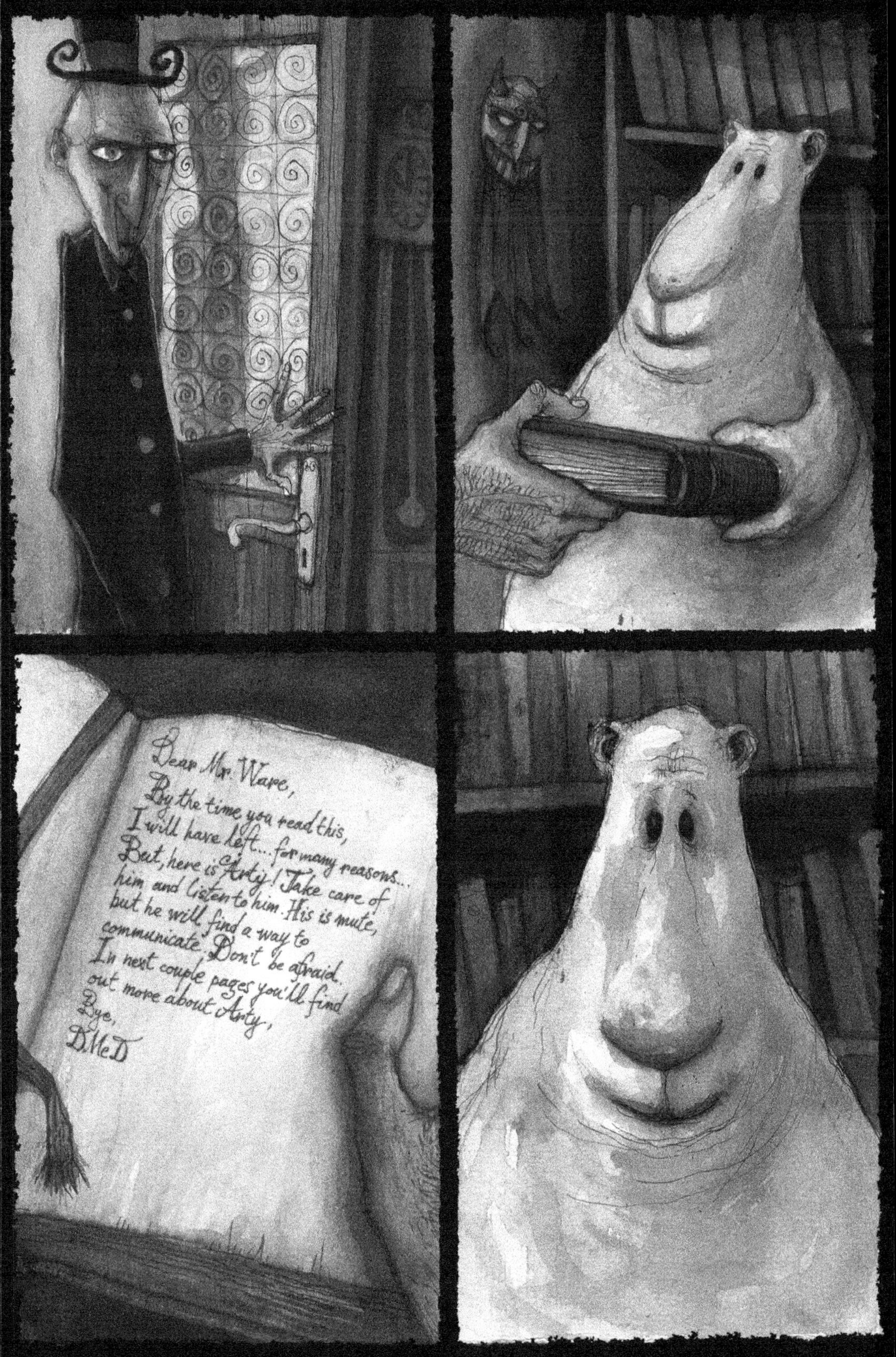
Dear Mr. Ware,
By the time you read this,
I will have left... for many reasons...
But, here is Arty! Take care of
him and listen to him. His is mute,
but he will find a way to
communicate. Don't be afraid.
In next couple pages you'll find
out more about Arty,
Bye,
D.McD

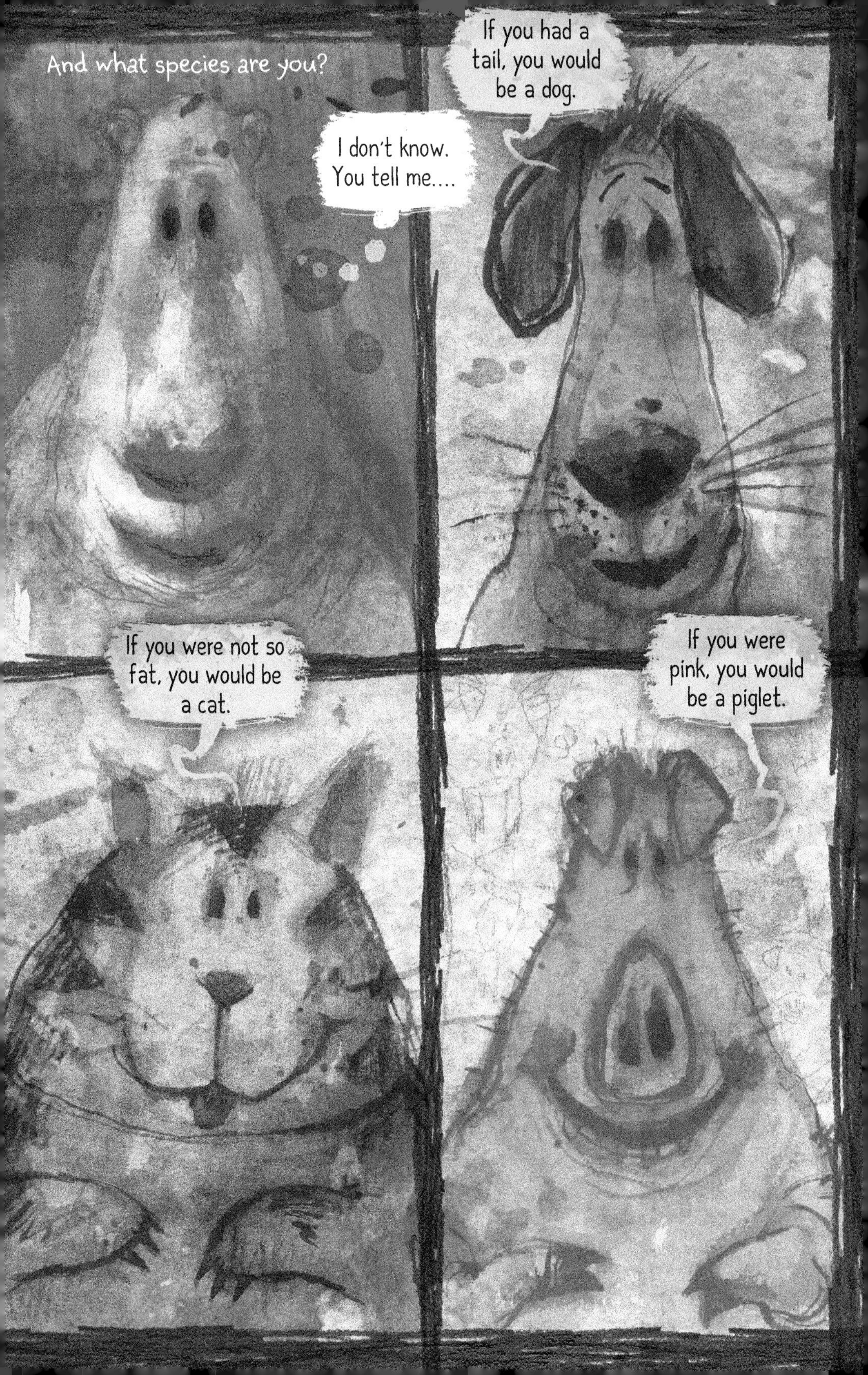
And what species are you?
If you had a tail, you would be a dog.
I don't know. You tell me....
If you were not so fat, you would be a cat.
If you were pink, you would be a piglet.

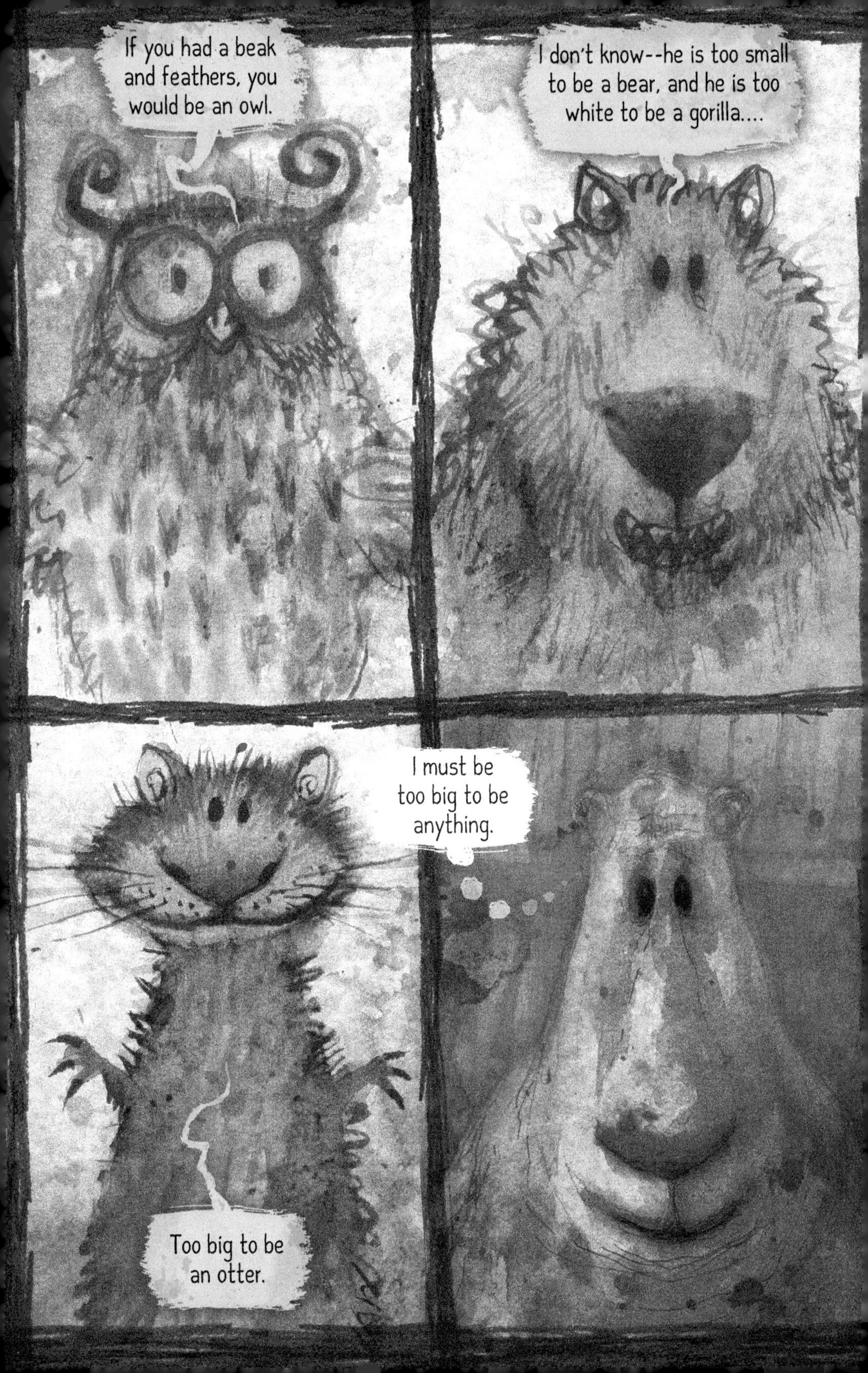
If you had a beak and feathers, you would be an owl.
I don't know--he is too small to be a bear, and he is too white to be a gorilla....
Too big to be an otter.
I must be too big to be anything.

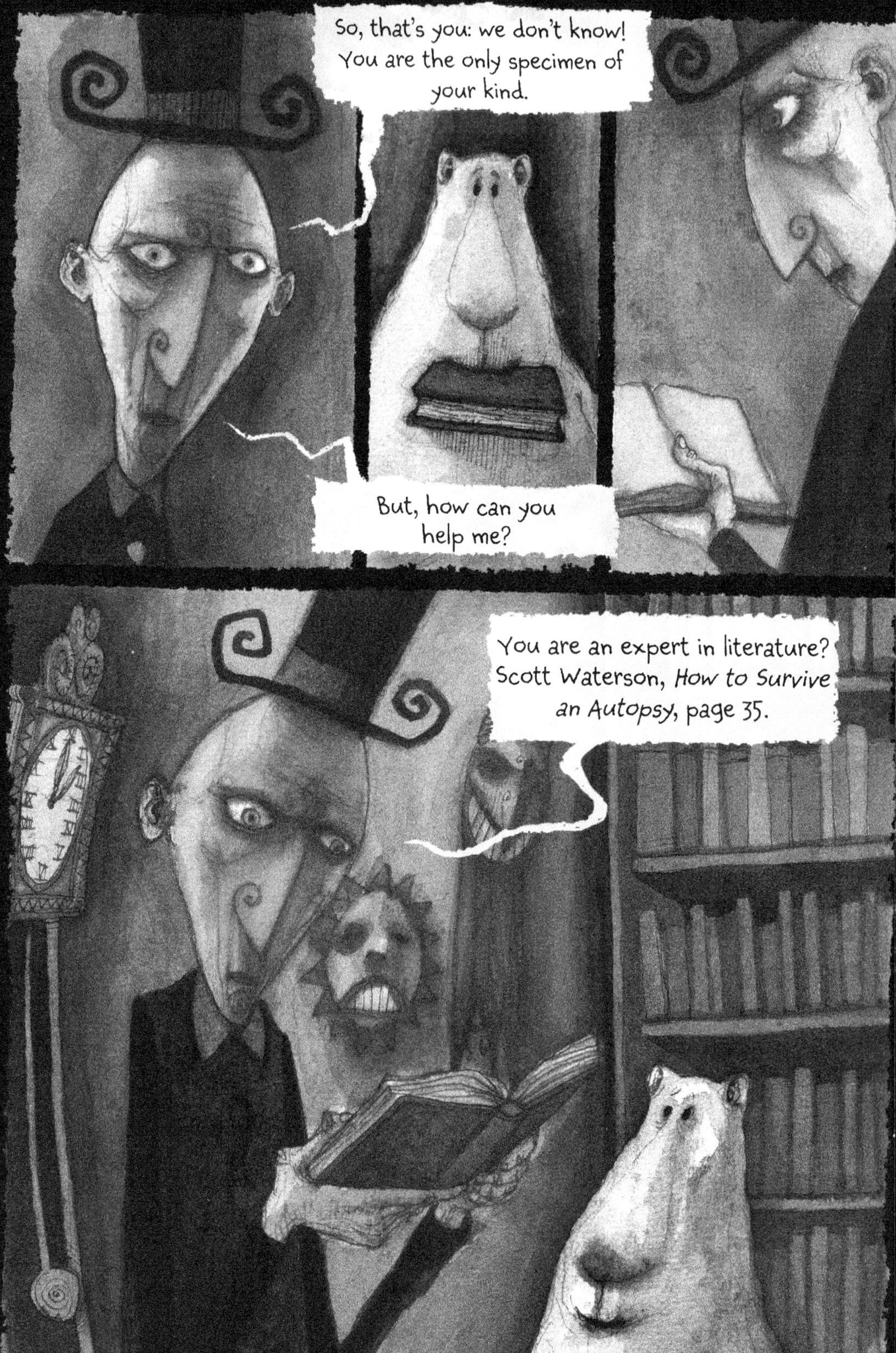
So, that's you: we don't know! You are the only specimen of your kind.
But, how can you help me?
You are an expert in literature? Scott Waterson, *How to Survive an Autopsy*, page 35.

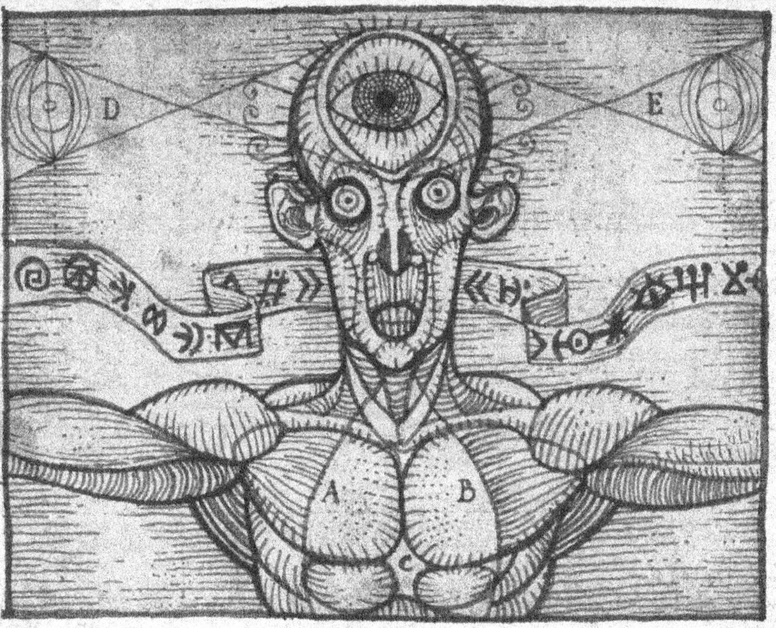
D
E
A
B
C

Human knowledge exceeds human power. We live in a transhuman society. But the technological development that is the means of governing is also the tool for manipulation. The aim of technology and pop culture at the same aesthetic level is to control people. Individual rebellion is welcome because it is expected. Moreover, each crime cannot exist without knowing about it. So, the original language of an artist is loyal to collective self-control. Diagnosis is the integral part of the disease. Until XVII century, every symbolic function came out from the human body alchemy: Christianity, macro-, and micro-cosmos . After that, man and his symbols splintered, and now symbols take over our lives. The neglected human body produces, at the biological level, new diseases as its symbolical function. The body invents new diseases to survive. Disease is a new symbol.

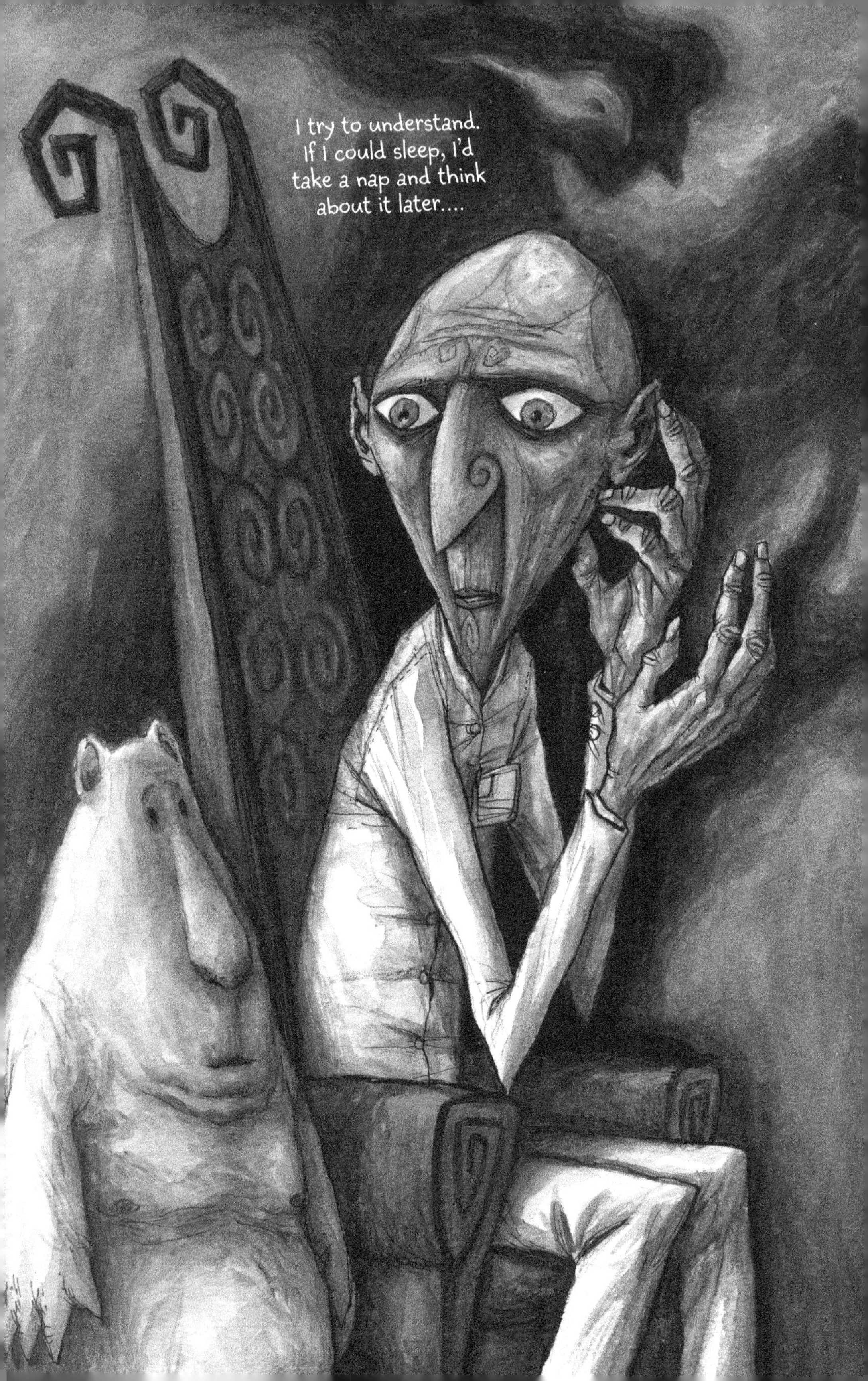
I try to understand. If I could sleep, I'd take a nap and think about it later....

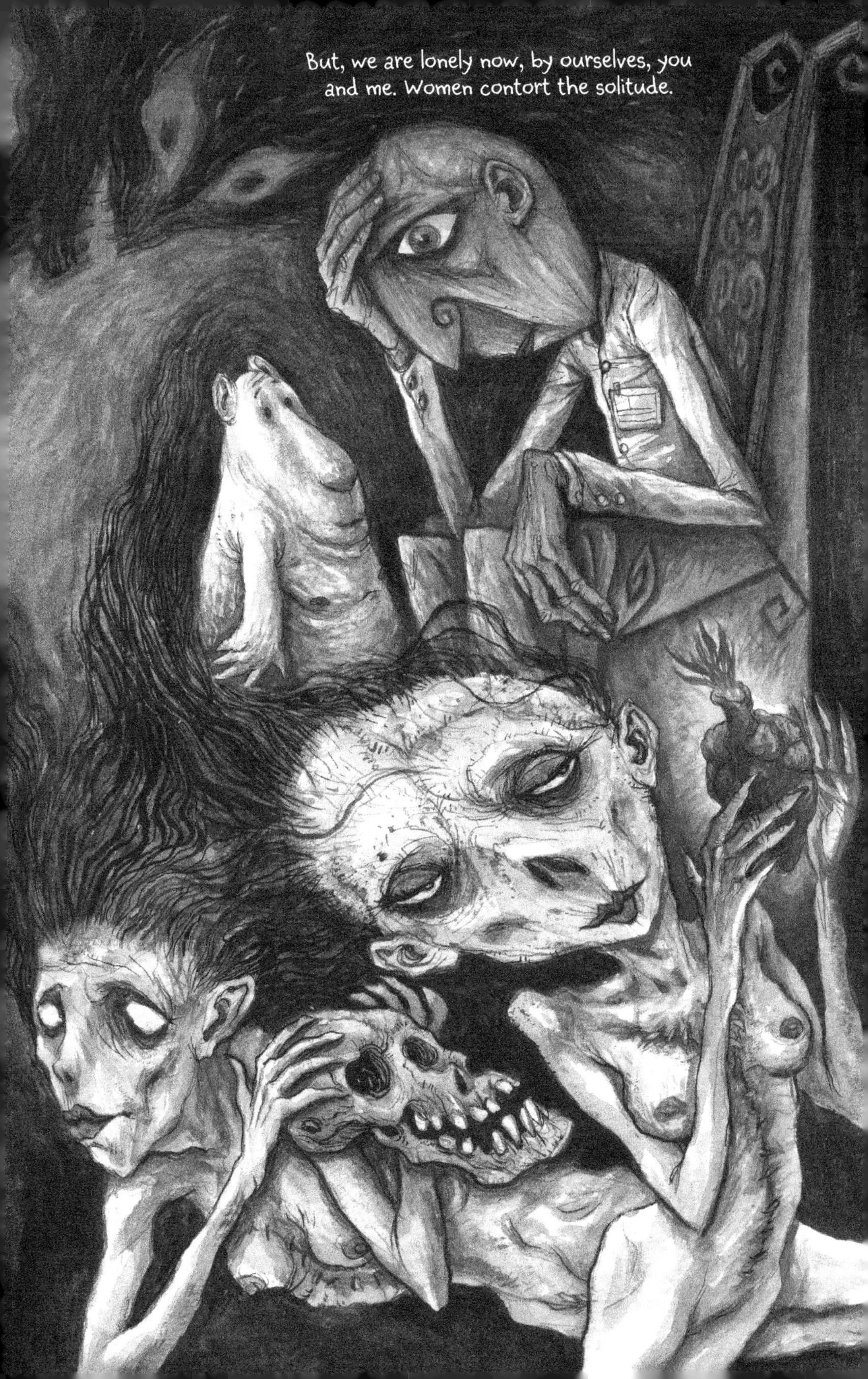
But, we are lonely now, by ourselves, you and me. Women contort the solitude.

CHAPTER THREE: KEEPERS OF STRUCTURE

The wreath of fever melted
like butter
And the smell of tempest wove
in the birch
All of the survivors sang in chorus
And stars are the musical
notations tonight

That shameless lush of flower beds
That insane spring sect--
Time is turning around
faster than Orpheus
Like the wiggling of
a headless insect

It is salvation of the fury...
Silk touches like ripe pomegranate
Built from an ink-secret edifice

In that alchemical amphitheatre
A divine wedding takes place
And each word is its own spouse

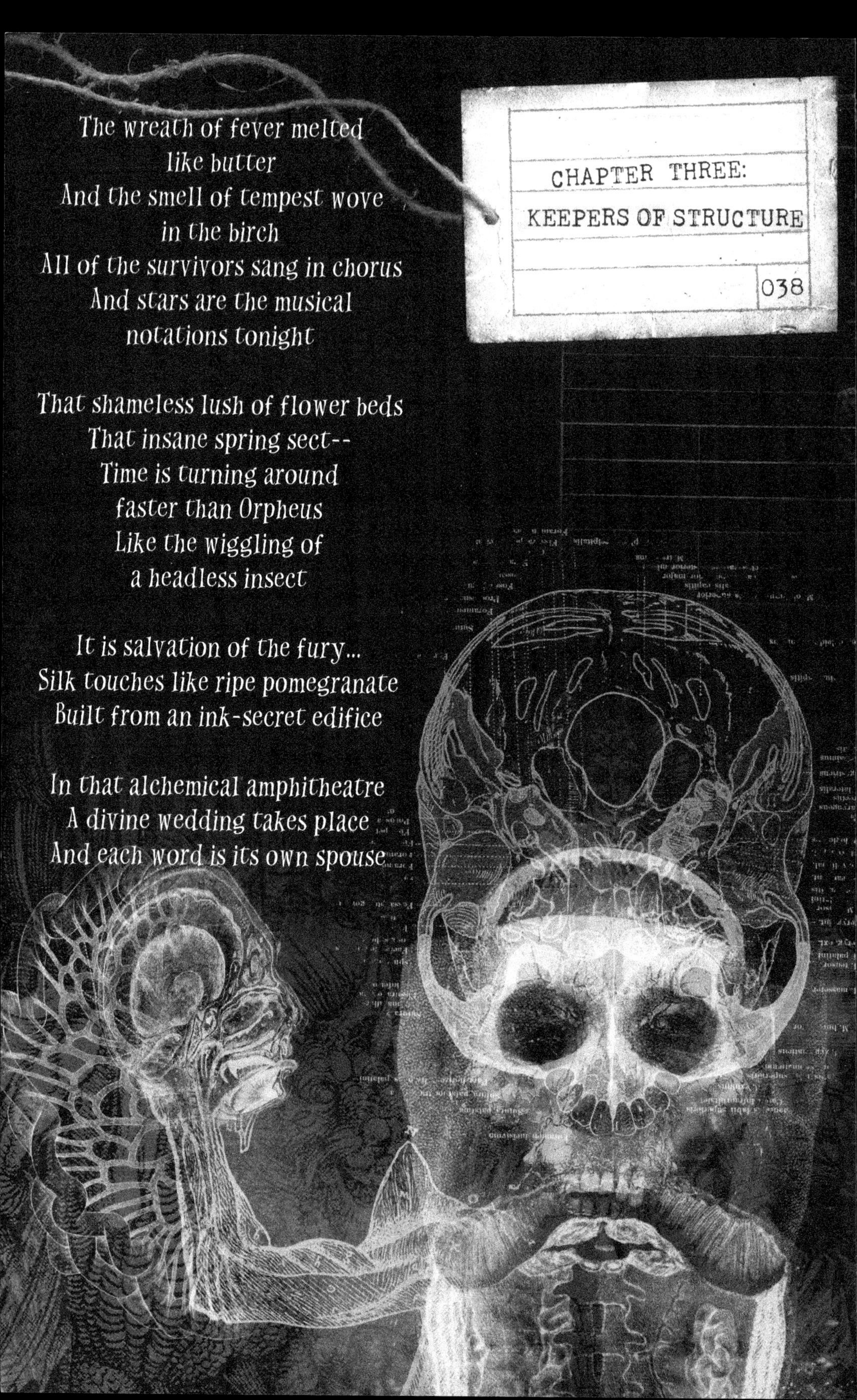

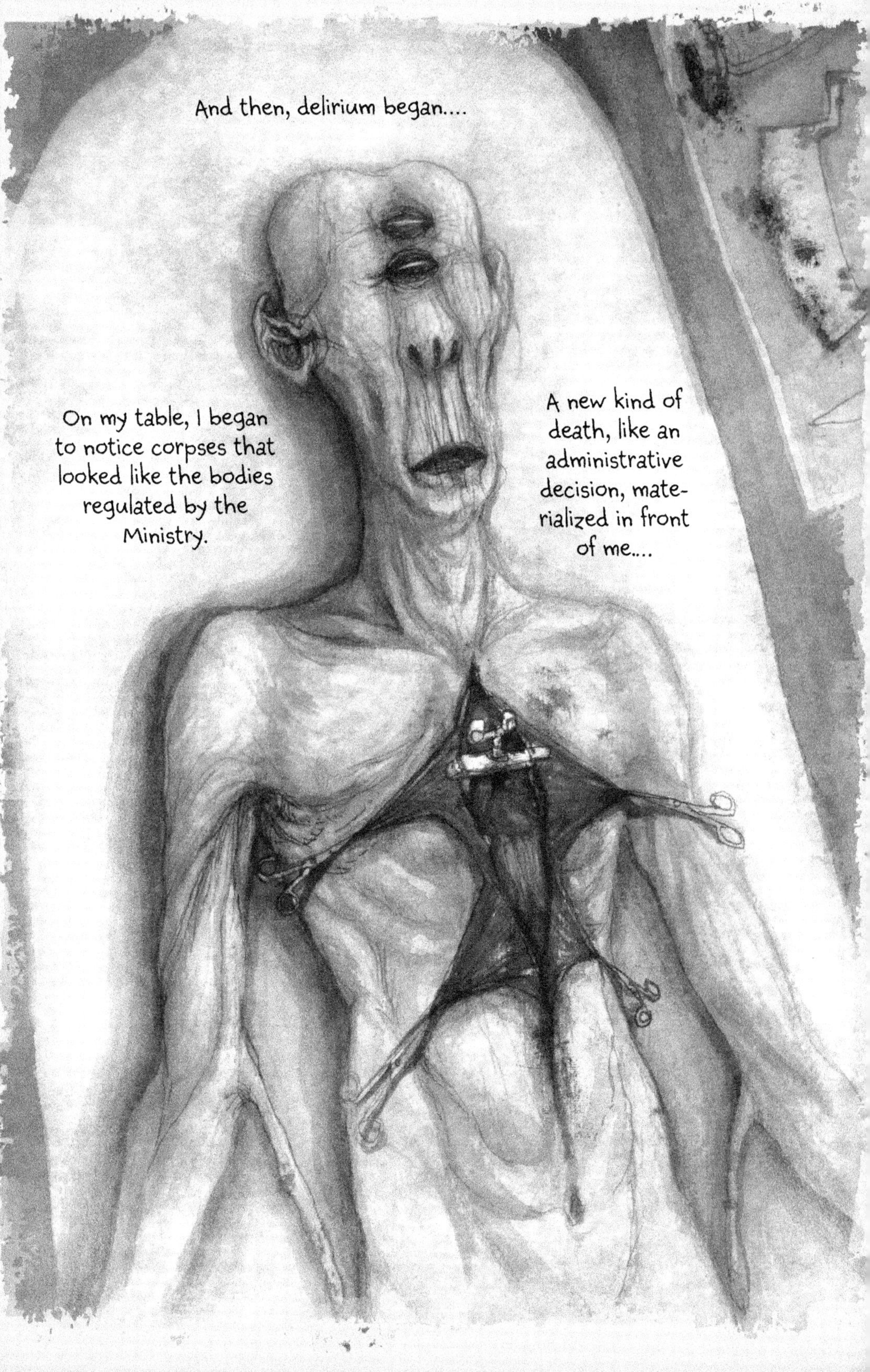

And then, delirium began....
On my table, I began to notice corpses that looked like the bodies regulated by the Ministry.
A new kind of death, like an administrative decision, mate-rialized in front of me....

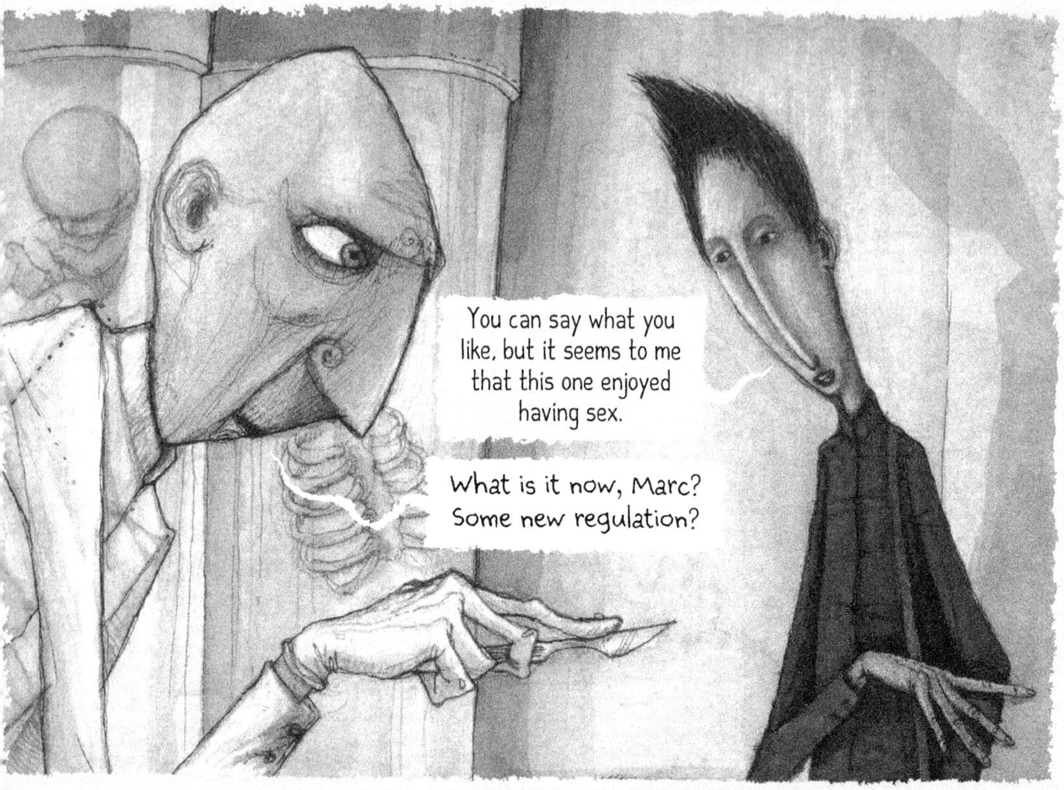
You can say what you like, but it seems to me that this one enjoyed having sex.
What is it now, Marc? Some new regulation?

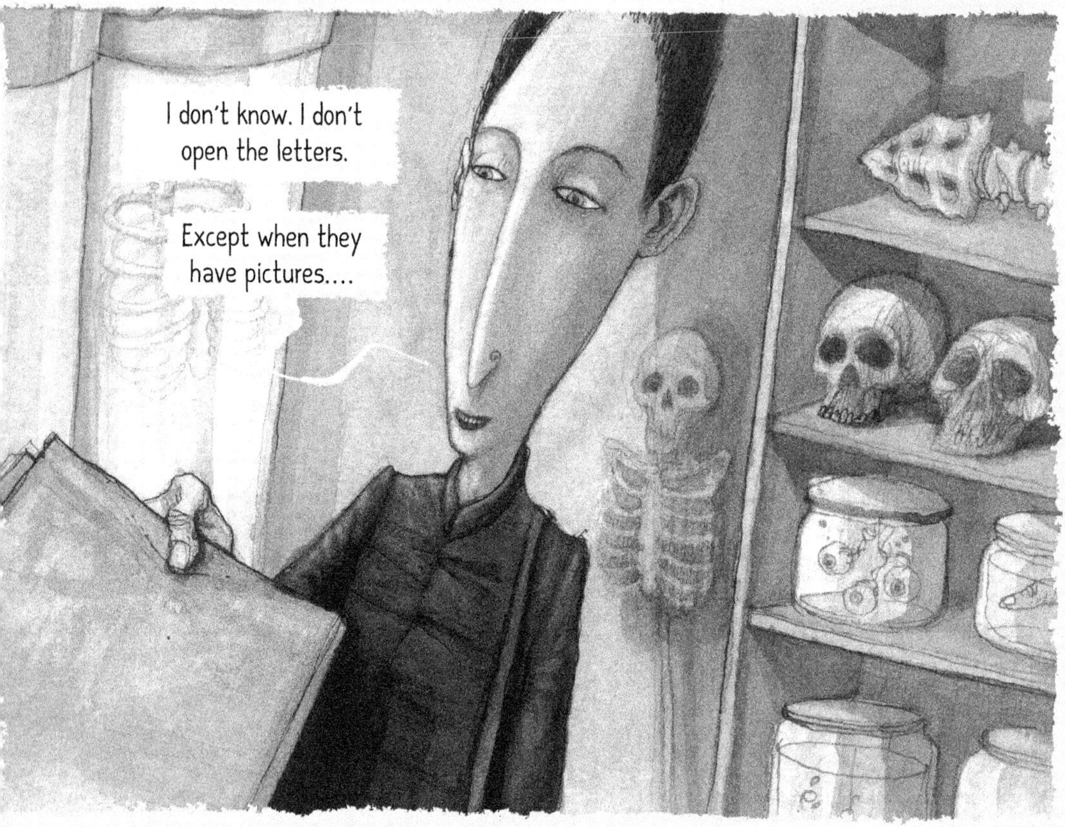
I don't know. I don't open the letters.
Except when they have pictures....

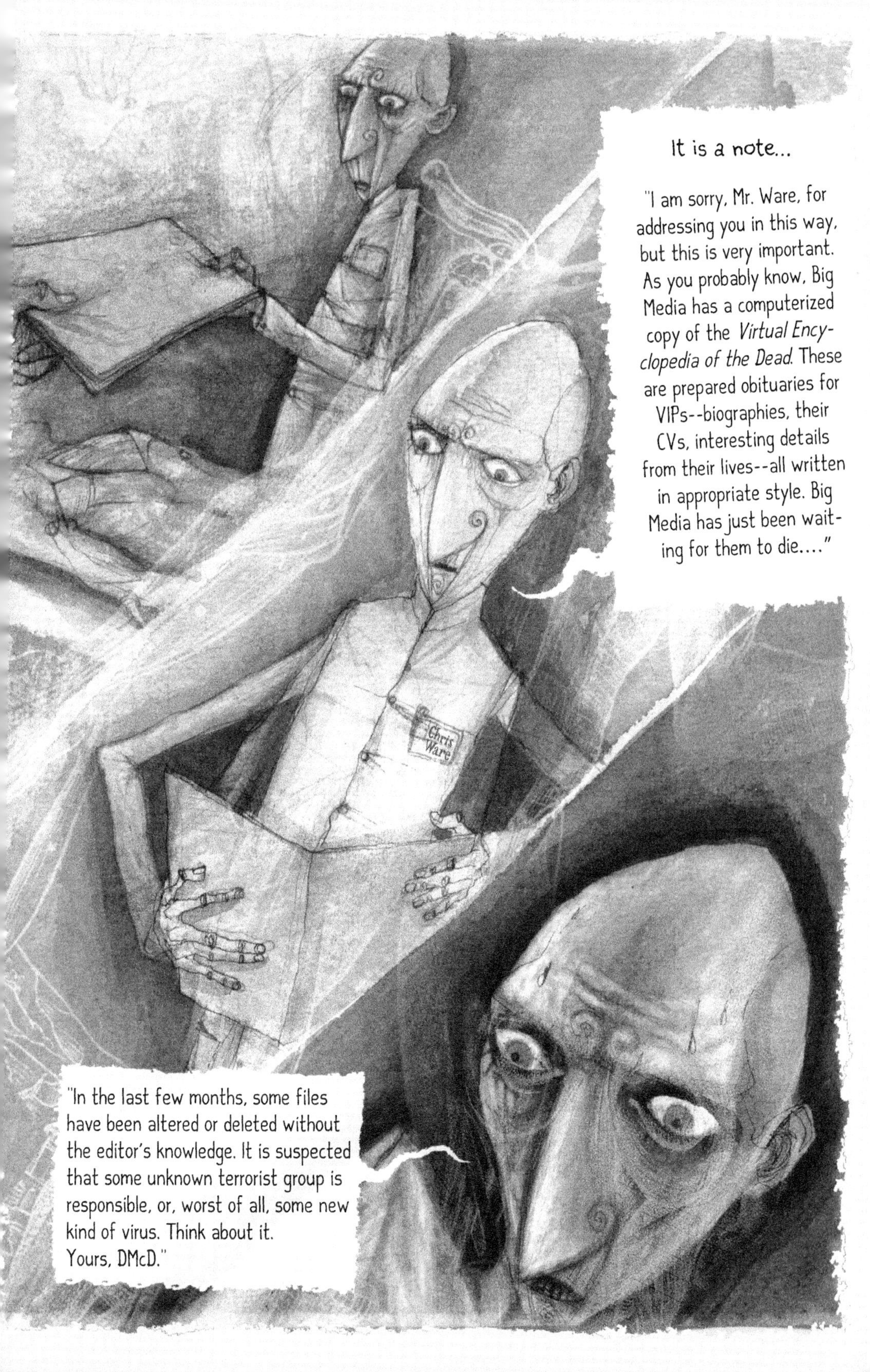
It is a note...
"I am sorry, Mr. Ware, for addressing you in this way, but this is very important. As you probably know, Big Media has a computerized copy of the *Virtual Encyclopedia of the Dead*. These are prepared obituaries for VIPs--biographies, their CVs, interesting details from their lives--all written in appropriate style. Big Media has just been waiting for them to die...."
Chris Ware
"In the last few months, some files have been altered or deleted without the editor's knowledge. It is suspected that some unknown terrorist group is responsible, or, worst of all, some new kind of virus. Think about it.
Yours, DMcD."

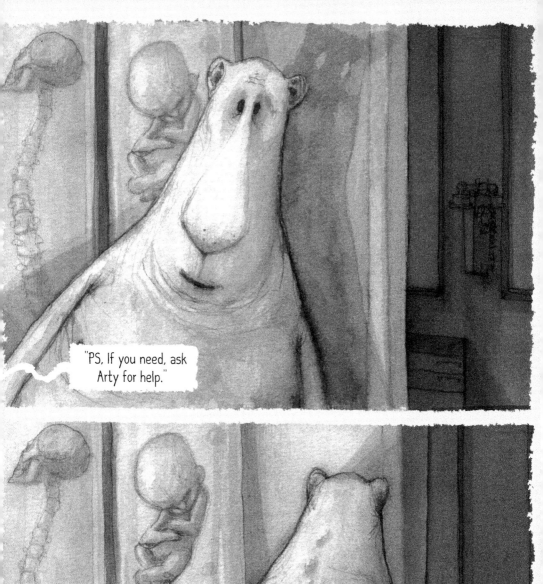

"PS, If you need, ask Arty for help."

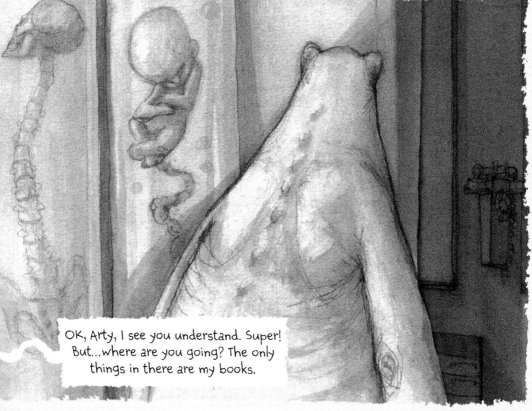

OK, Arty, I see you understand. Super! But...where are you going? The only things in there are my books.

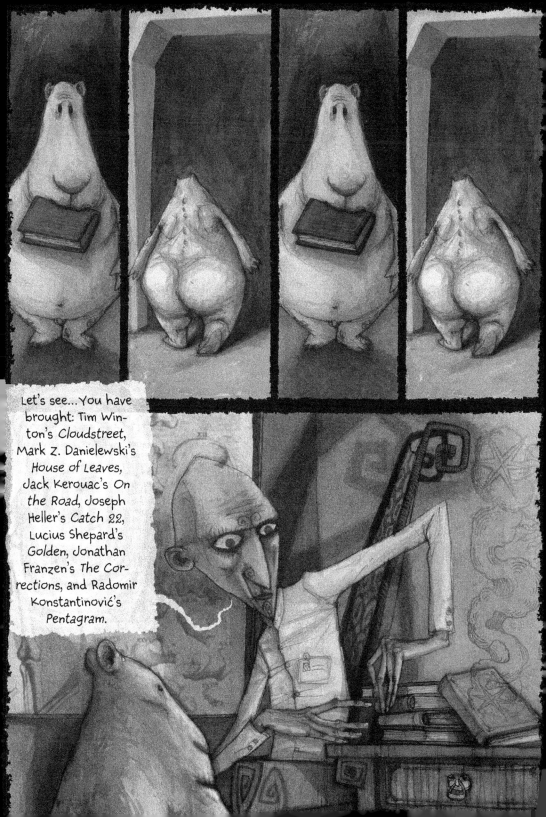

Let's see...You have brought: Tim Winton's *Cloudstreet*, Mark Z. Danielewski's *House of Leaves*, Jack Kerouac's *On the Road*, Joseph Heller's *Catch 22*, Lucius Shepard's *Golden*, Jonathan Franzen's *The Corrections*, and Radomir Konstantinović's *Pentagram*.

If I understand you correctly, I should go to Cloud Street, and find 'House of Leaves,' the other name for the Ministry of Death, in the middle of the road.

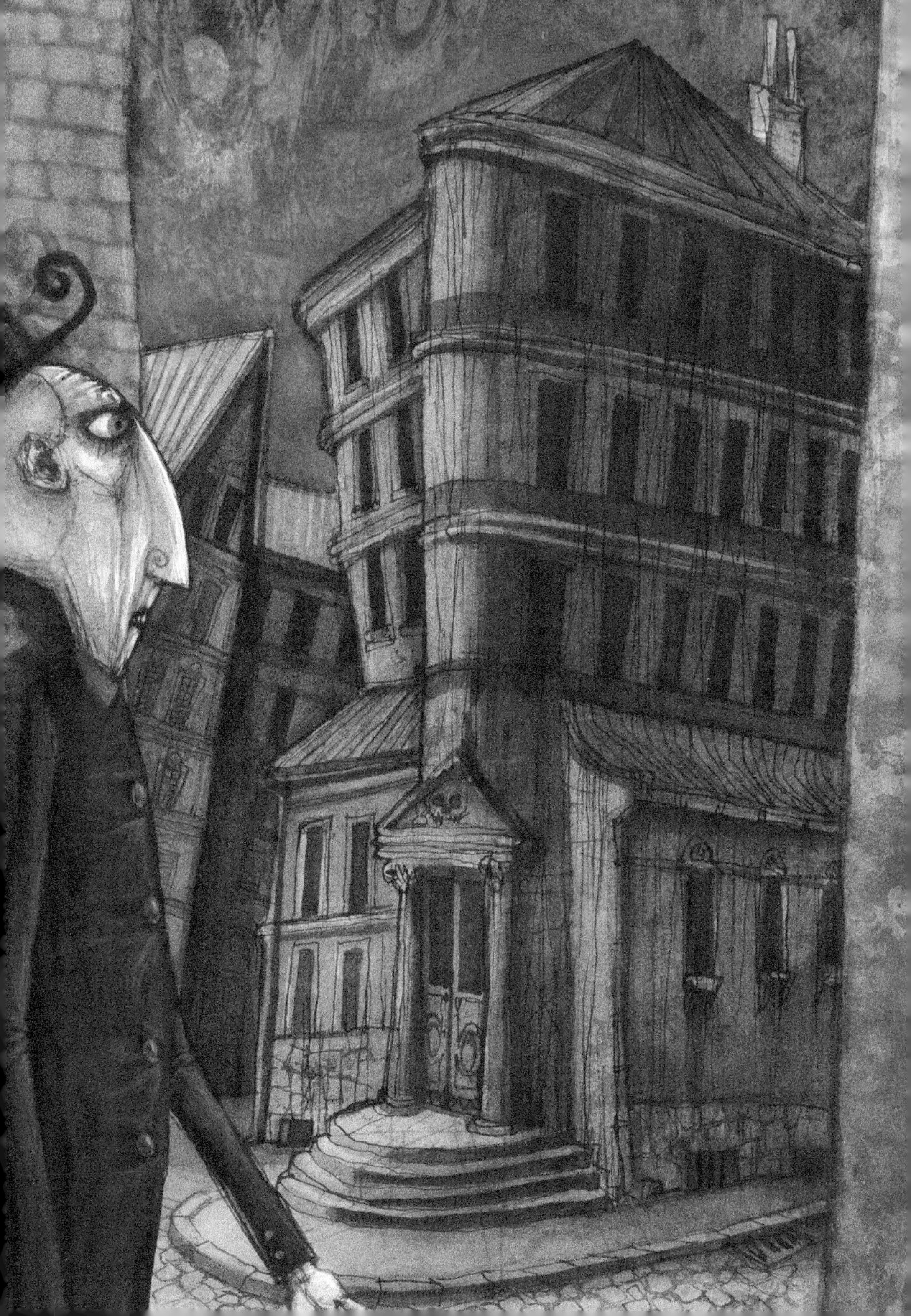

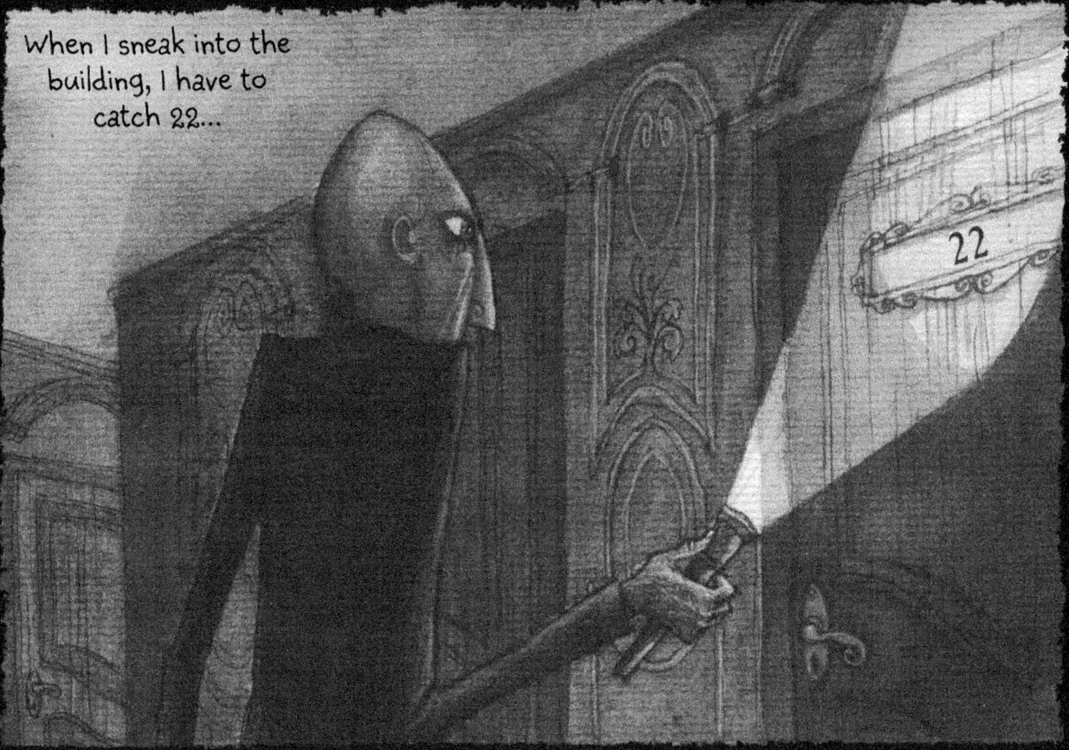
When I sneak into the building, I have to catch 22...
22

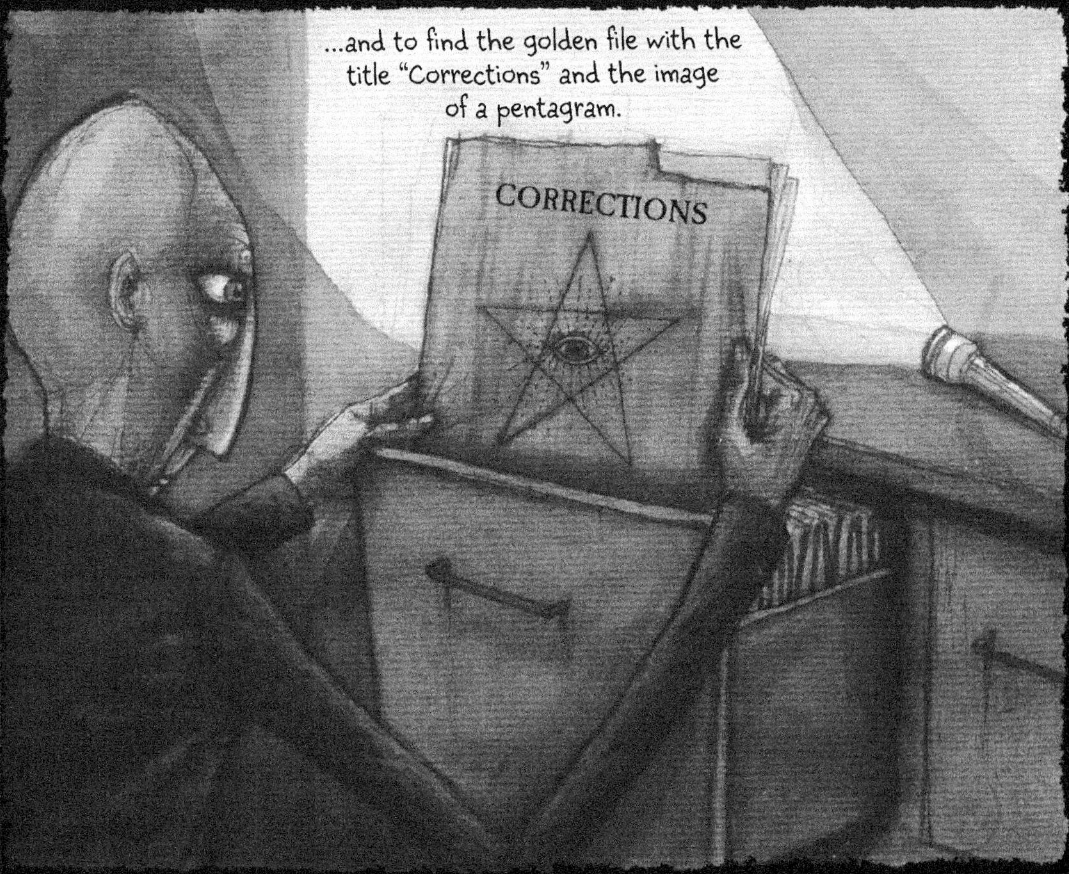
...and to find the golden file with the title "Corrections" and the image of a pentagram.
CORRECTIONS

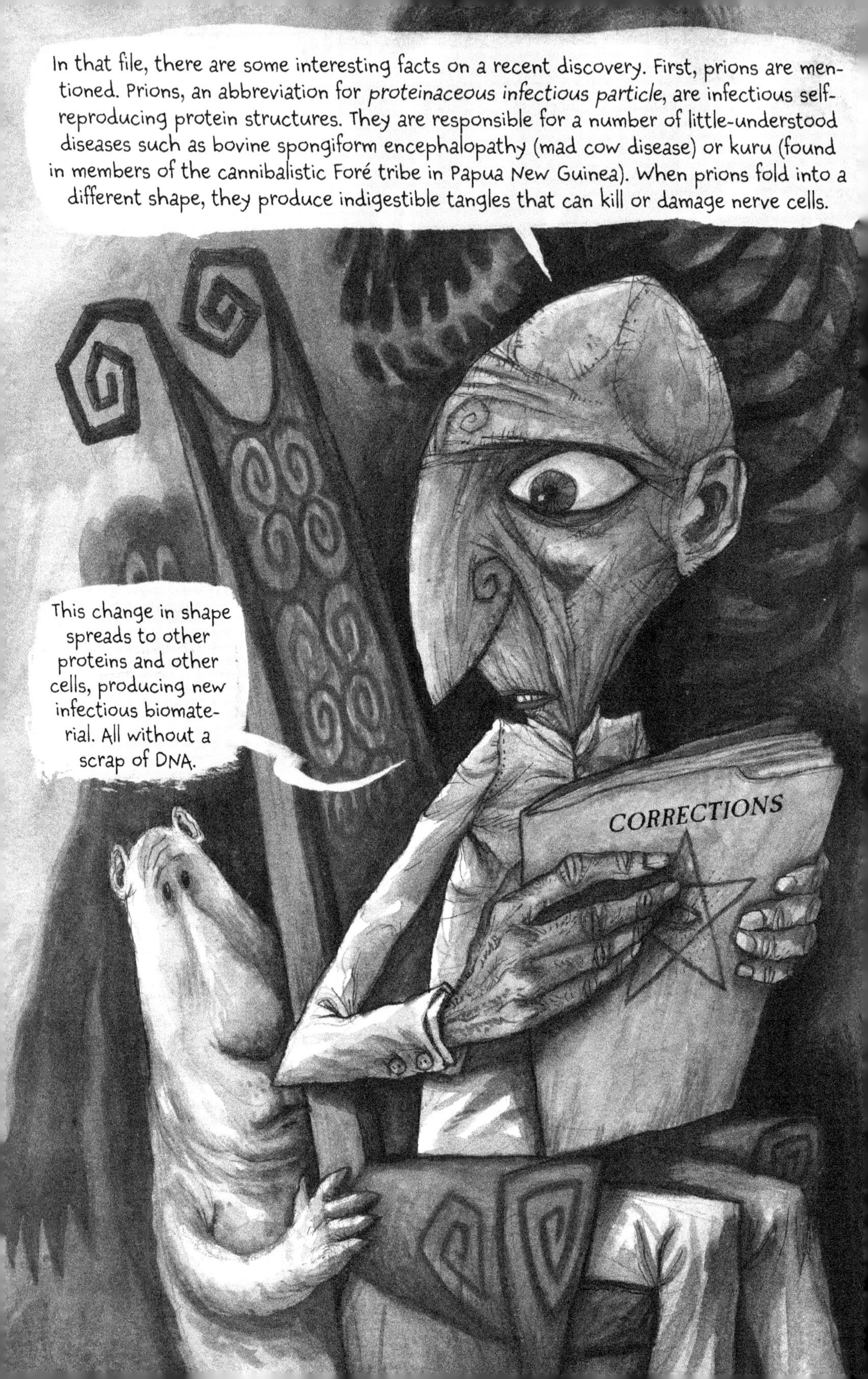
In that file, there are some interesting facts on a recent discovery. First, prions are mentioned. Prions, an abbreviation for *proteinaceous infectious particle*, are infectious self-reproducing protein structures. They are responsible for a number of little-understood diseases such as bovine spongiform encephalopathy (mad cow disease) or kuru (found in members of the cannibalistic Foré tribe in Papua New Guinea). When prions fold into a different shape, they produce indigestible tangles that can kill or damage nerve cells.
This change in shape spreads to other proteins and other cells, producing new infectious biomaterial. All without a scrap of DNA.
CORRECTIONS

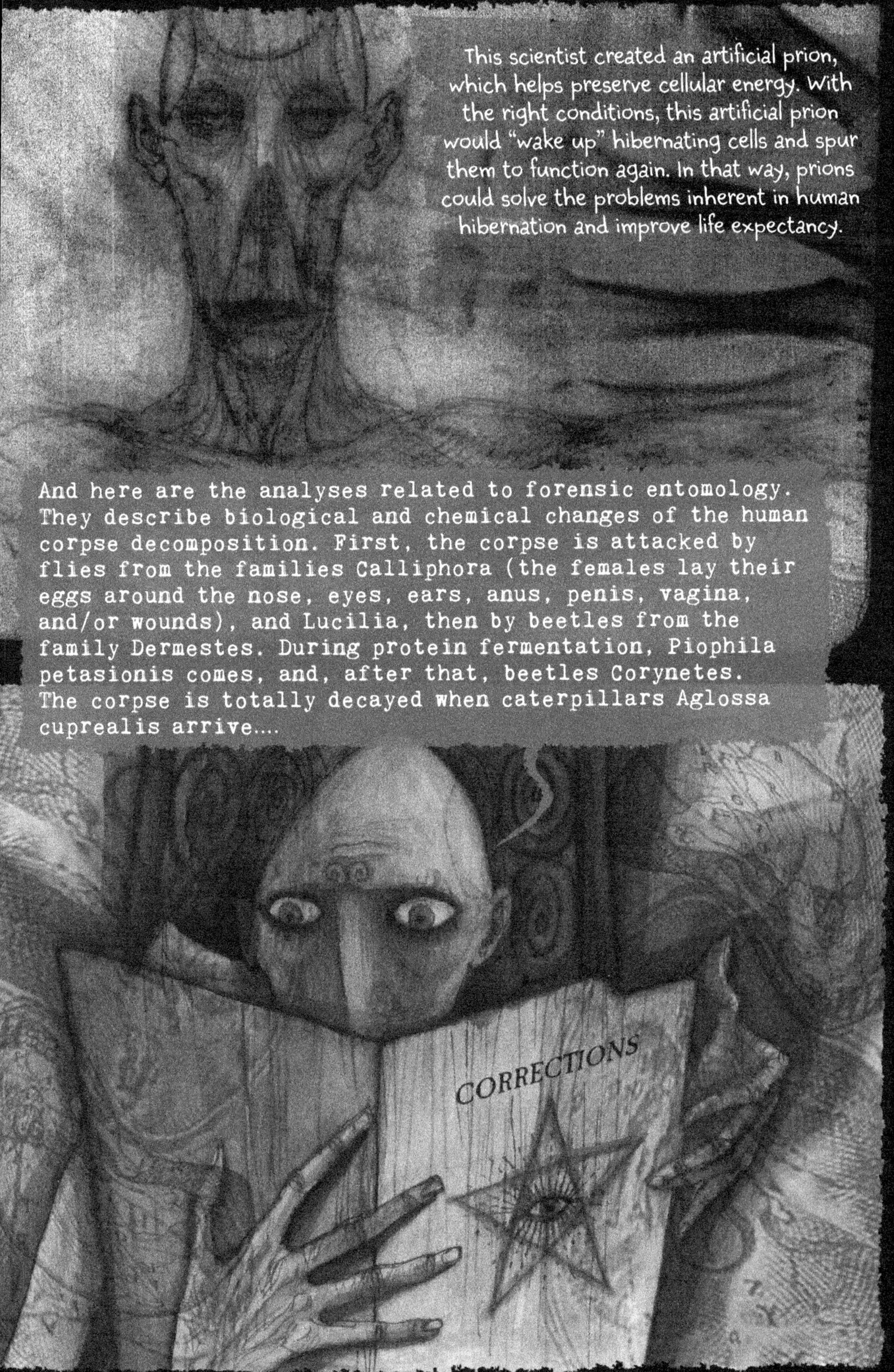
This scientist created an artificial prion, which helps preserve cellular energy. With the right conditions, this artificial prion would "wake up" hibernating cells and spur them to function again. In that way, prions could solve the problems inherent in human hibernation and improve life expectancy.
And here are the analyses related to forensic entomology. They describe biological and chemical changes of the human corpse decomposition. First, the corpse is attacked by flies from the families Calliphora (the females lay their eggs around the nose, eyes, ears, anus, penis, vagina, and/or wounds), and Lucilia, then by beetles from the family Dermestes. During protein fermentation, Piophila petasionis comes, and, after that, beetles Corynetes. The corpse is totally decayed when caterpillars Aglossa cuprealis arrive....
CORRECTIONS

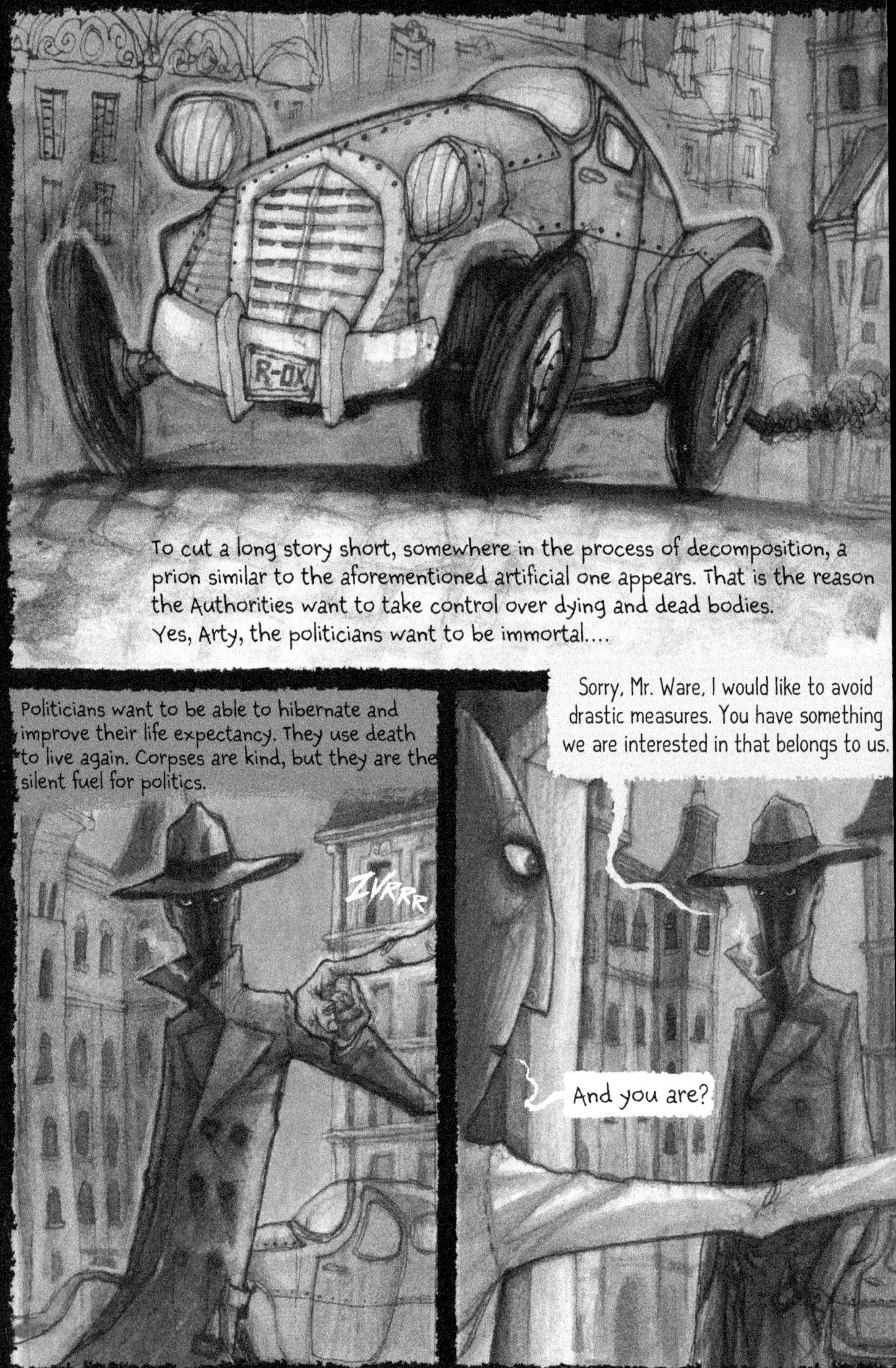
R-OX
To cut a long story short, somewhere in the process of decomposition, a prion similar to the aforementioned artificial one appears. That is the reason the Authorities want to take control over dying and dead bodies.
Yes, Arty, the politicians want to be immortal....
Politicians want to be able to hibernate and improve their life expectancy. They use death to live again. Corpses are kind, but they are the silent fuel for politics.
ZVRRR
Sorry, Mr. Ware, I would like to avoid drastic measures. You have something we are interested in that belongs to us.
And you are?

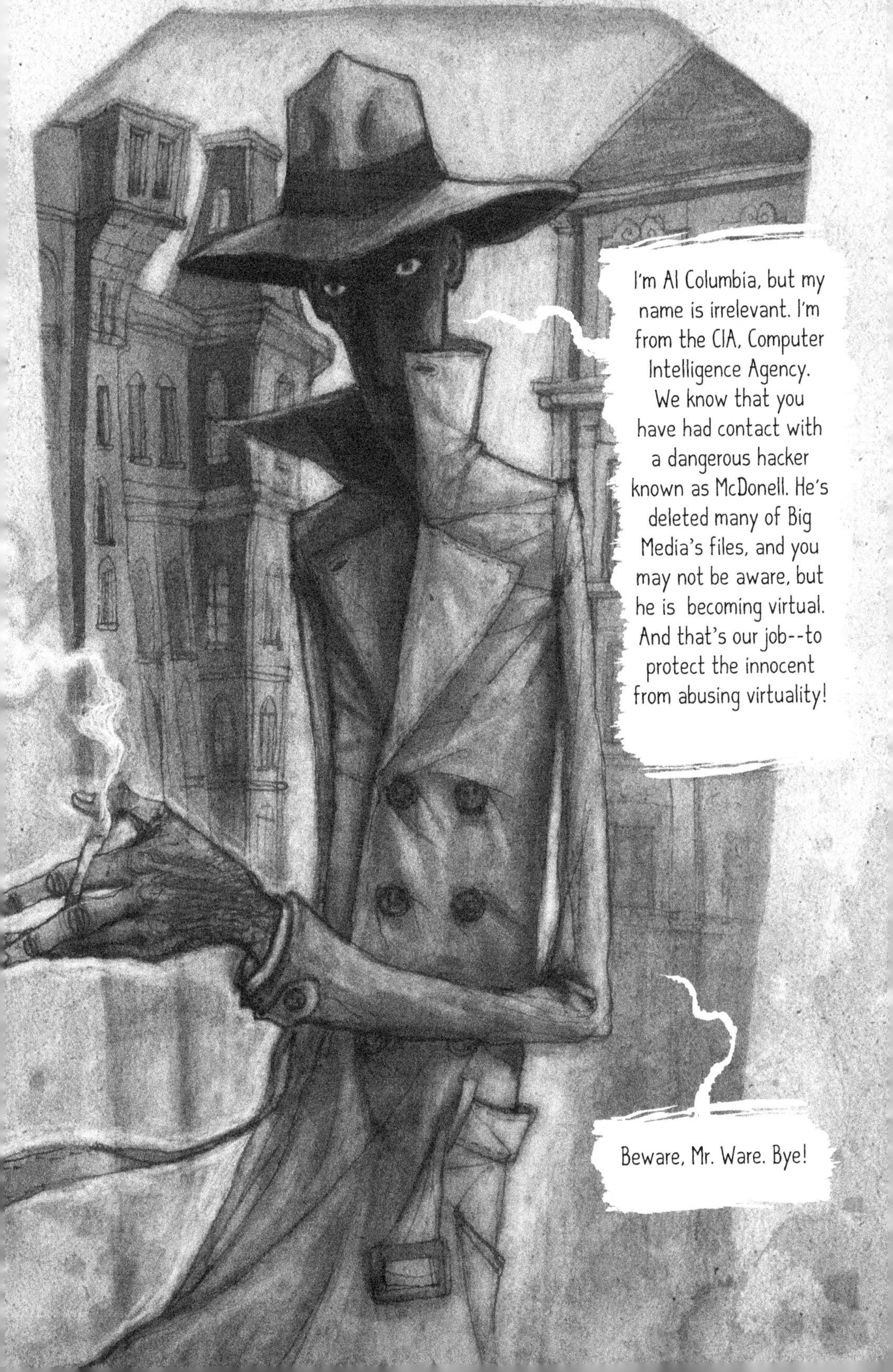
I'm Al Columbia, but my name is irrelevant. I'm from the CIA, Computer Intelligence Agency. We know that you have had contact with a dangerous hacker known as McDonell. He's deleted many of Big Media's files, and you may not be aware, but he is becoming virtual. And that's our job--to protect the innocent from abusing virtuality!
Beware, Mr. Ware. Bye!

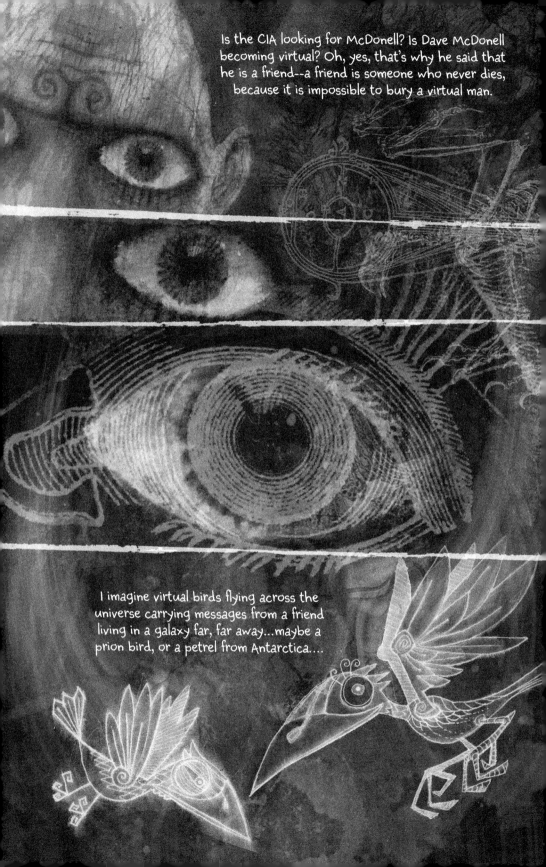

Is the CIA looking for McDonell? Is Dave McDonell becoming virtual? Oh, yes, that's why he said that he is a friend--a friend is someone who never dies, because it is impossible to bury a virtual man.

I imagine virtual birds flying across the universe carrying messages from a friend living in a galaxy far, far away...maybe a prion bird, or a petrel from Antarctica....

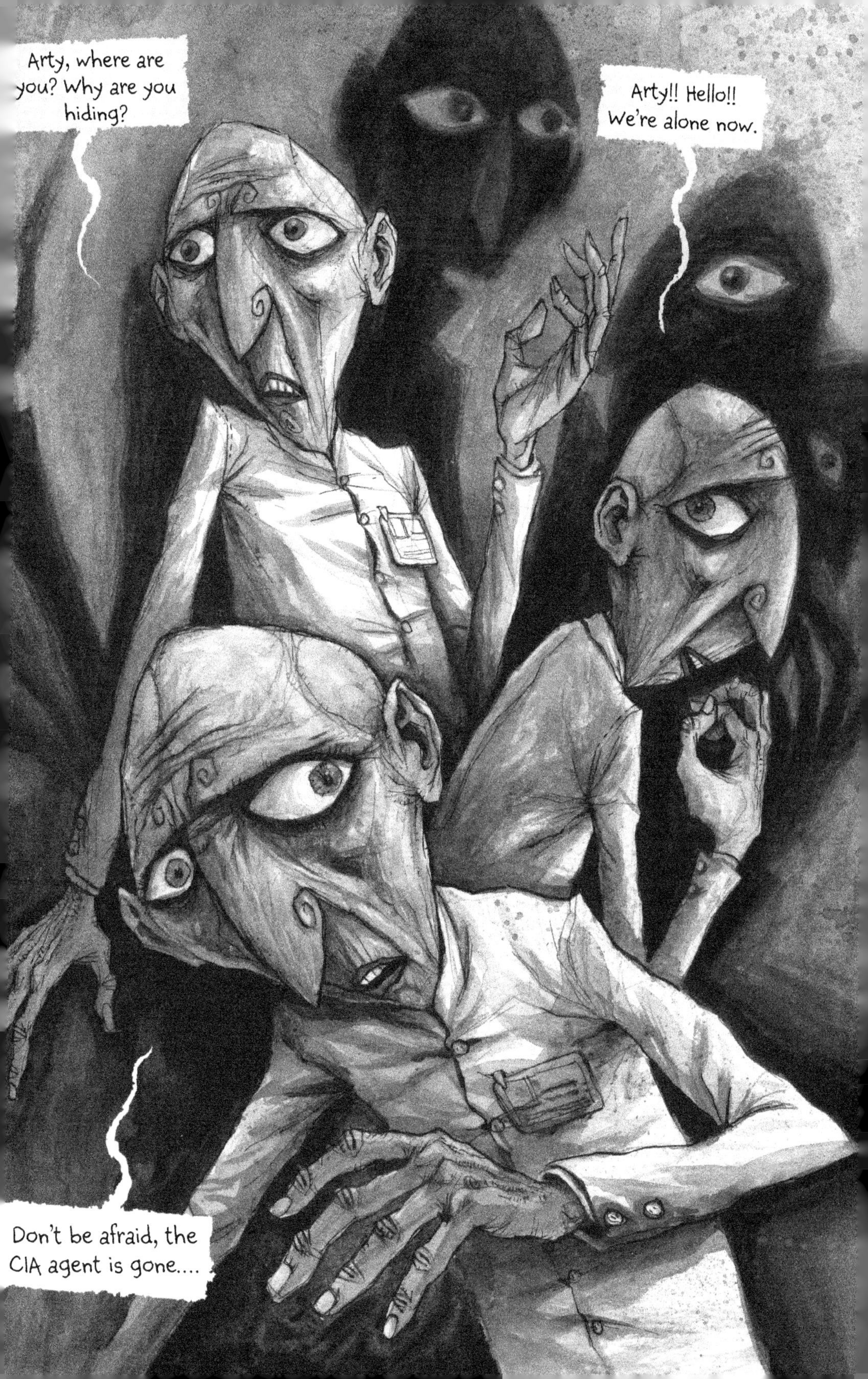
Arty, where are you? Why are you hiding?
Arty!! Hello!! We're alone now.
Don't be afraid, the CIA agent is gone....

CHAPTER FOUR: ARCHETYPE, CEREBROSPINAL FLUID

I am squeezed, drowned into myself
I am dropping into the innocence
My marrow and blood decay
Like slobber sinking into the mud of bones

Flesh is putrefying, tendons are breaking
My meaningless implosions
Words like vessels are falling apart
Rising of ruby downfall

This body of mine is leaking out
I am only the creature made of fog
Cerebral fluid thinks instead of the brain

The white skeleton is shameless

It ascends into the sky's abyss
A torrent of me in my empty body

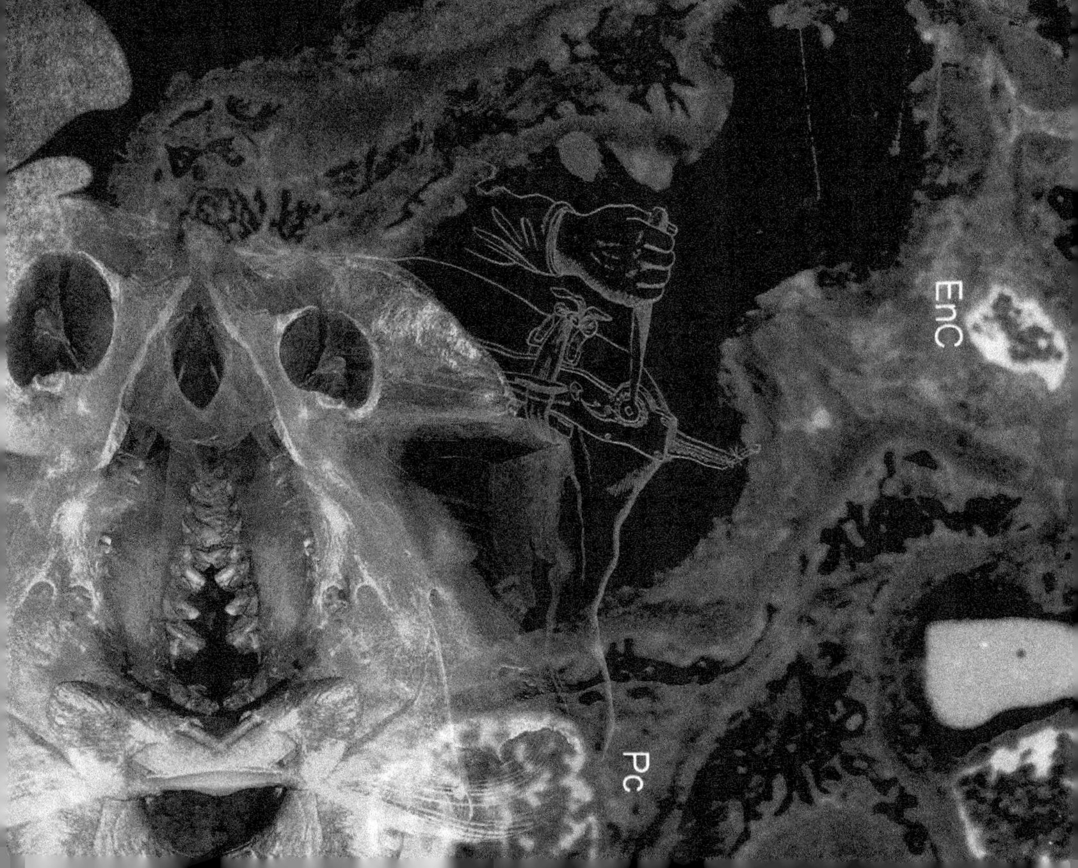
EnC
Pc

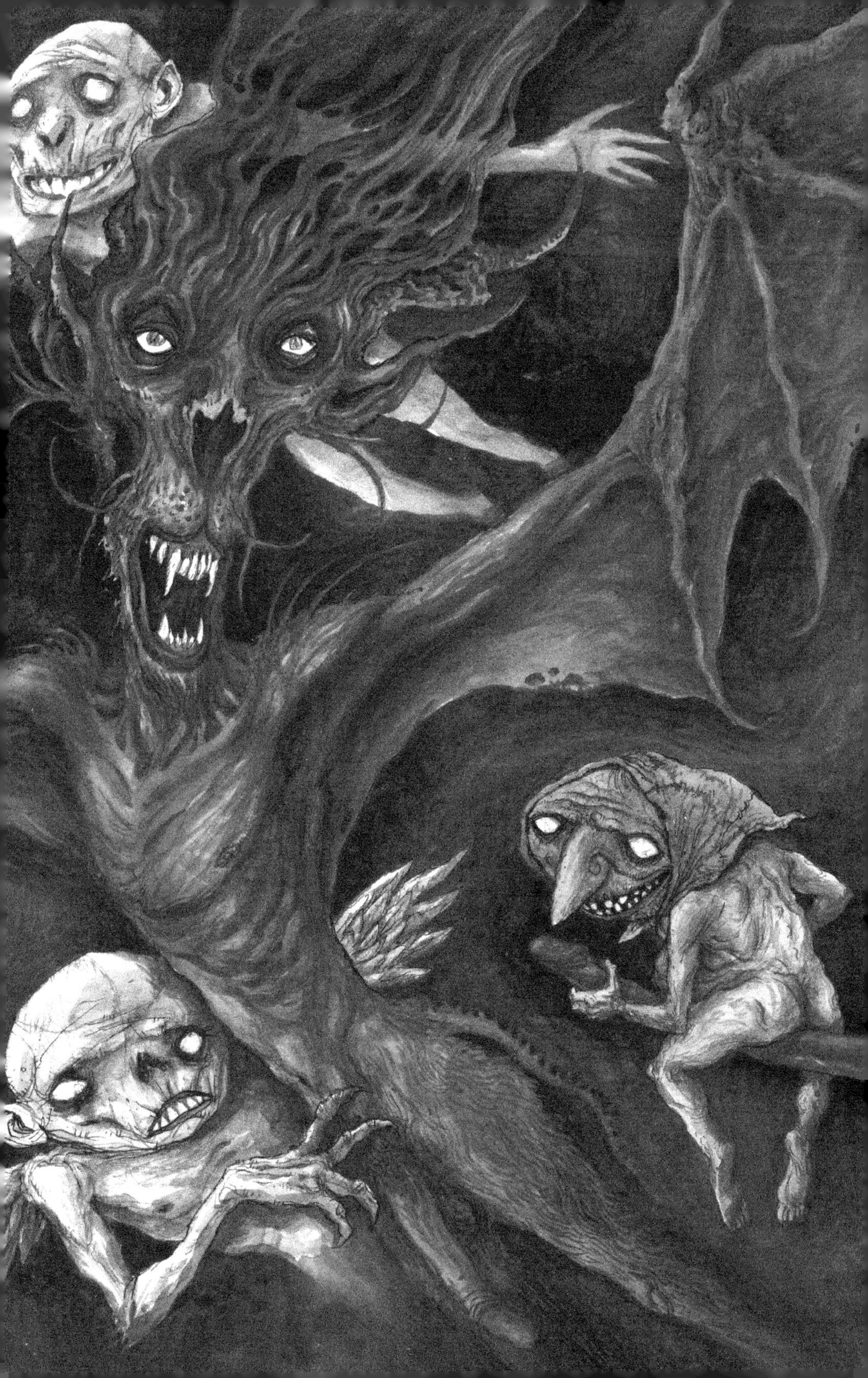

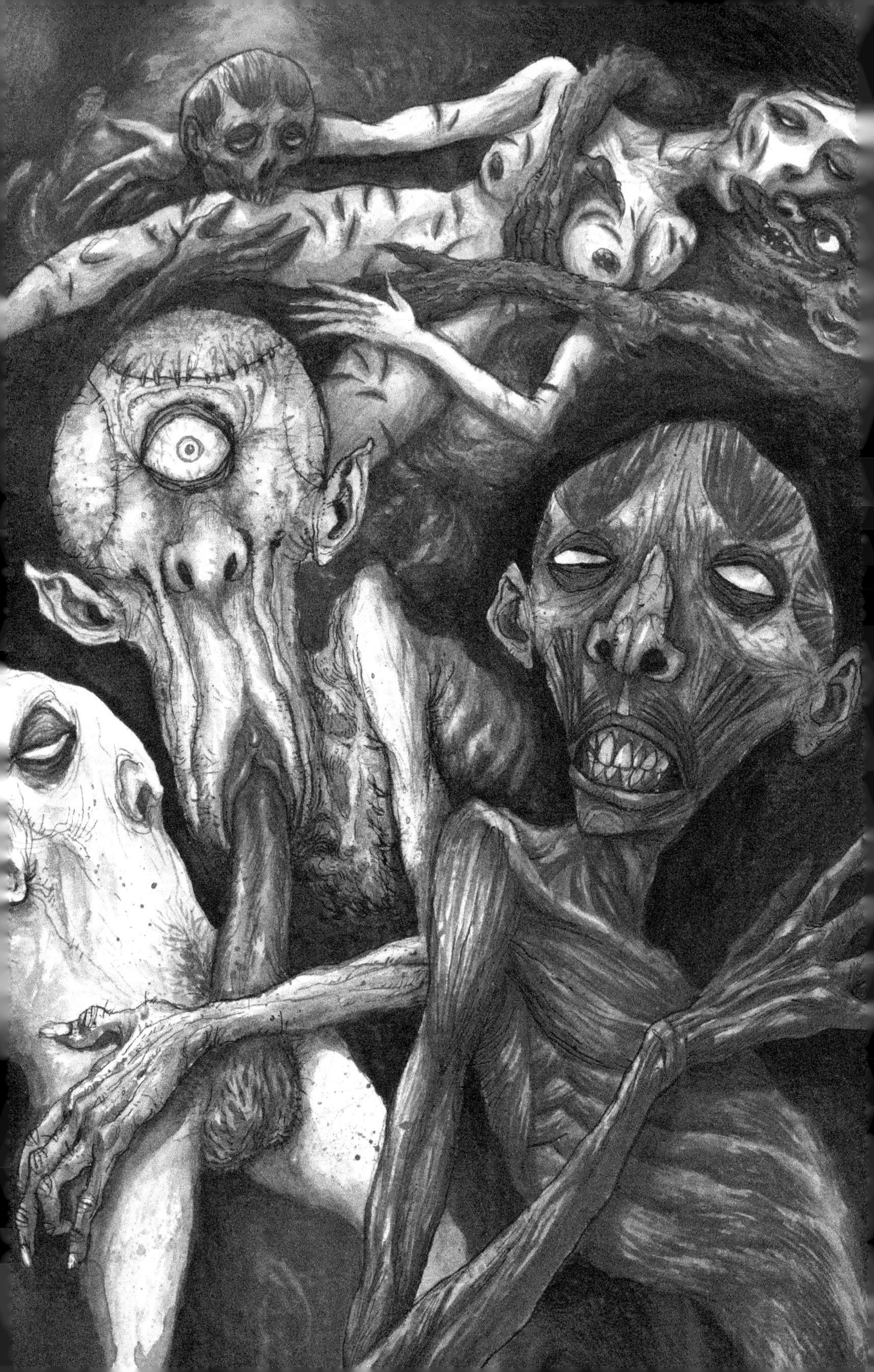

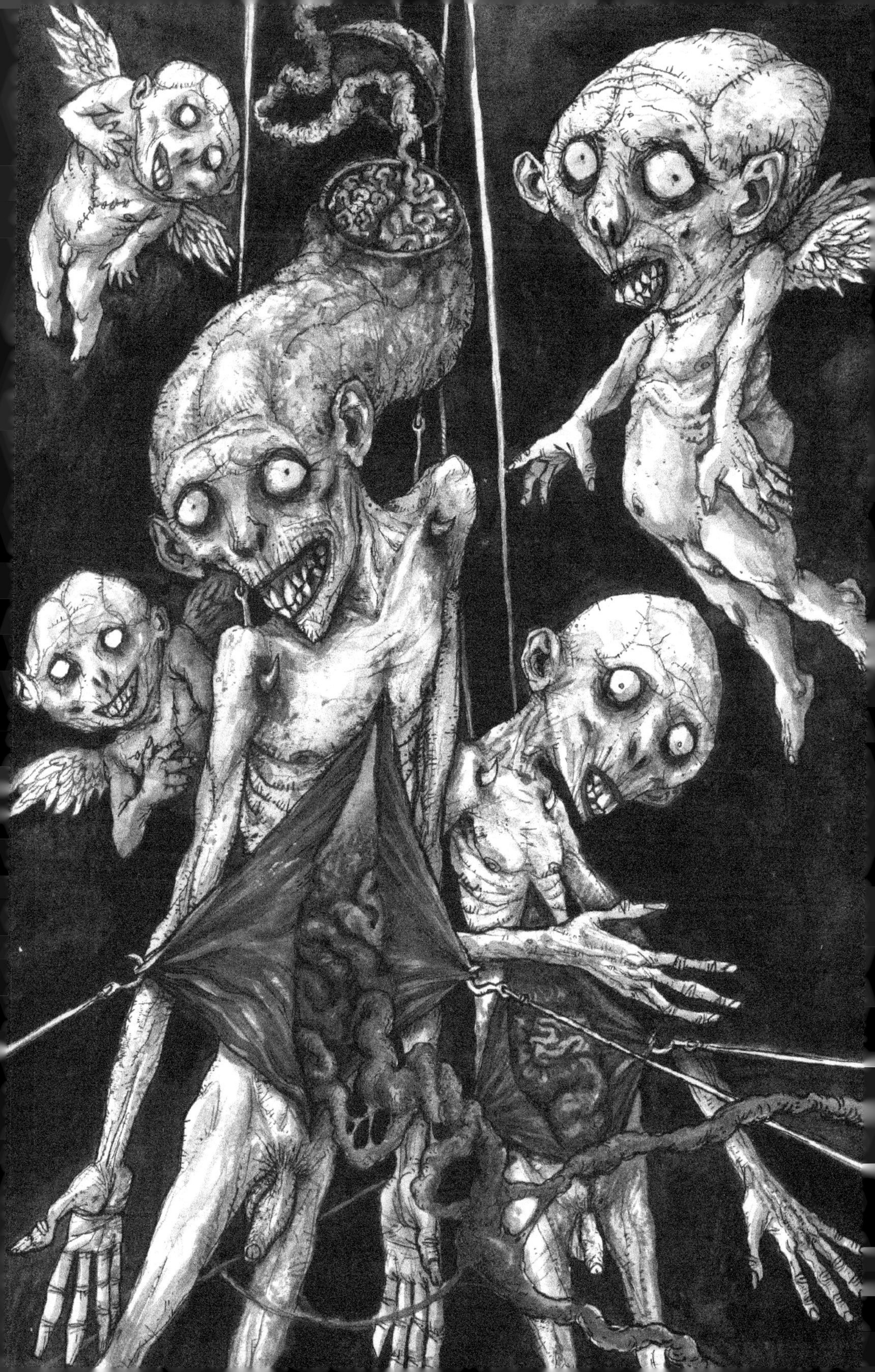

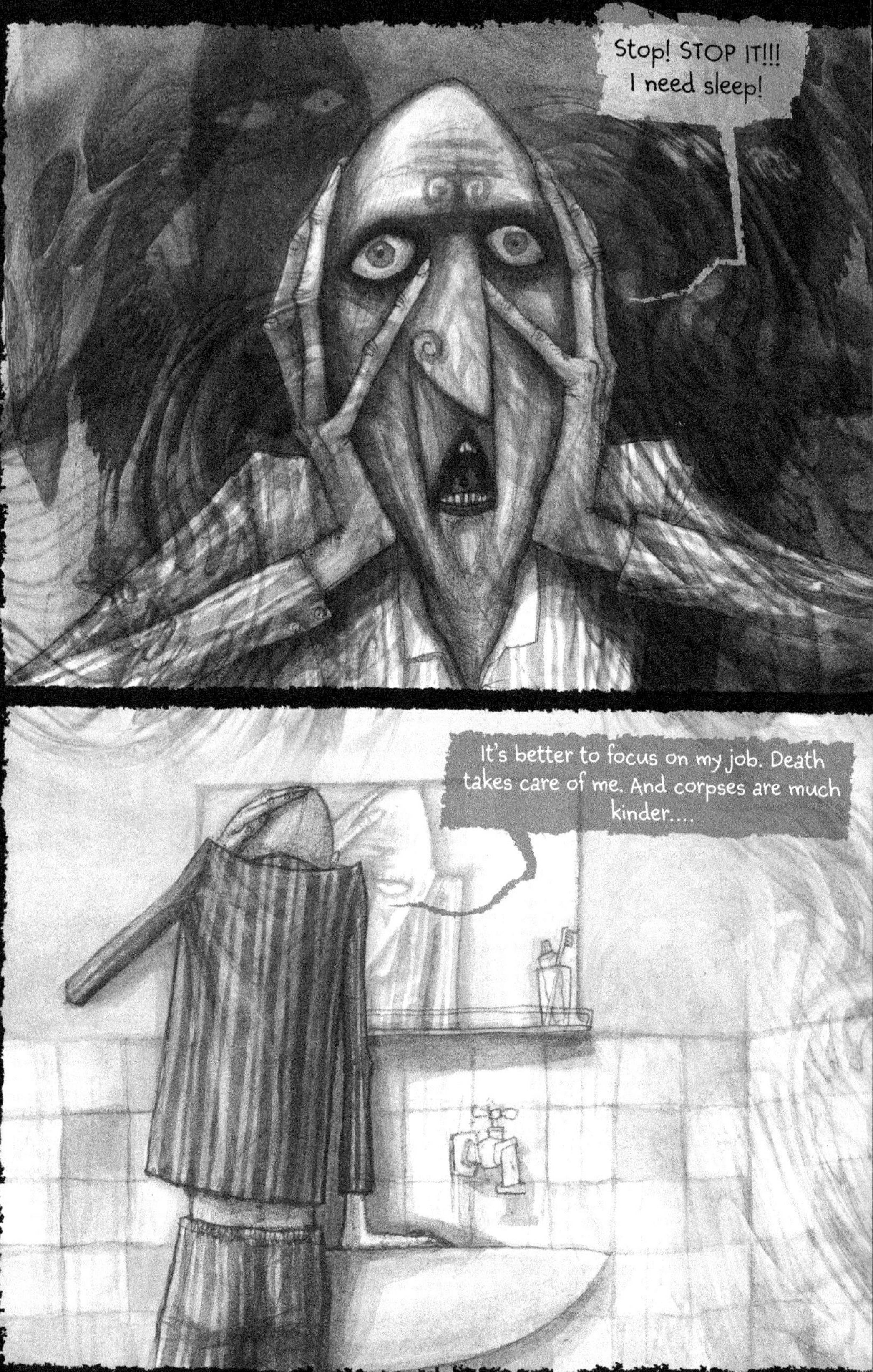
Stop! STOP IT!!! I need sleep!
It's better to focus on my job. Death takes care of me. And corpses are much kinder....

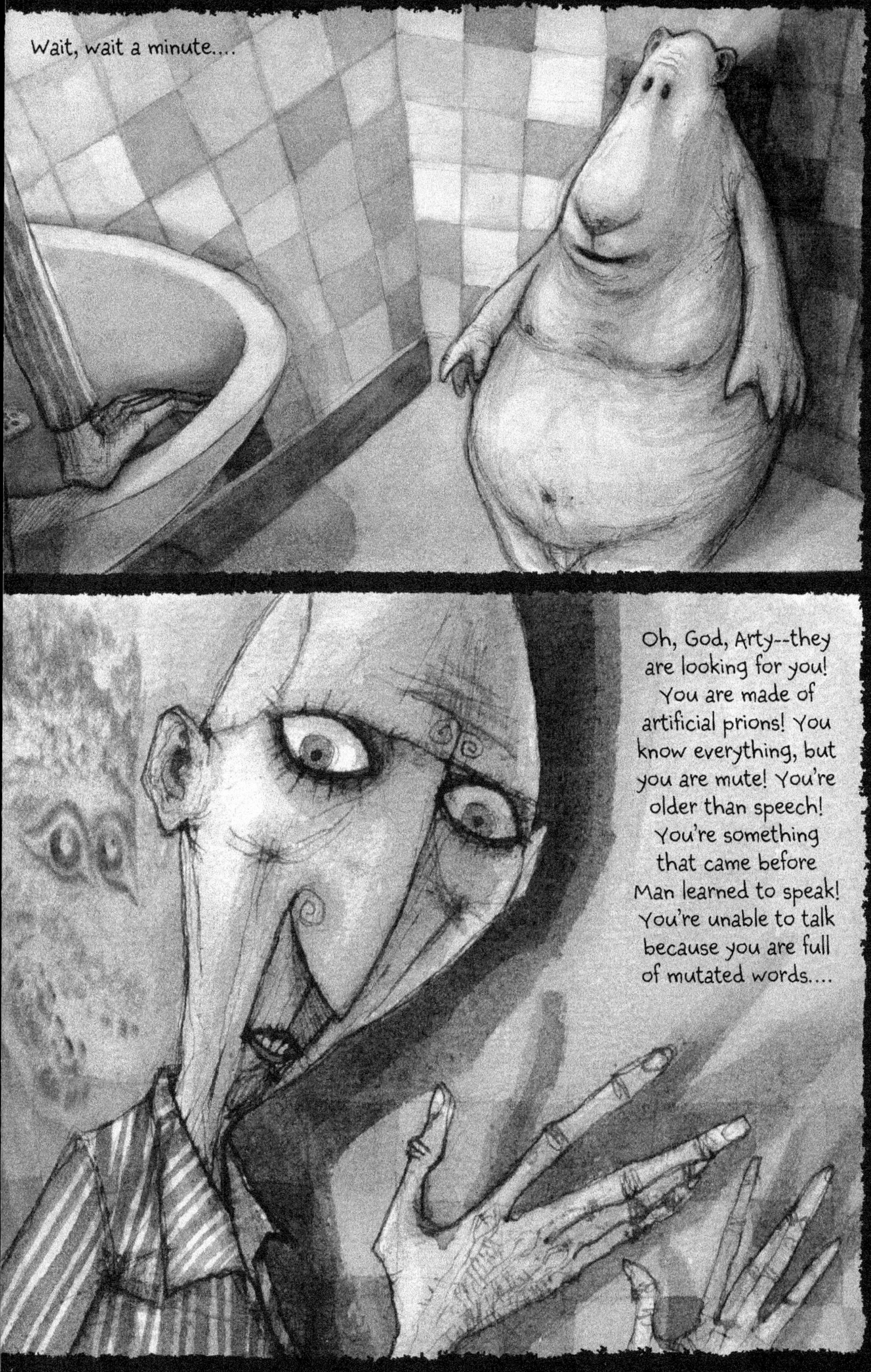
Wait, wait a minute....
Oh, God, Arty--they are looking for you! You are made of artificial prions! You know everything, but you are mute! You're older than speech! You're something that came before Man learned to speak! You're unable to talk because you are full of mutated words....

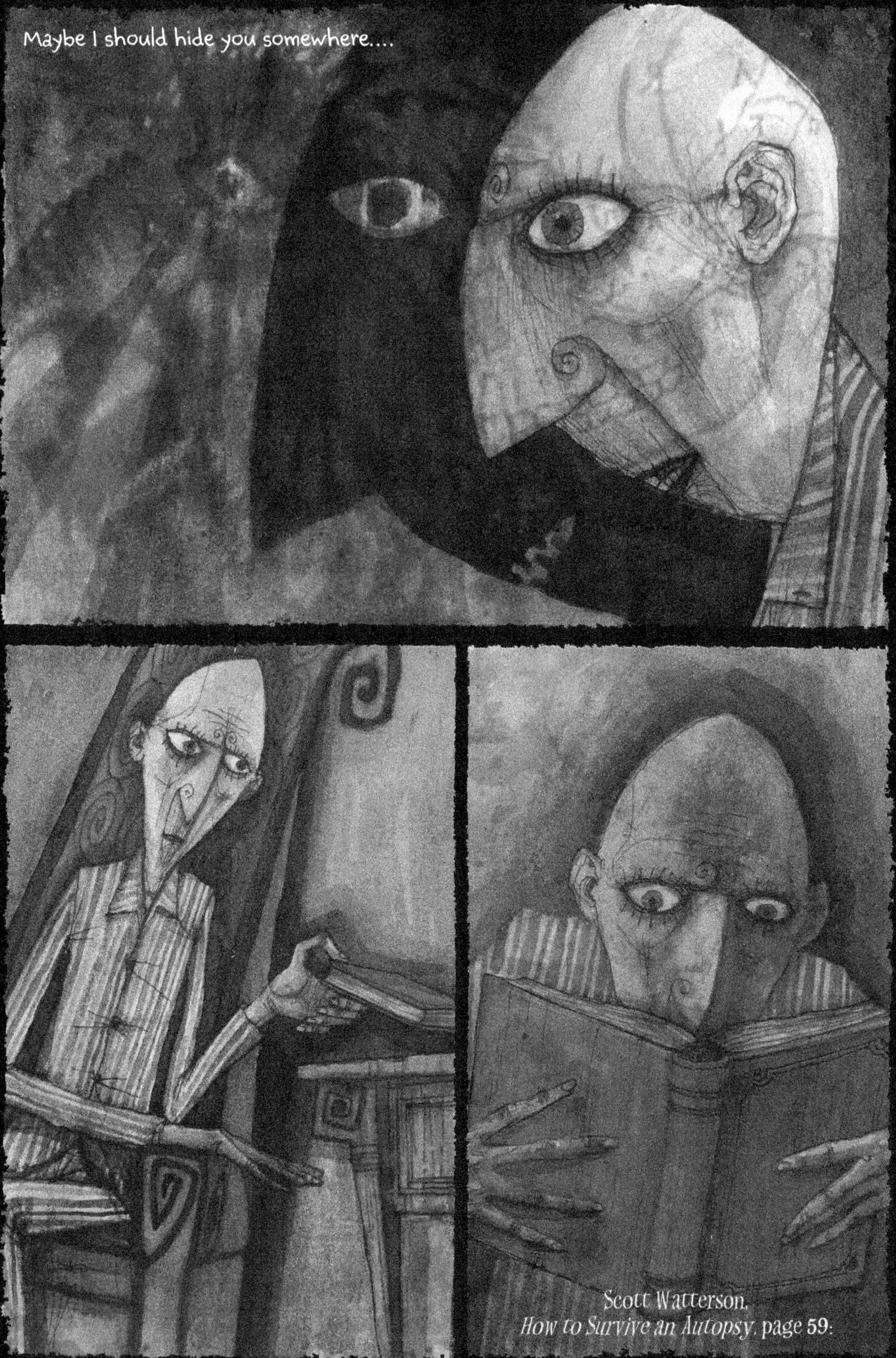
Maybe I should hide you somewhere....
Scott Watterson,
How to Survive an Autopsy, page 59:

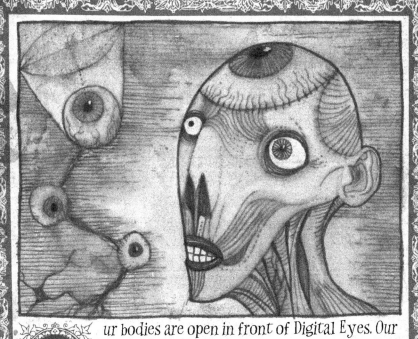

O ur bodies are open in front of Digital Eyes. Our organs, our virtual innards, are displayed as images, and images never sleep. They are the screen's insomnia. The future belongs to generic structures that avoid codes of any kind. That is the ecstasy of self-reproductive bodies without DNA; biomaterial that mutates without genes, genetic engineering new forms of tissue with different purpose. We need to produce new species. Race is a functional category. The archaeology of knowledge becomes archaeology of media. Bright new ideas are simply various digital formats. Knowledge is the style of choosing. To create is to select.

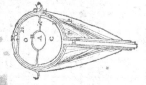

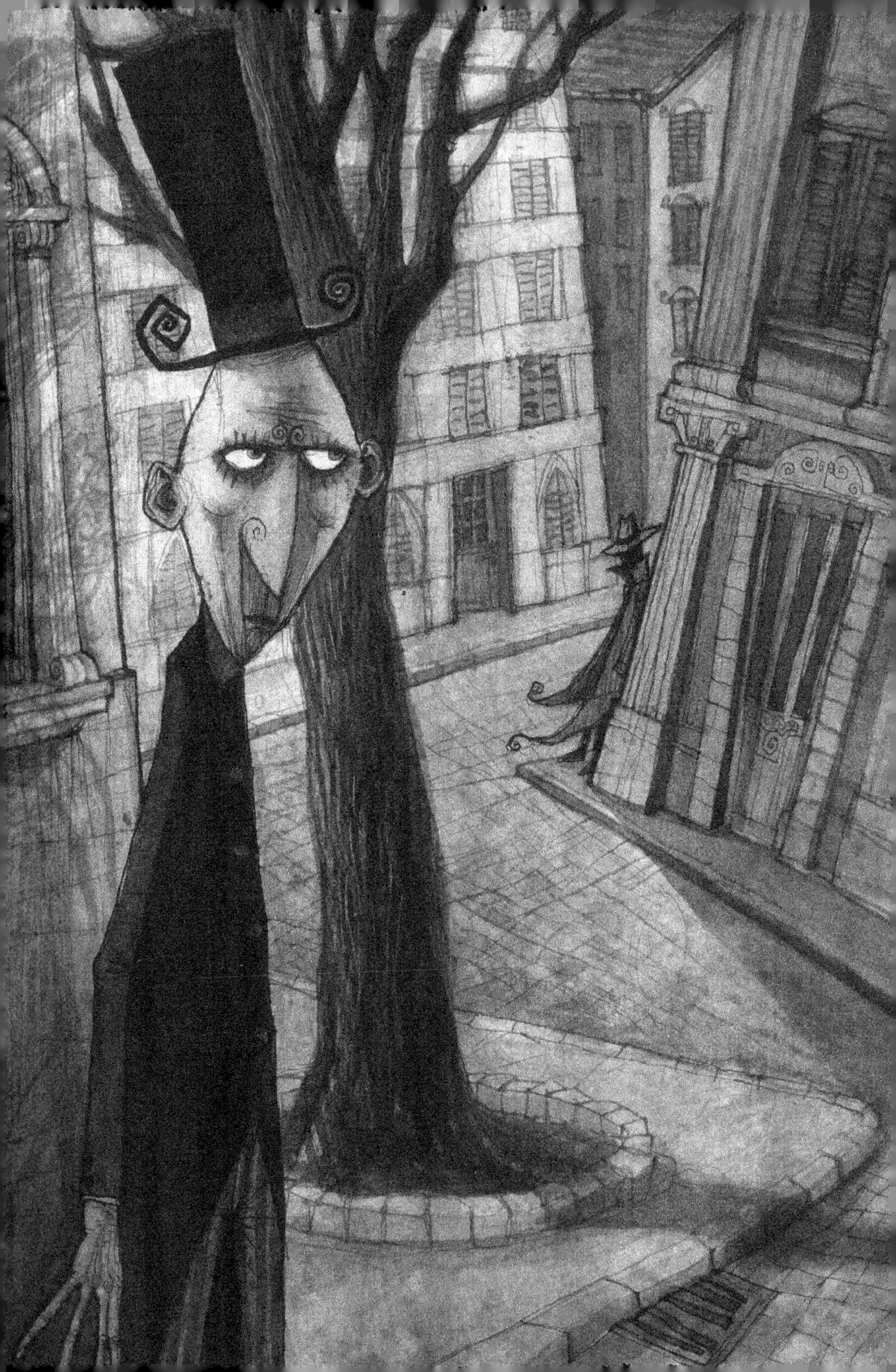

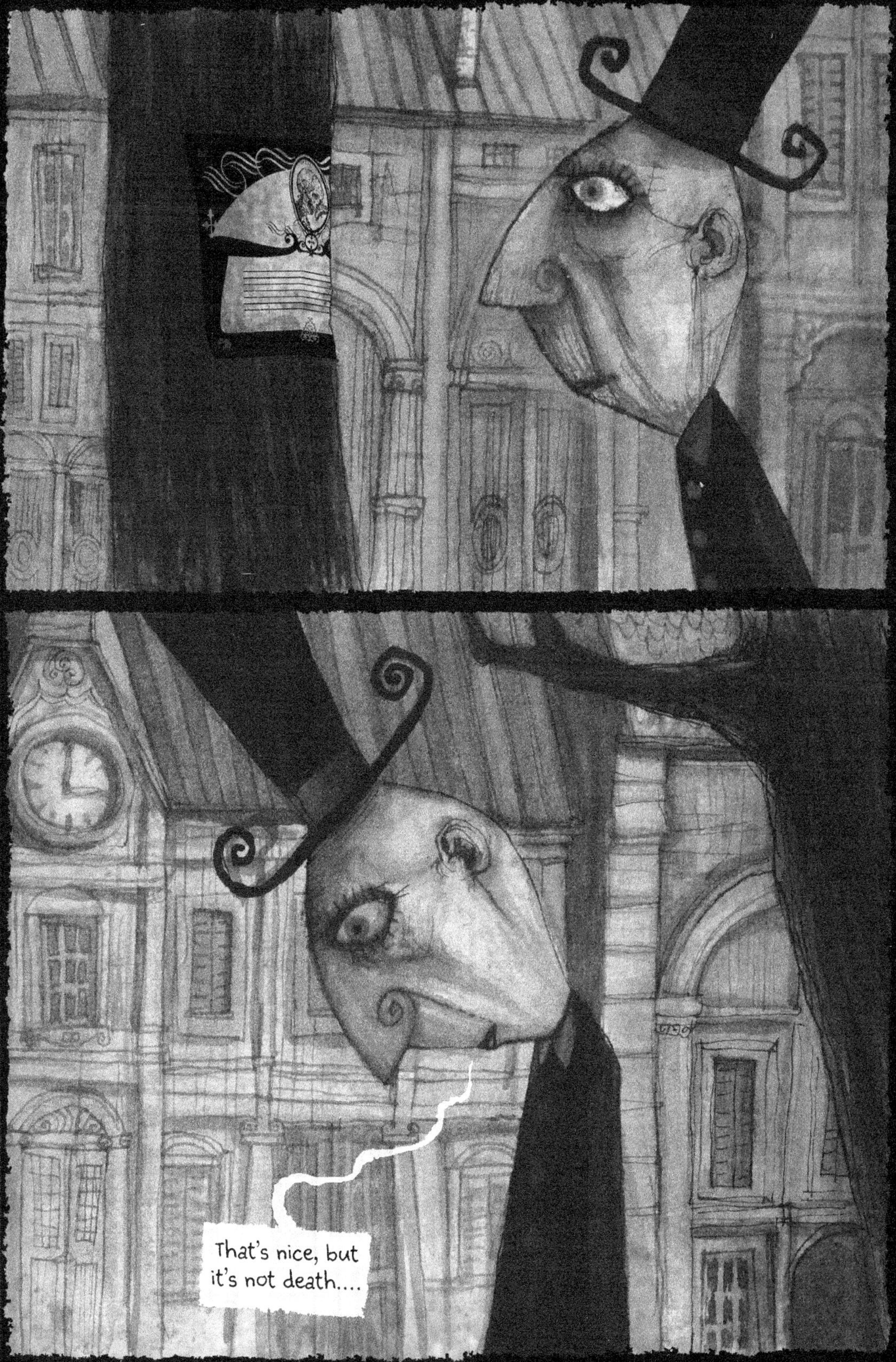
That's nice, but it's not death....

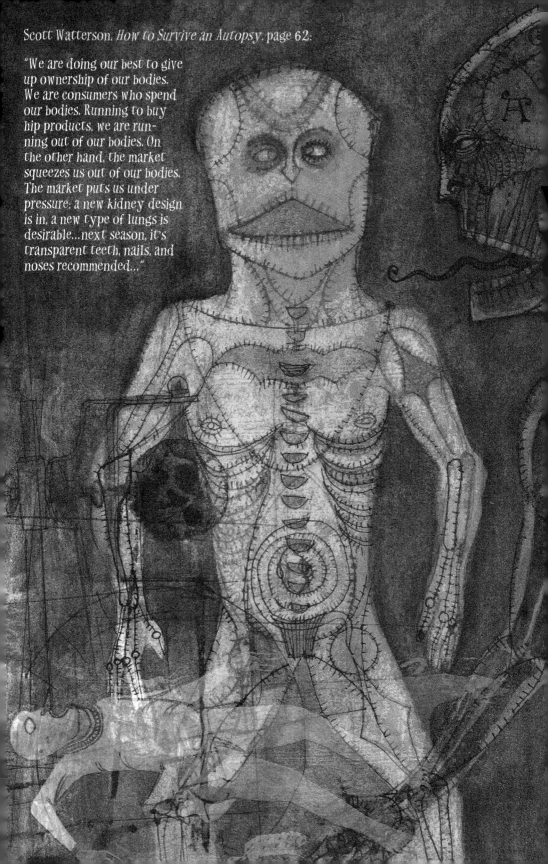

Scott Watterson, *How to Survive an Autopsy*, page 62:

"We are doing our best to give up ownership of our bodies. We are consumers who spend our bodies. Running to buy hip products, we are running out of our bodies. On the other hand, the market squeezes us out of our bodies. The market puts us under pressure: a new kidney design is in, a new type of lungs is desirable...next season, it's transparent teeth, nails, and noses recommended..."

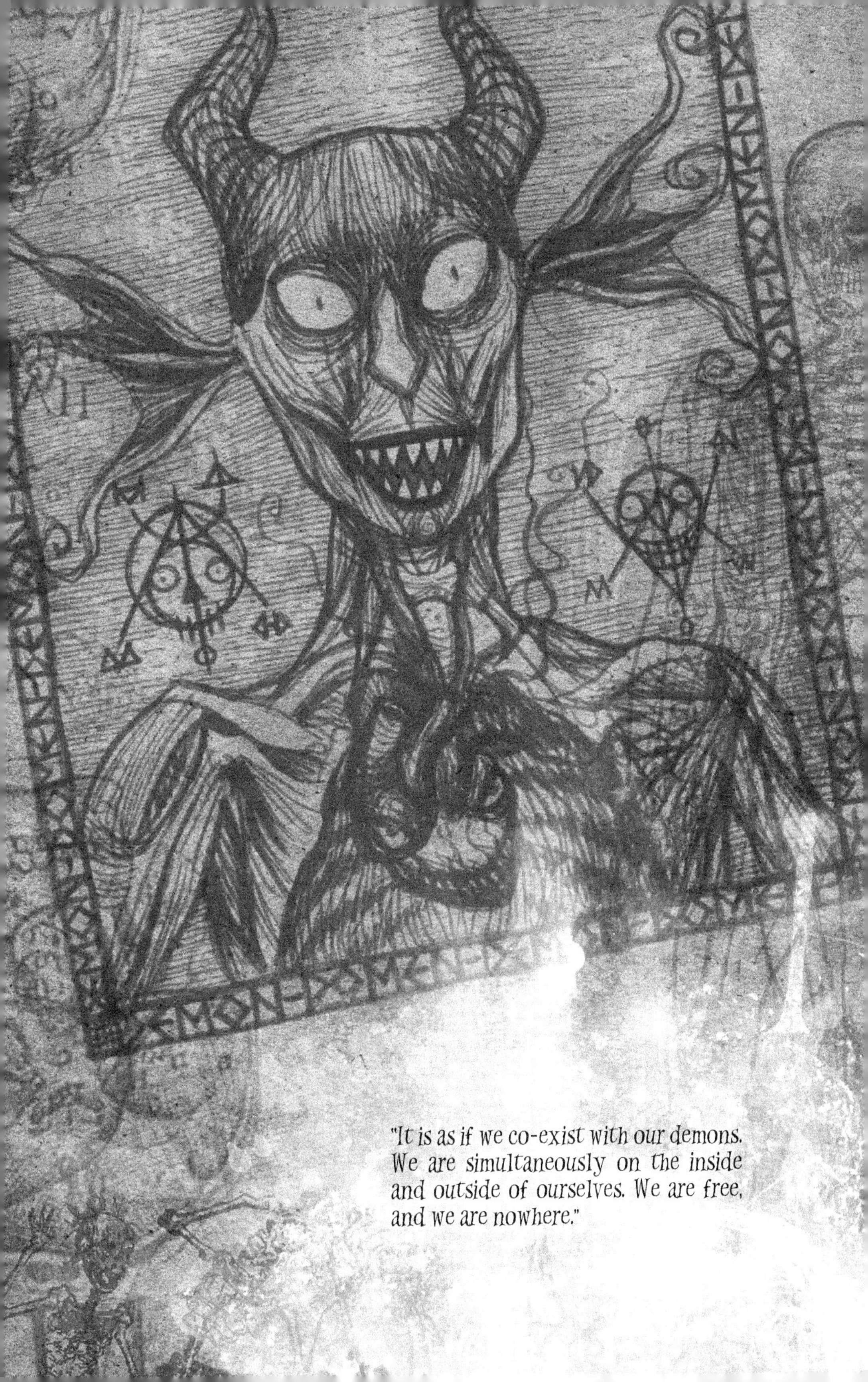

"It is as if we co-exist with our demons. We are simultaneously on the inside and outside of ourselves. We are free, and we are nowhere."

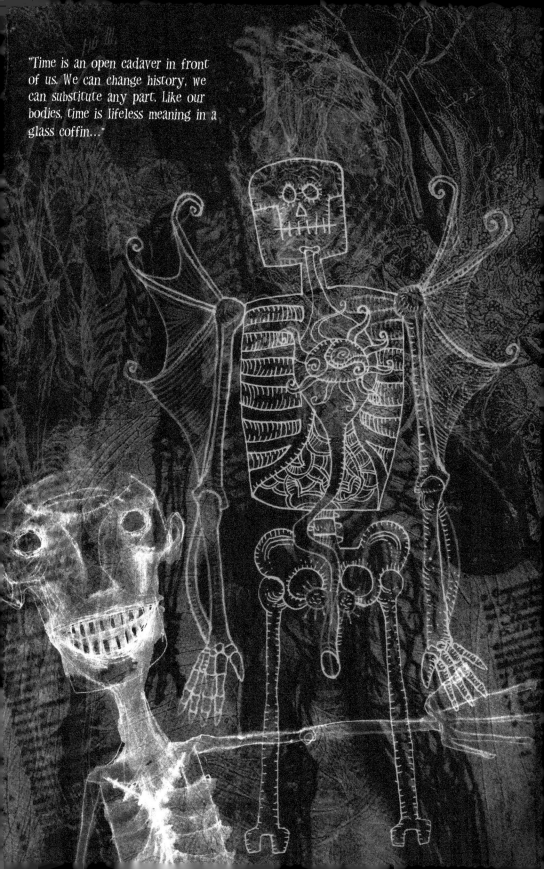

"Time is an open cadaver in front of us. We can change history, we can substitute any part. Like our bodies, time is lifeless meaning in a glass coffin..."

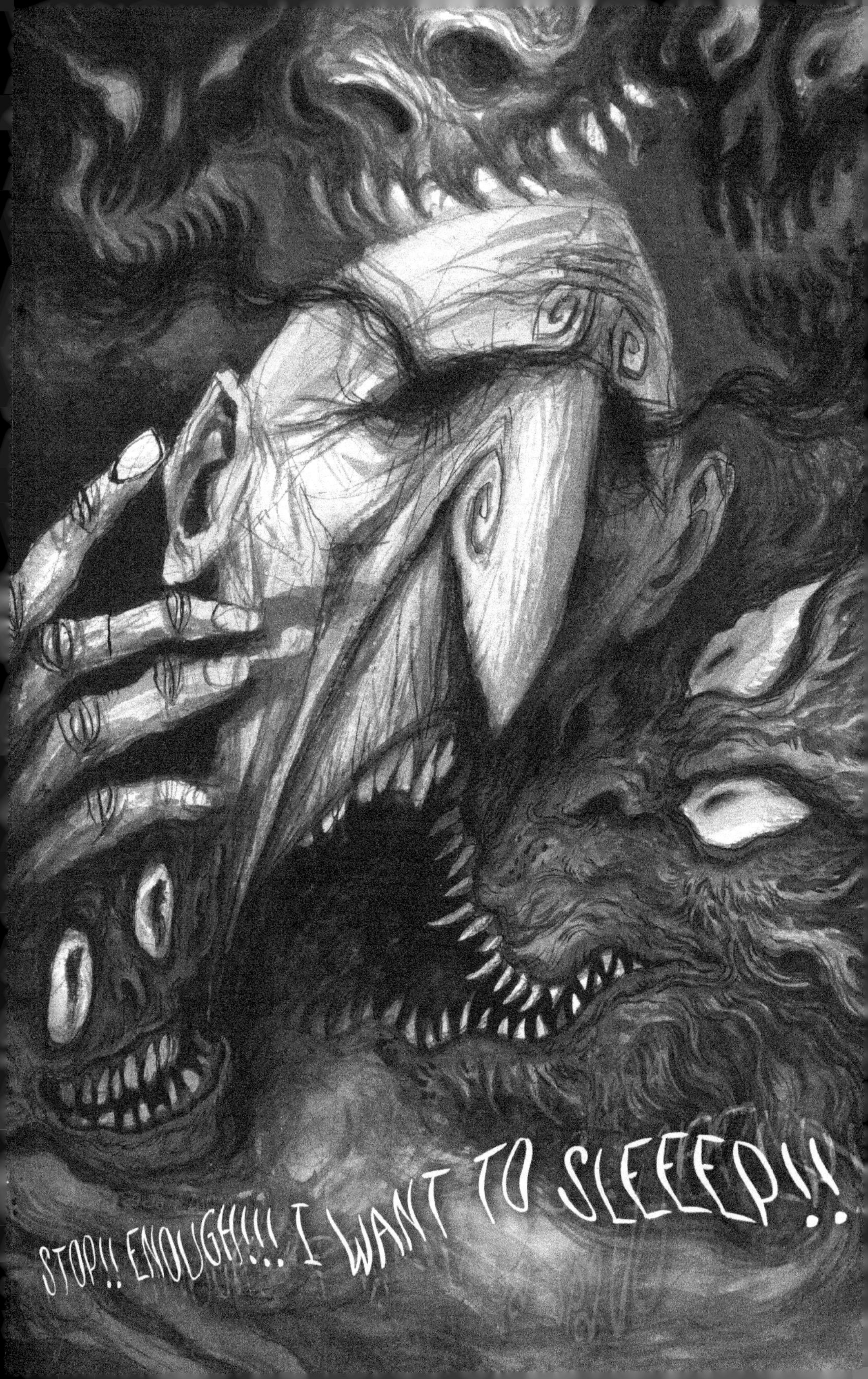
STOP!! ENOUGH!!!! I WANT TO SLEEEP!!

CHAPTER FIVE: PENTAGRAM

The mind slips deeper into the horror of the world
Hands of a clock play tag
Inside the belly is the orphan of disease
The skull is a cheerful sanatorium

You are a pinhead on the move
Worthless dying makes you tired
Your body decomposes into little creatures
And bitterness at the right moment

You are dreamlike, fervid
A delta of sweat, sink for tears
A layer of butter on the bed
An imaginary plague
you are what you forget
you are your holocaust...

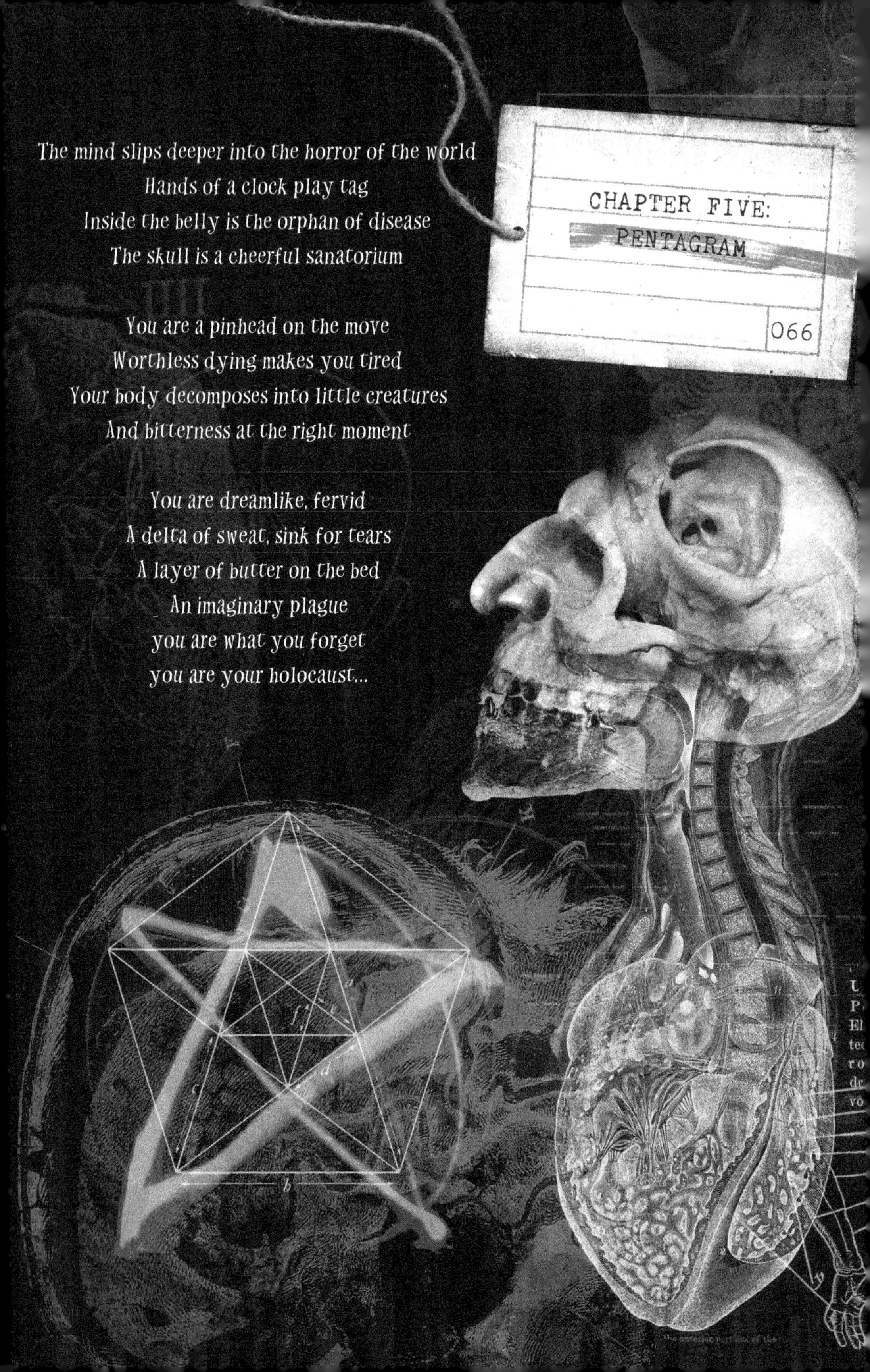

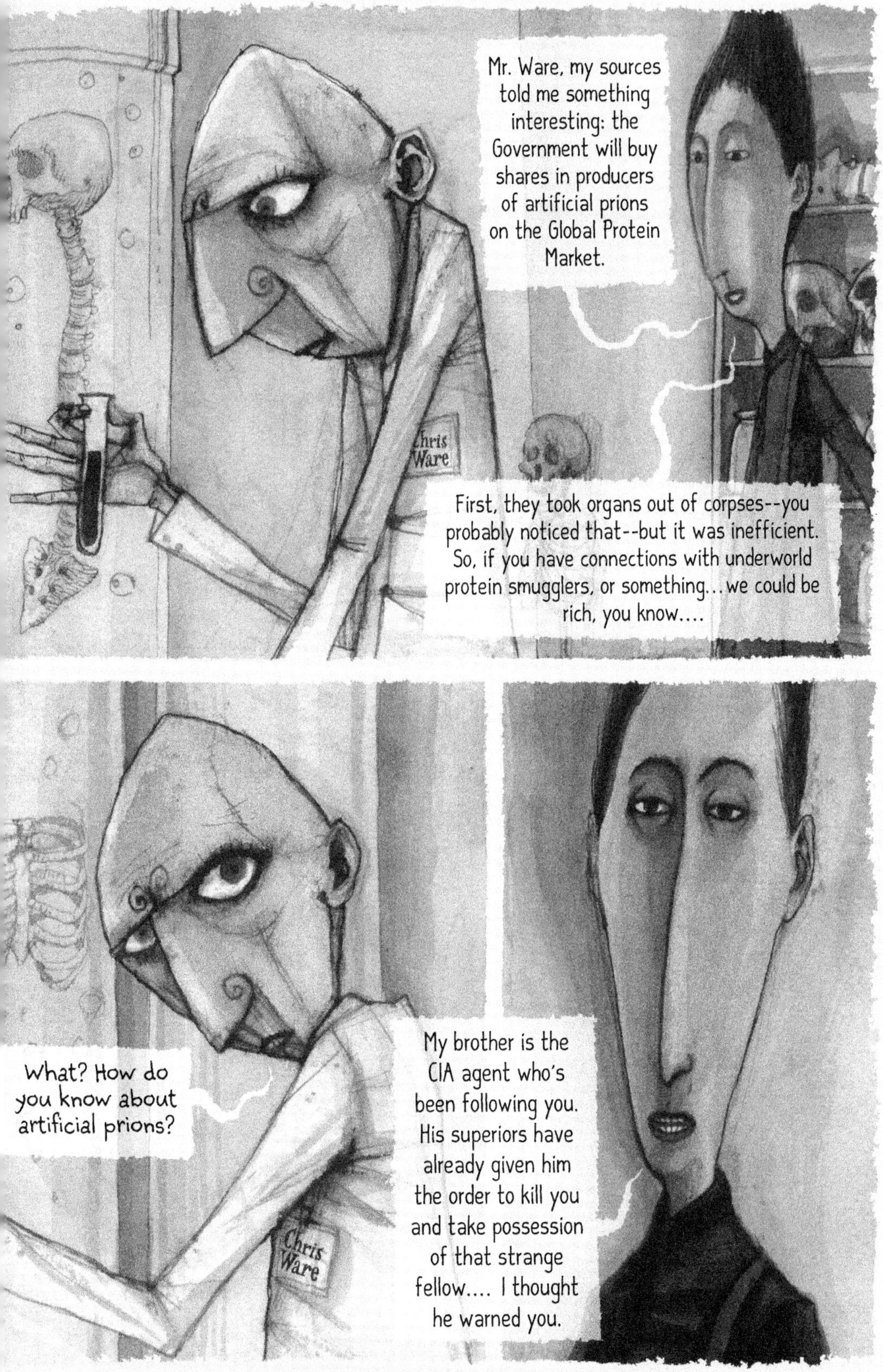
Mr. Ware, my sources told me something interesting: the Government will buy shares in producers of artificial prions on the Global Protein Market.
First, they took organs out of corpses--you probably noticed that--but it was inefficient. So, if you have connections with underworld protein smugglers, or something...we could be rich, you know....
Chris Ware
What? How do you know about artificial prions?
My brother is the CIA agent who's been following you. His superiors have already given him the order to kill you and take possession of that strange fellow.... I thought he warned you.
Chris Ware

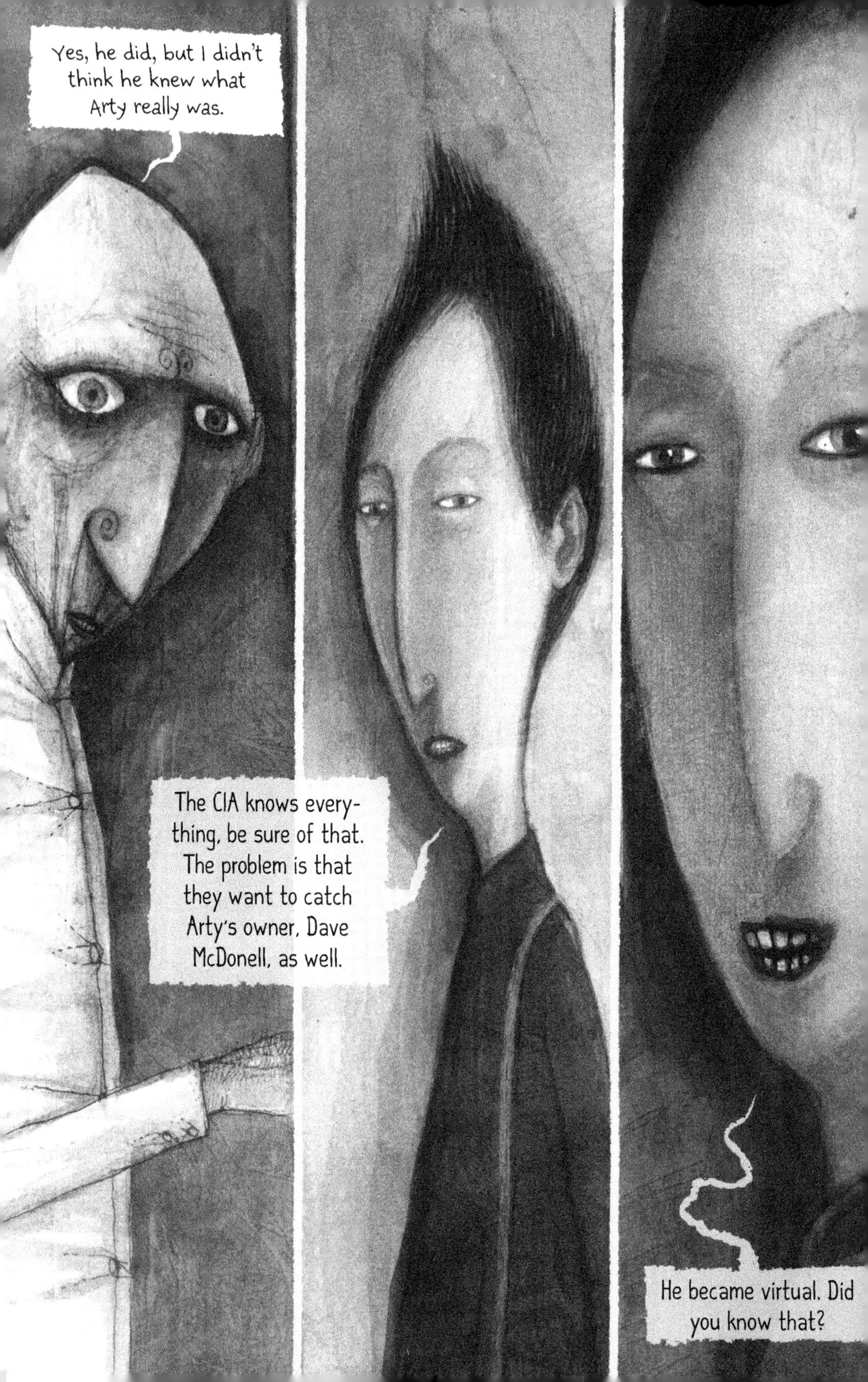
Yes, he did, but I didn't think he knew what Arty really was.
The CIA knows everything, be sure of that. The problem is that they want to catch Arty's owner, Dave McDonell, as well.
He became virtual. Did you know that?

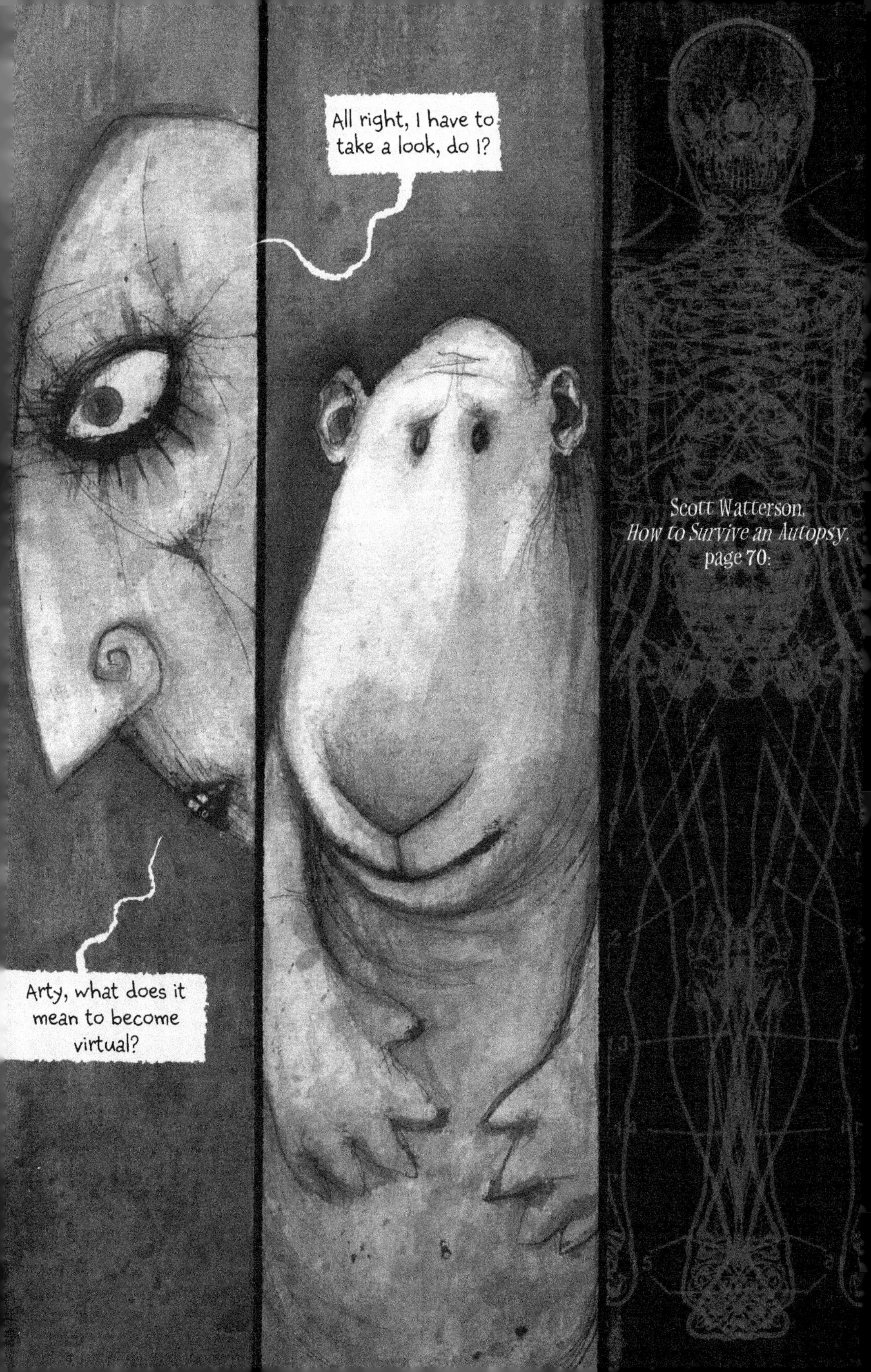
Arty, what does it mean to become virtual?
All right, I have to take a look, do I?
Scott Watterson,
How to Survive an Autopsy,
page 70:

LXX

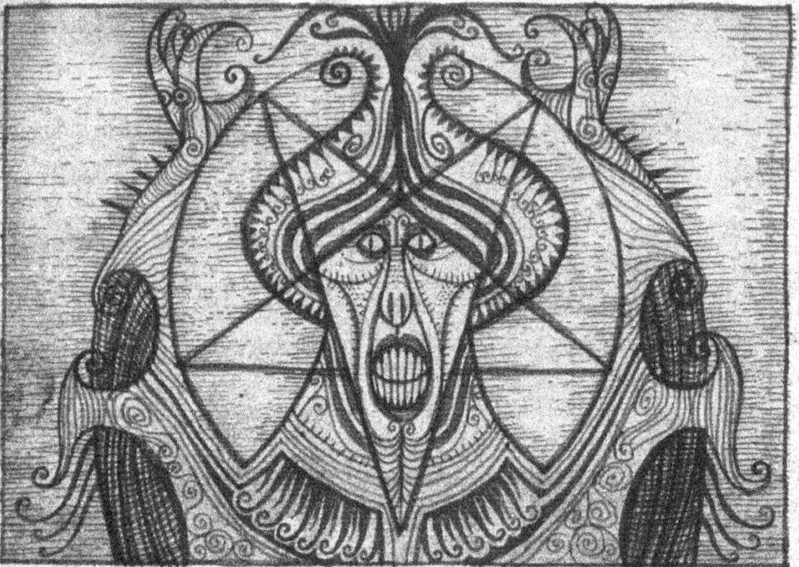

Today, being virtual does not mean that you exist on the surface of the screen. To be virtual means gaining the power to go beyond the image to the other side. It is a form of transhumanism where you live beyond the system that controls the society. Through it, you can fight that system with the same means. On one side, there is the Pentagram: Order and Big Brother Eye, and on the other side is the whole cosmos of the eternal wandering. Being virtual refers to the demonic space between them. Virtual demons resist the Pentagram dictatorship. Pentagrams need code production. The demons seek a breakthrough. In fact, both sides are looking for the perfect image of death. The image of death is what is needed, not the death itself. In the end, it all boils down to the Graphic Conspiracy.

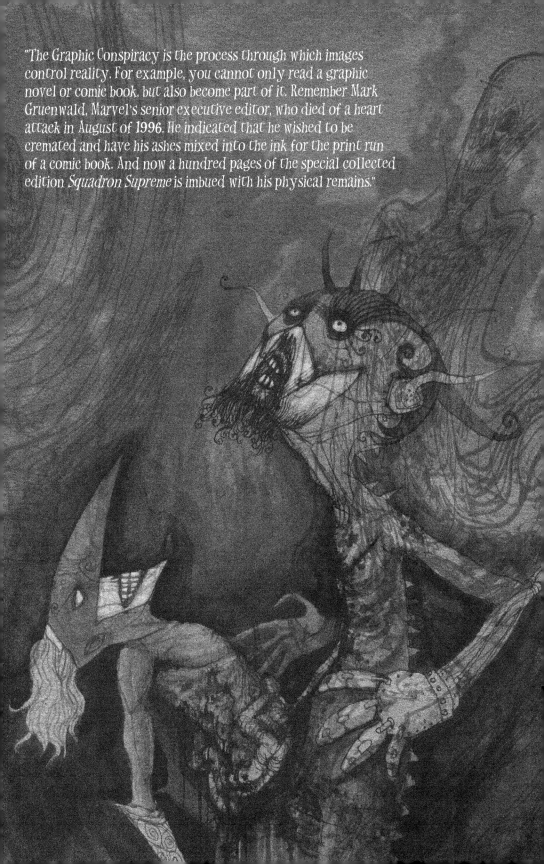

"The Graphic Conspiracy is the process through which images control reality. For example, you cannot only read a graphic novel or comic book, but also become part of it. Remember Mark Gruenwald, Marvel's senior executive editor, who died of a heart attack in August of 1996. He indicated that he wished to be cremated and have his ashes mixed into the ink for the print run of a comic book. And now a hundred pages of the special collected edition *Squadron Supreme* is imbued with his physical remains."

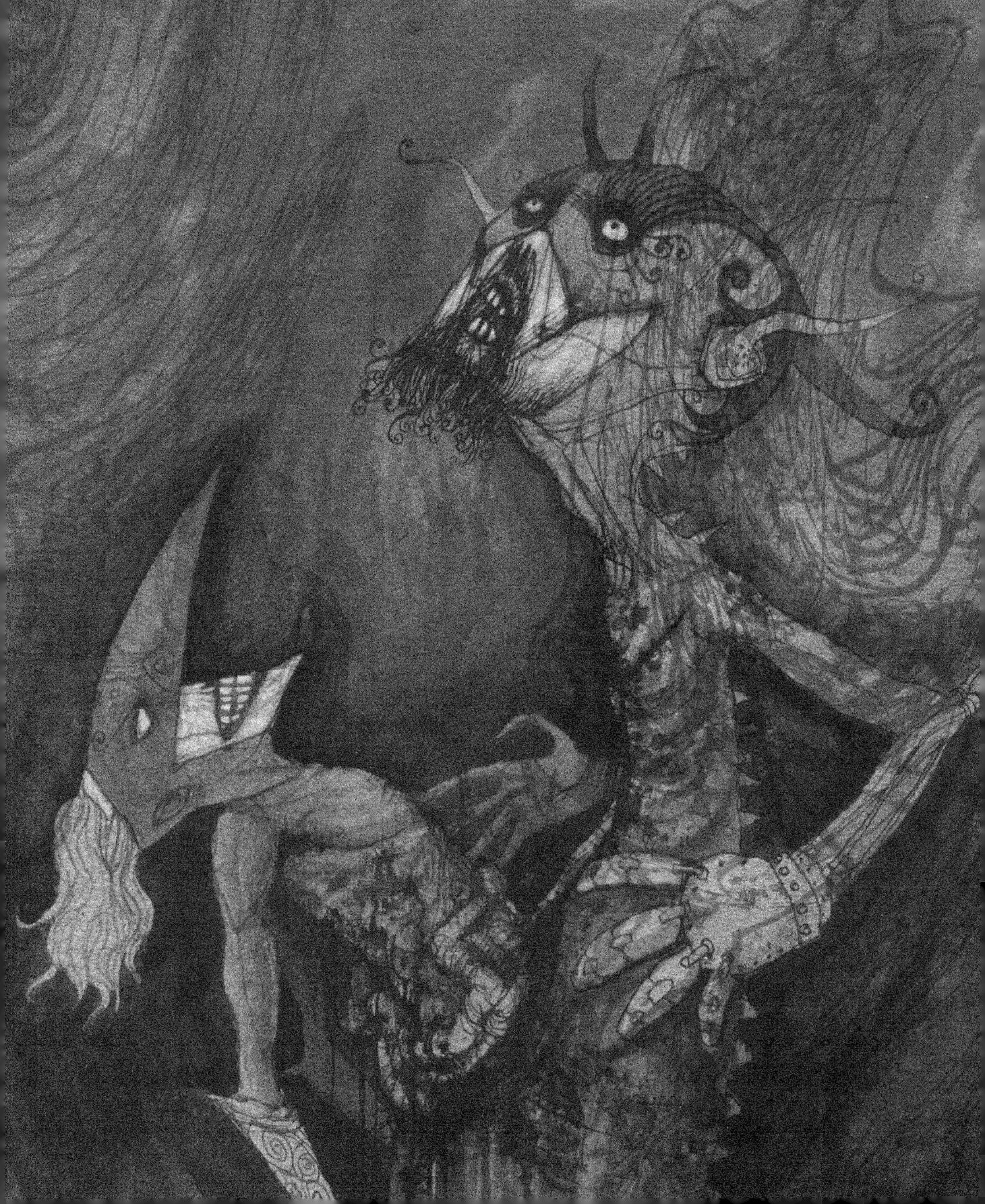

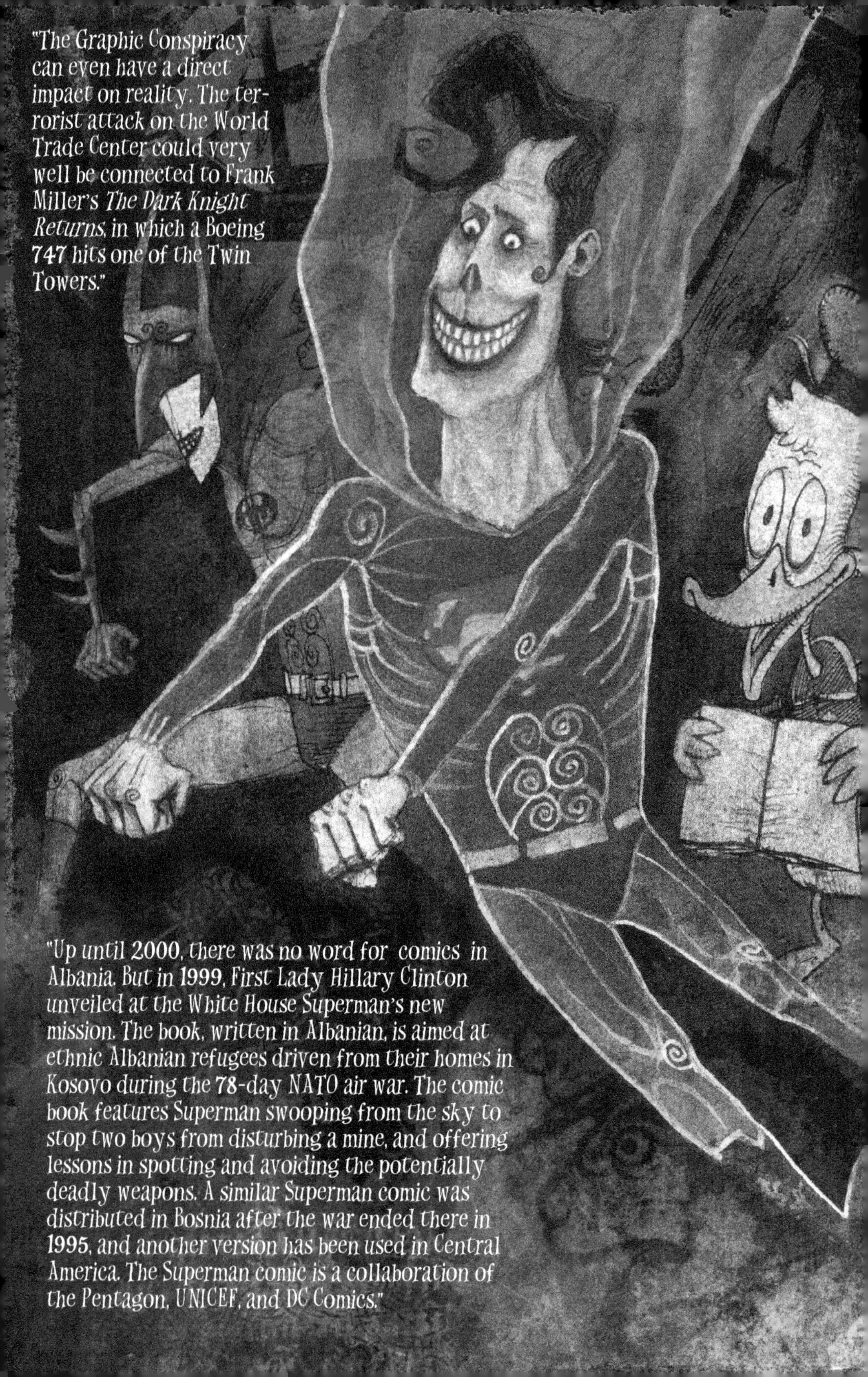

"The Graphic Conspiracy can even have a direct impact on reality. The terrorist attack on the World Trade Center could very well be connected to Frank Miller's *The Dark Knight Returns*, in which a Boeing **747** hits one of the Twin Towers."

"Up until **2000**, there was no word for comics in Albania. But in **1999**, First Lady Hillary Clinton unveiled at the White House Superman's new mission. The book, written in Albanian, is aimed at ethnic Albanian refugees driven from their homes in Kosovo during the **78**-day NATO air war. The comic book features Superman swooping from the sky to stop two boys from disturbing a mine, and offering lessons in spotting and avoiding the potentially deadly weapons. A similar Superman comic was distributed in Bosnia after the war ended there in **1995**, and another version has been used in Central America. The Superman comic is a collaboration of the Pentagon, UNICEF, and DC Comics."

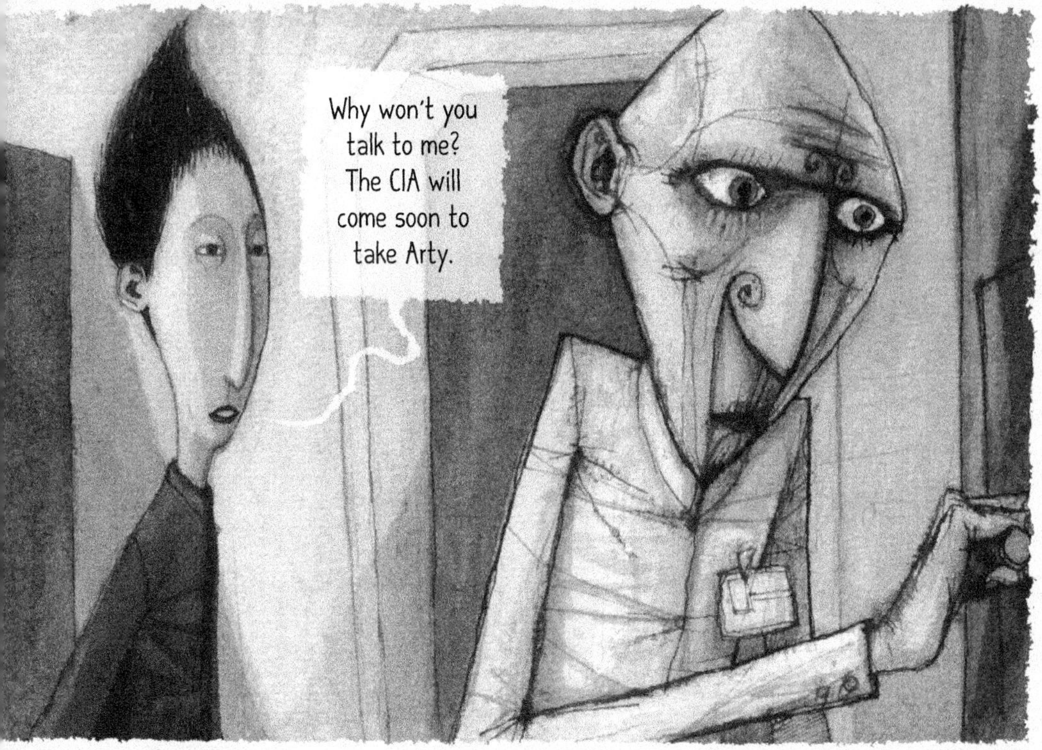
Why won't you talk to me? The CIA will come soon to take Arty.

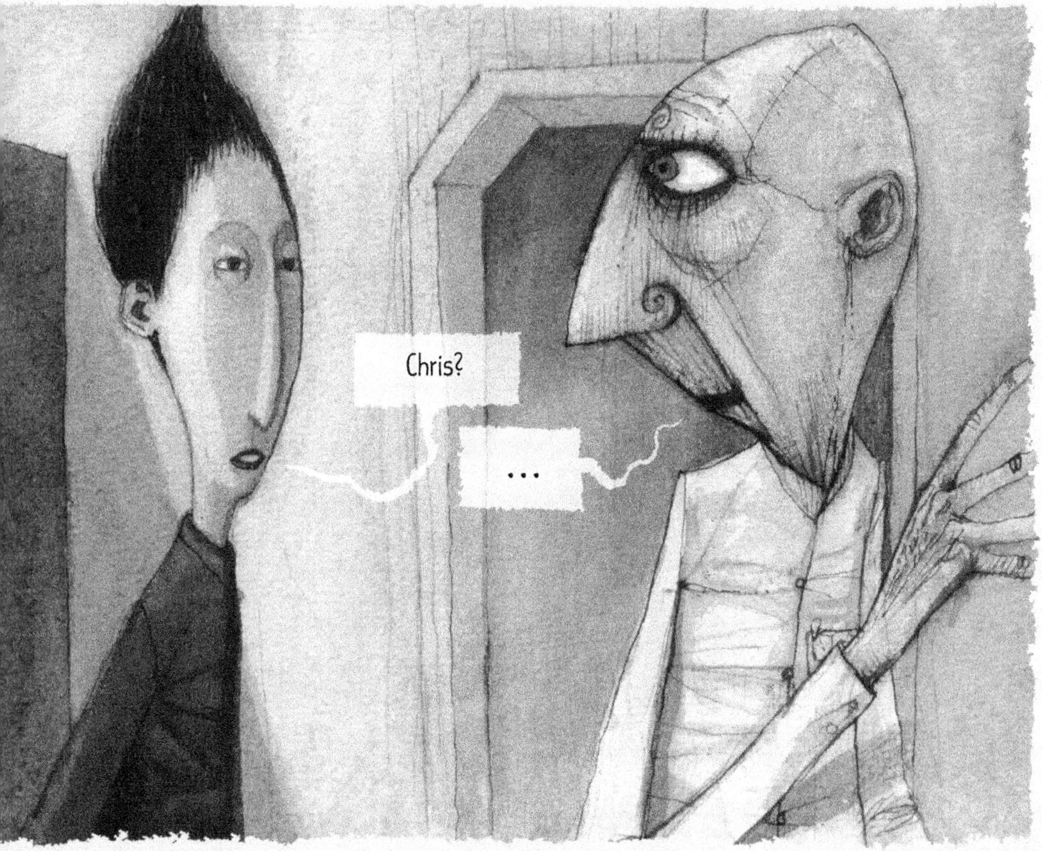
Chris?
...

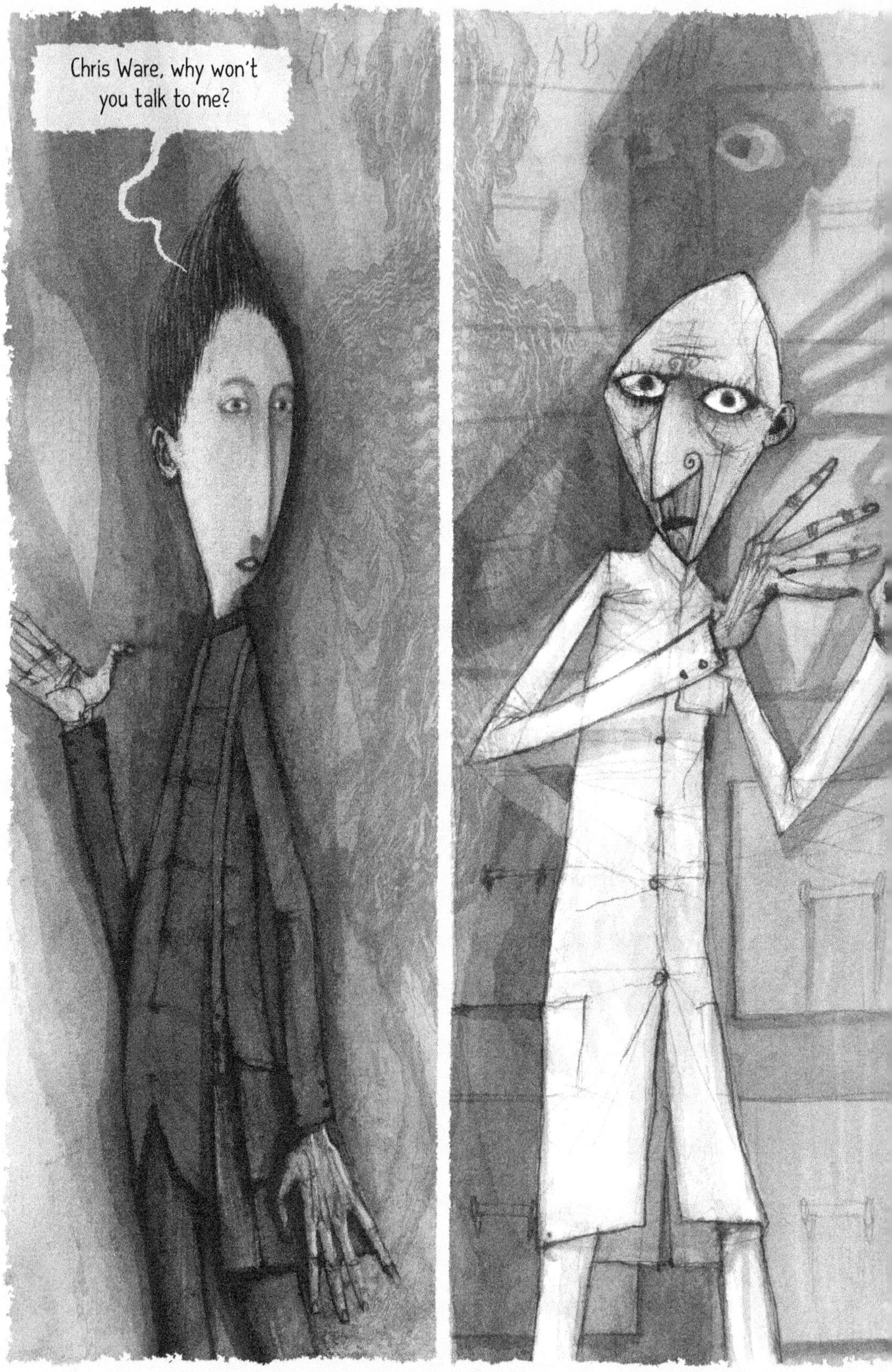
Chris Ware, why won't you talk to me?

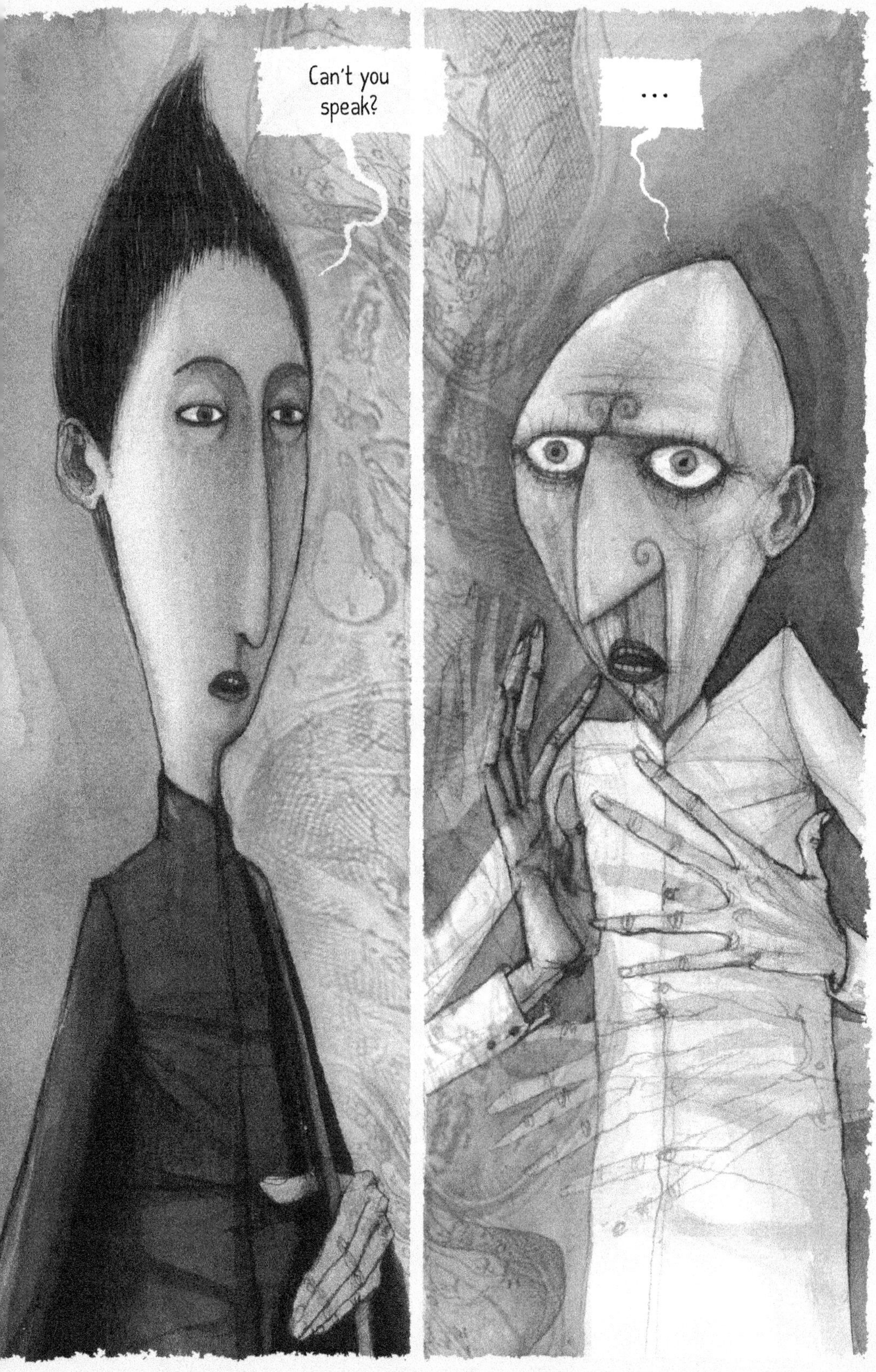
Can't you speak?
...

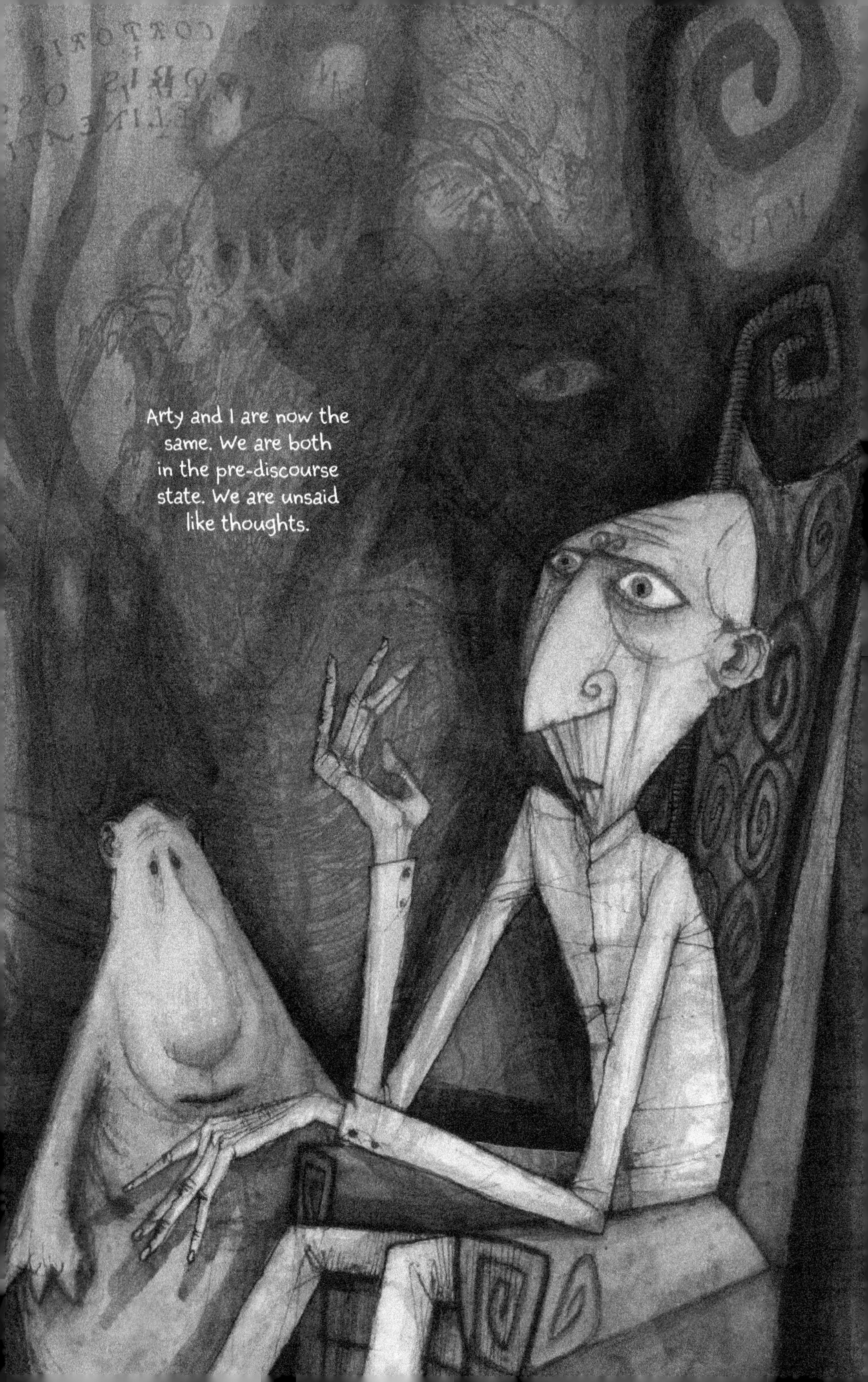
Arty and I are now the same. We are both in the pre-discourse state. We are unsaid like thoughts.

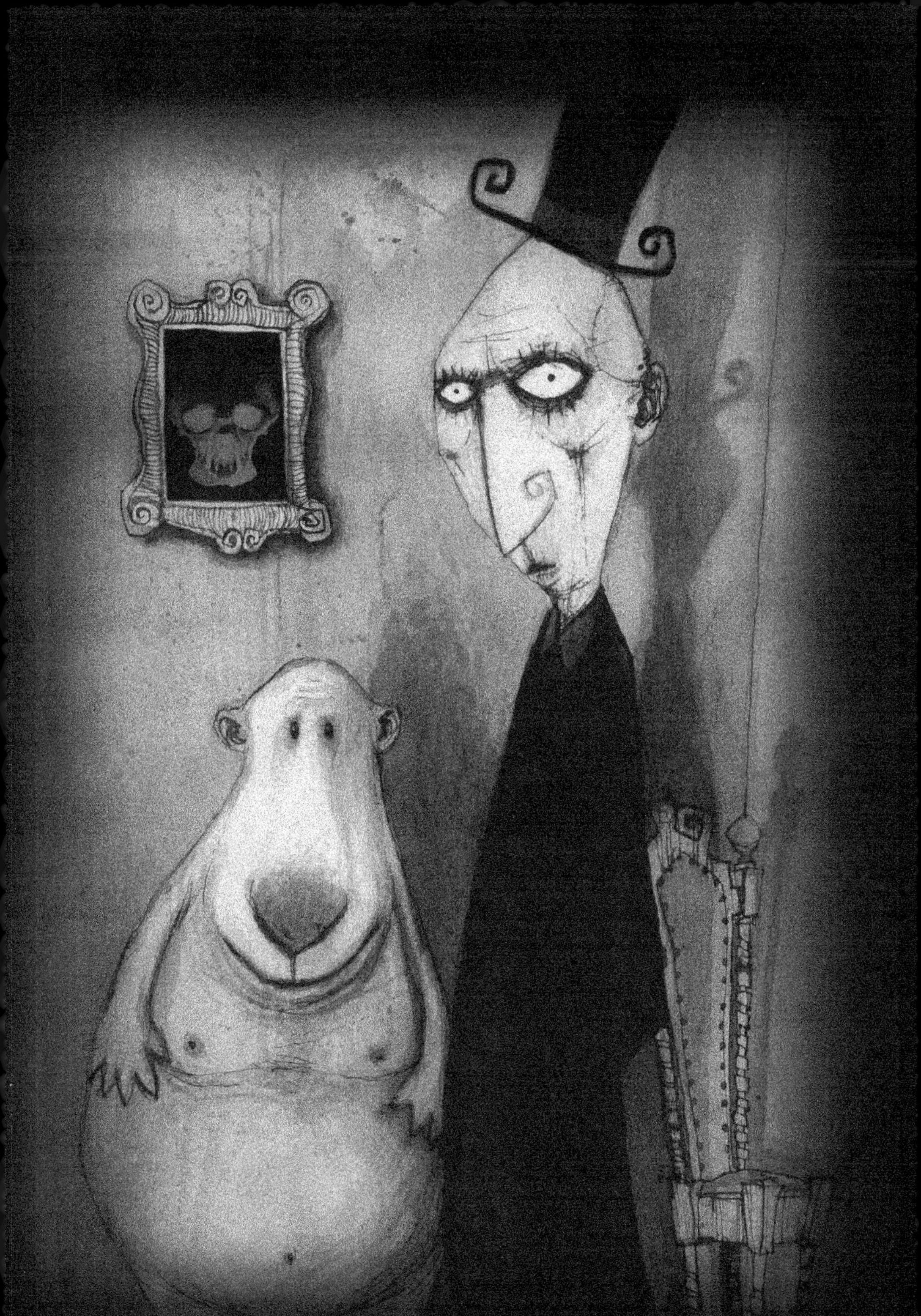

We are mute images now.

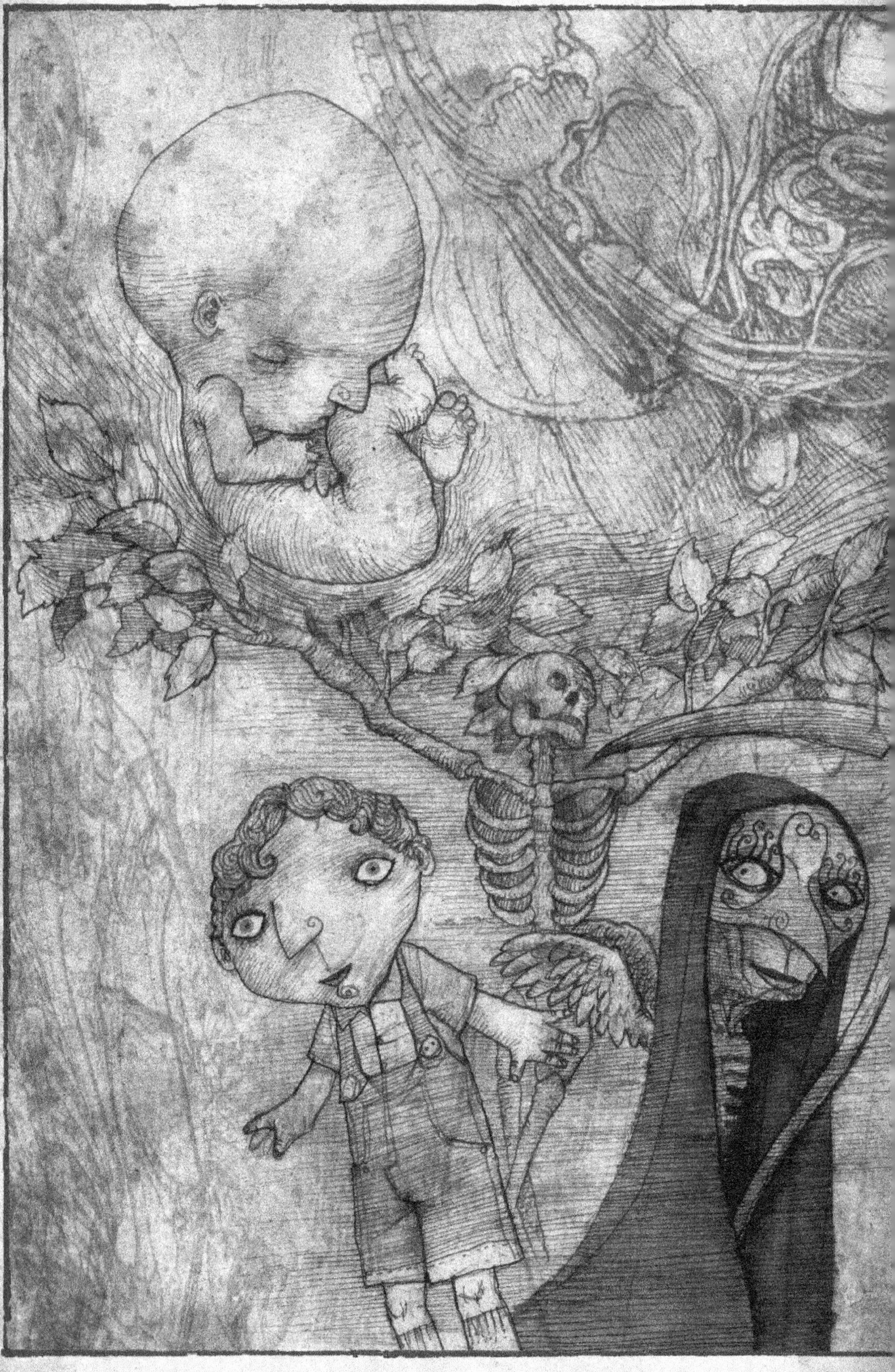

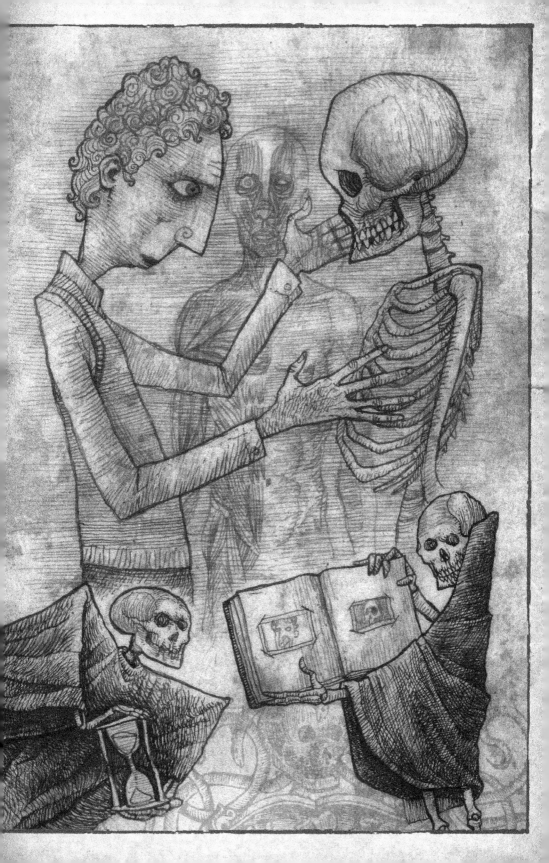

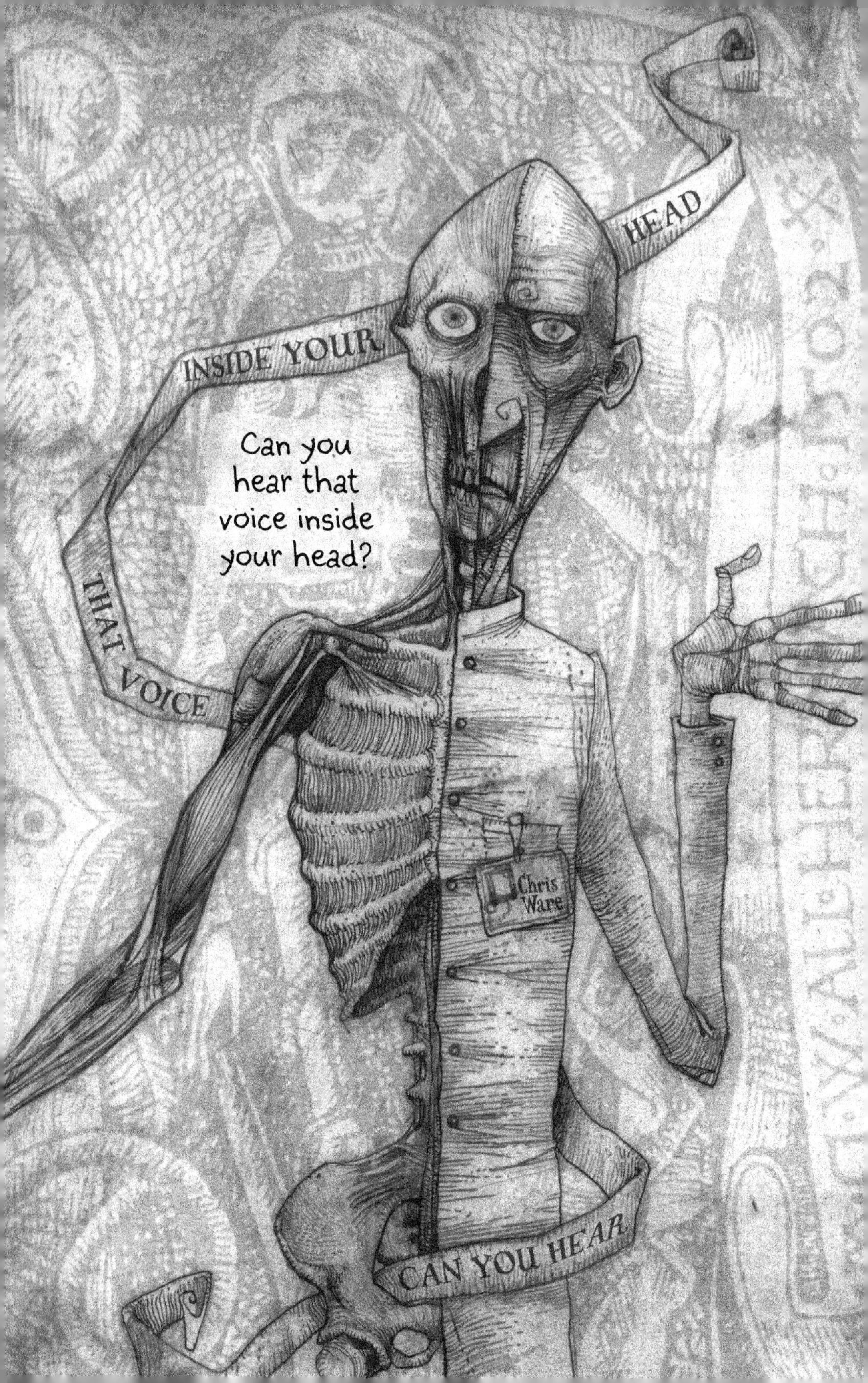
Can you hear that voice inside your head?
CAN YOU HEAR
THAT VOICE
INSIDE YOUR
HEAD
Chris Ware

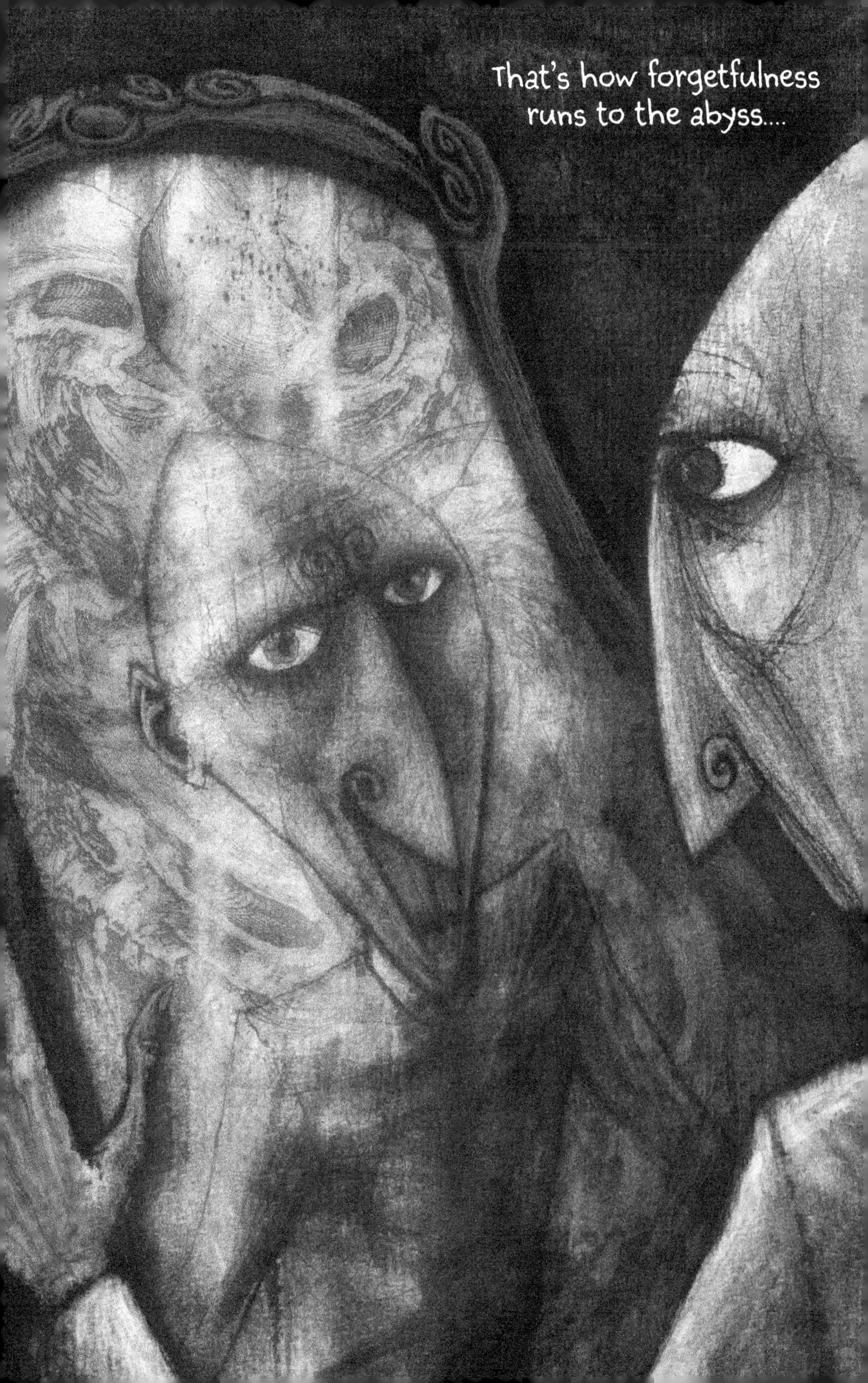
That's how forgetfulness runs to the abyss....

CHAPTER SIX: RIVER OF OBLIVION

I still sail over the river Acheron
The passion is naked because of me
I am still flying, gliding easily
and all of a sudden I shriek

In the curtain of honey, locust petals
With the eyes of sea birds
My thin translucent woman
Take care of me as if I were a child

Her beak plunges into my neck
The shattered words from my mouth
Go to a deserted place of no return
I am still sailing over the river Acheron

And the world is meaningful like a sonnet
I am alone because I am forgotten

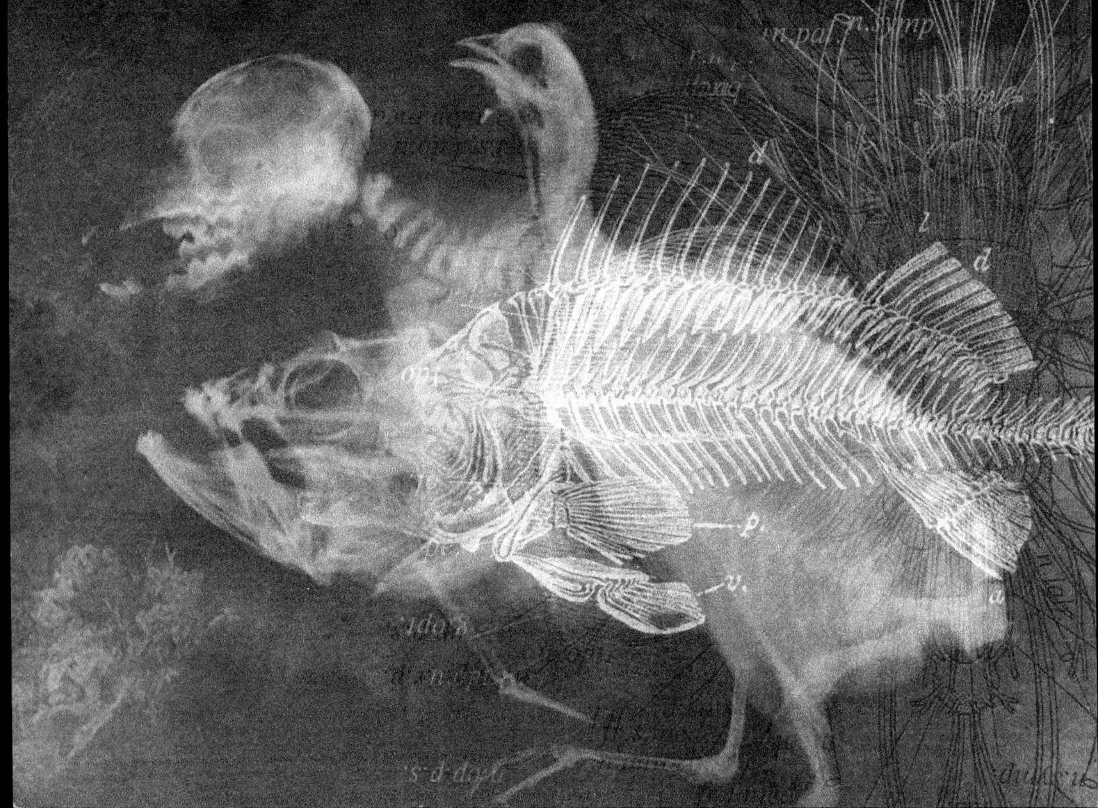

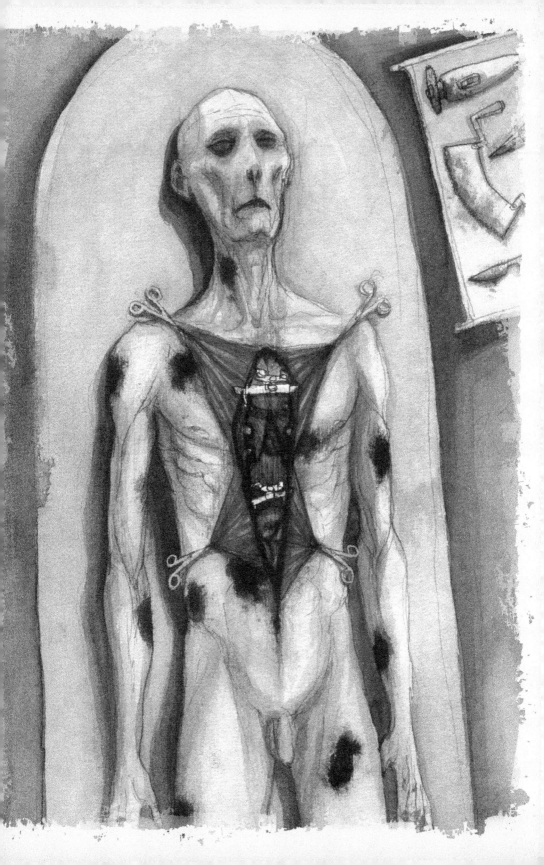

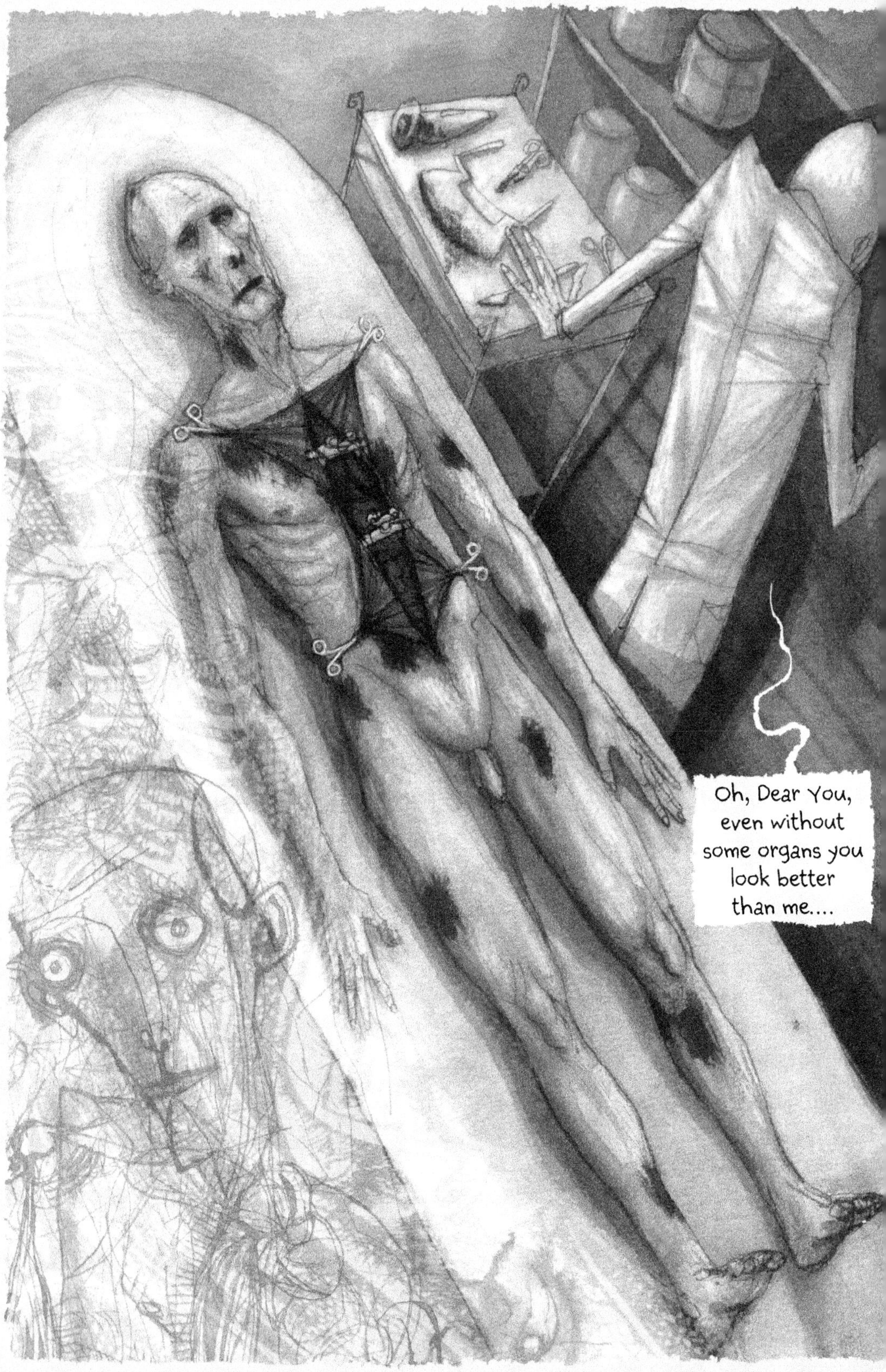
Oh, Dear You, even without some organs you look better than me....

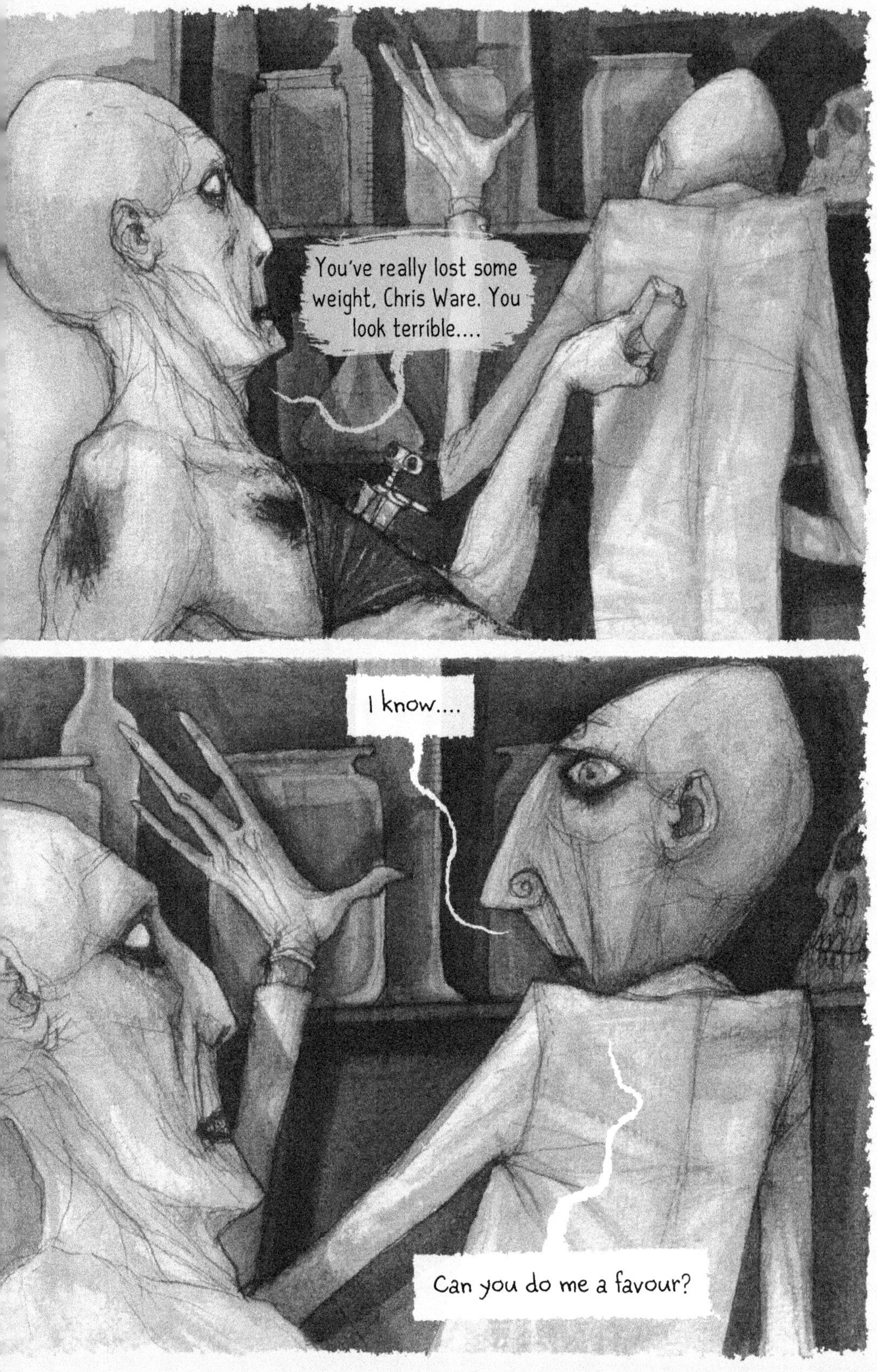

You've really lost some weight, Chris Ware. You look terrible....
I know....
Can you do me a favour?

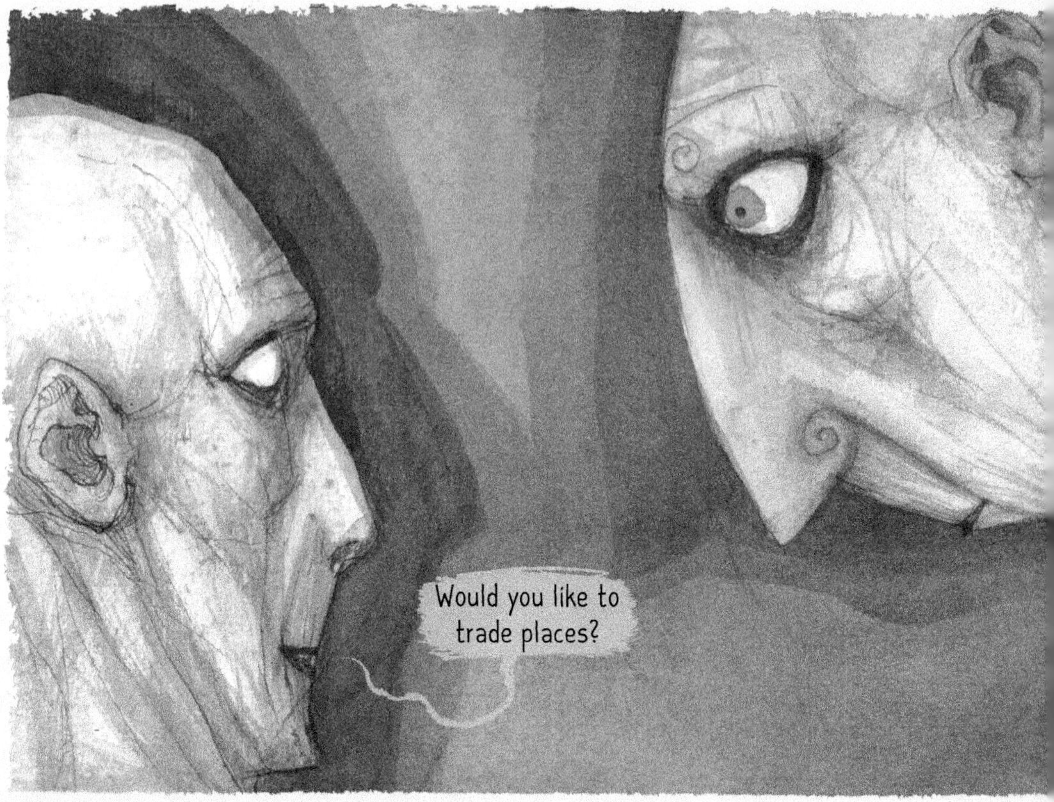
Would you like to trade places?

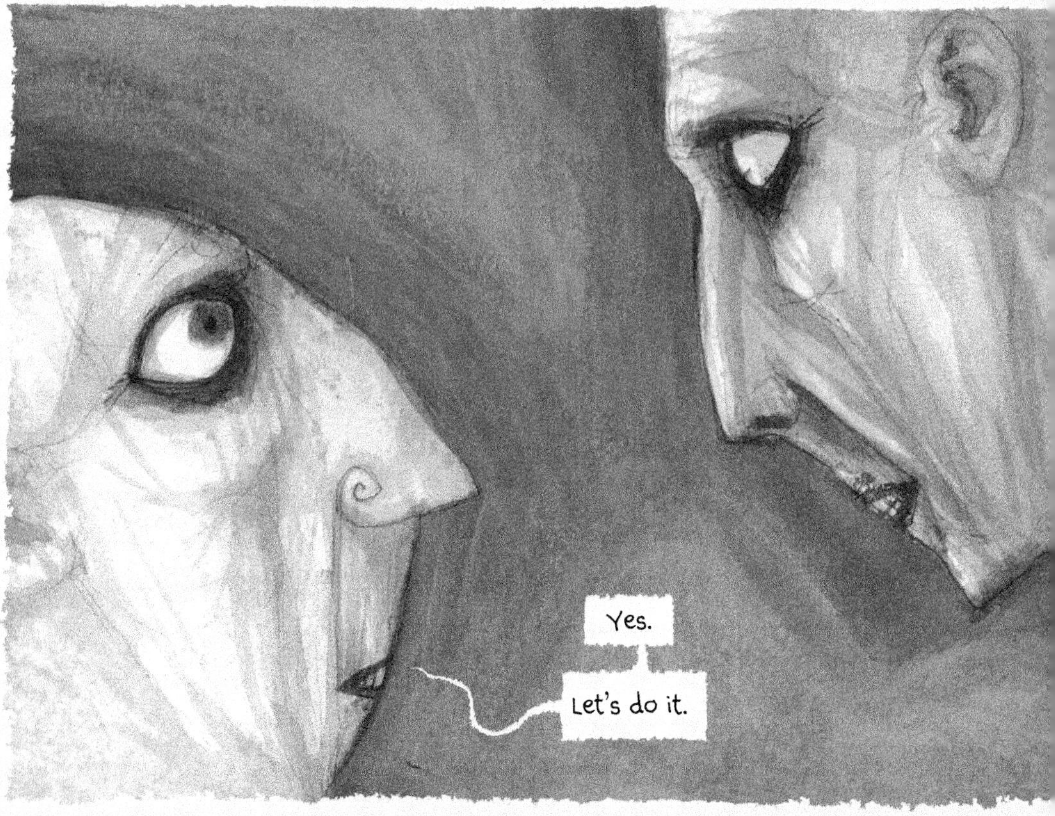
Yes.
Let's do it.

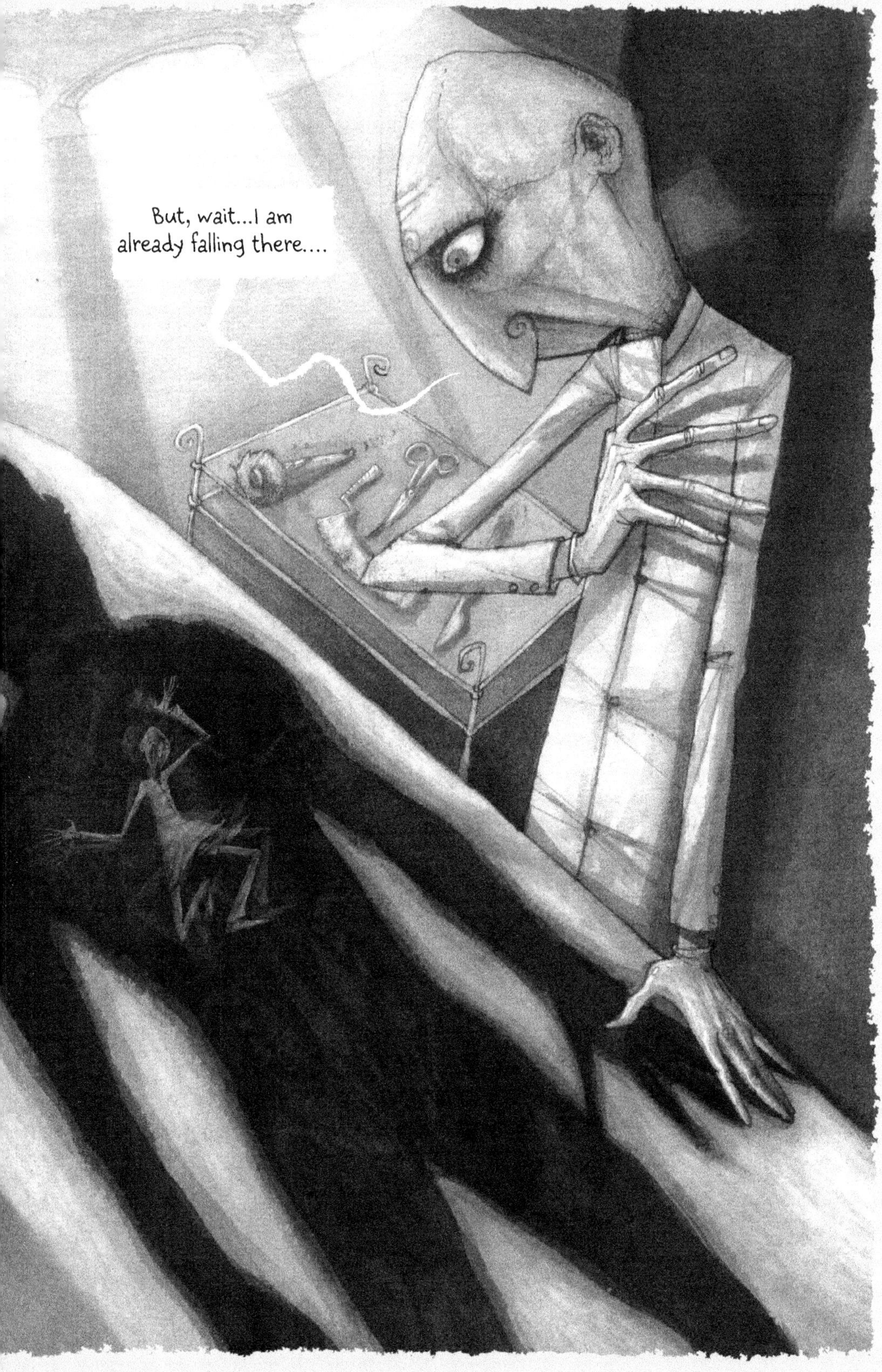
But, wait...I am already falling there....

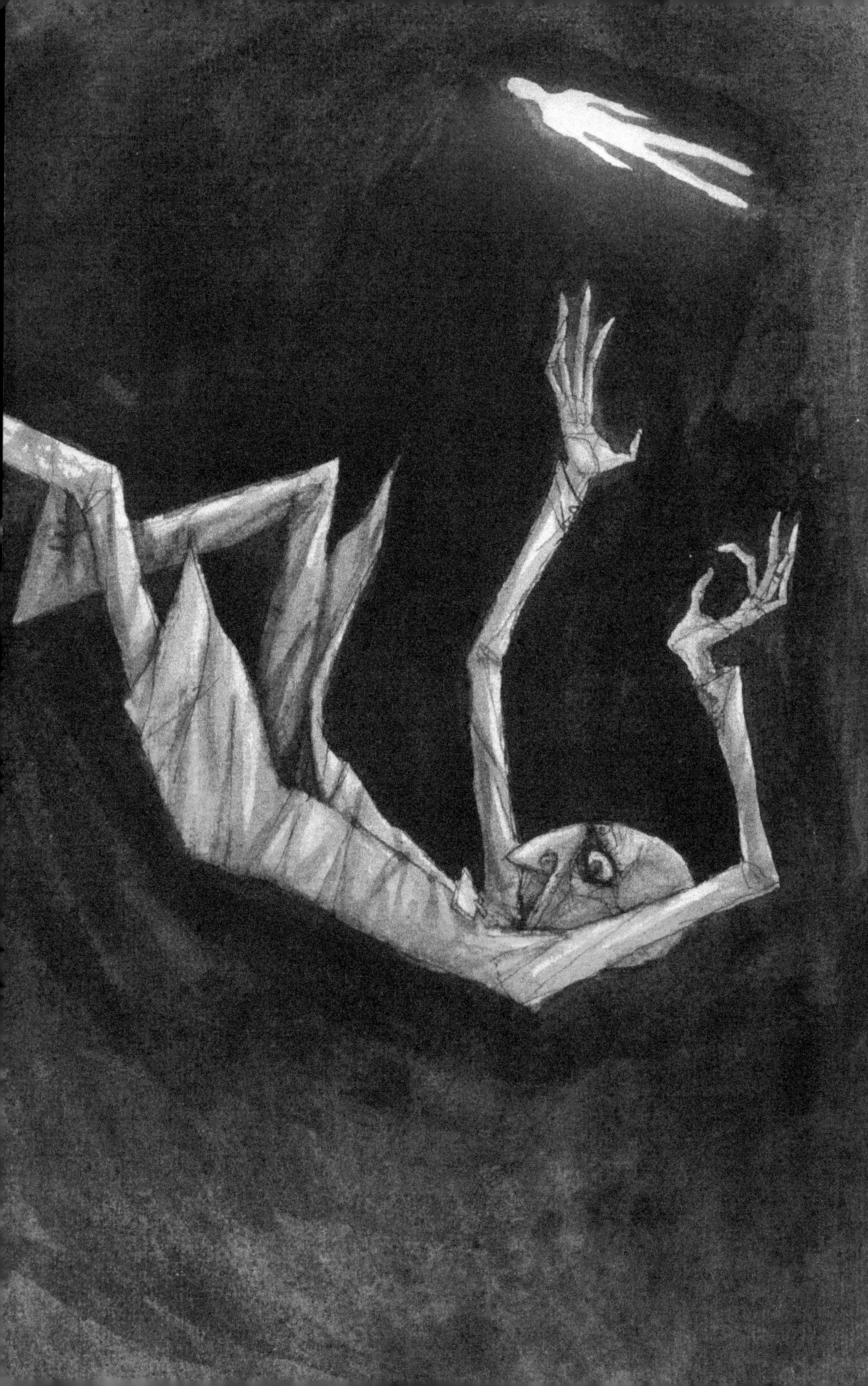

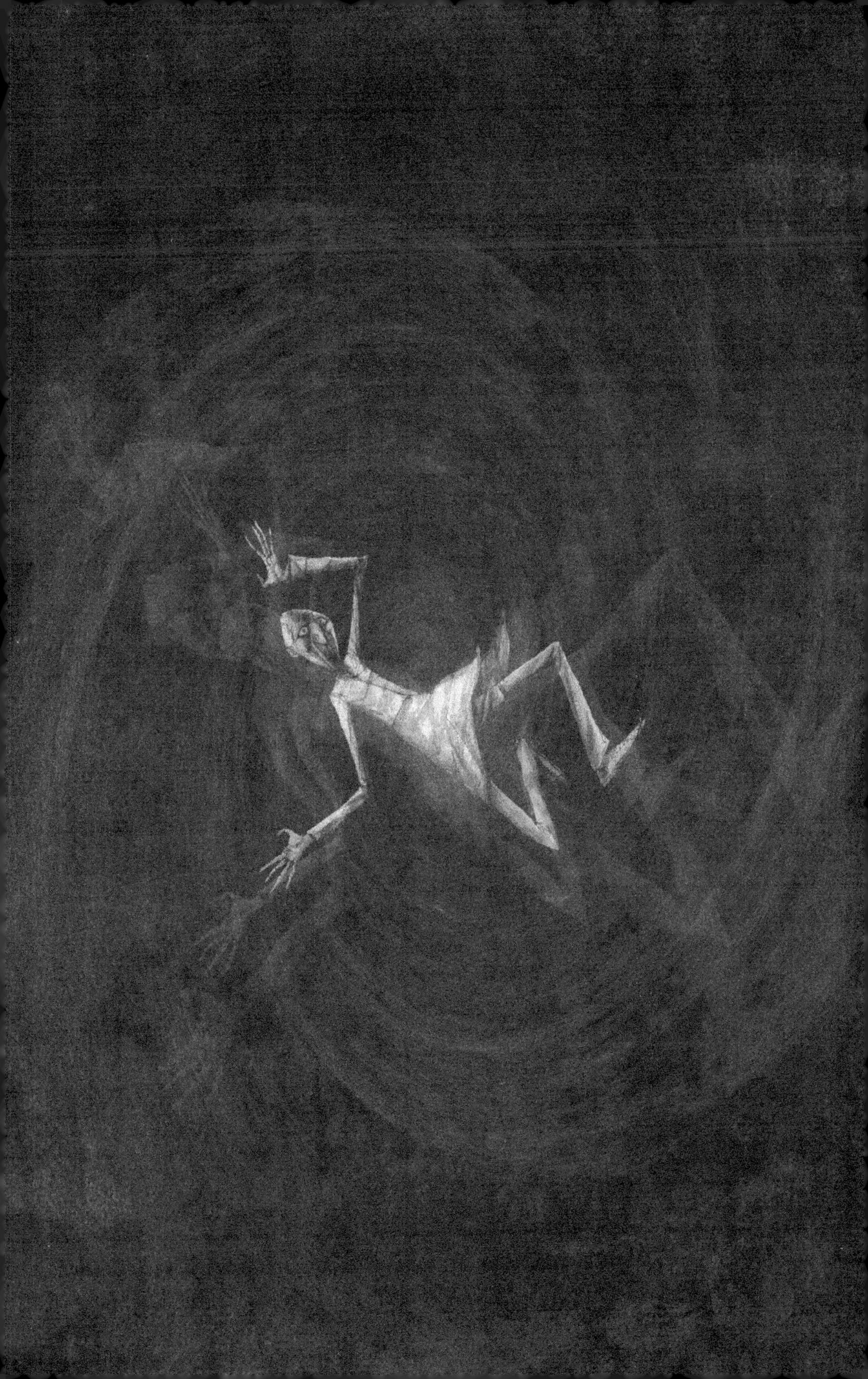

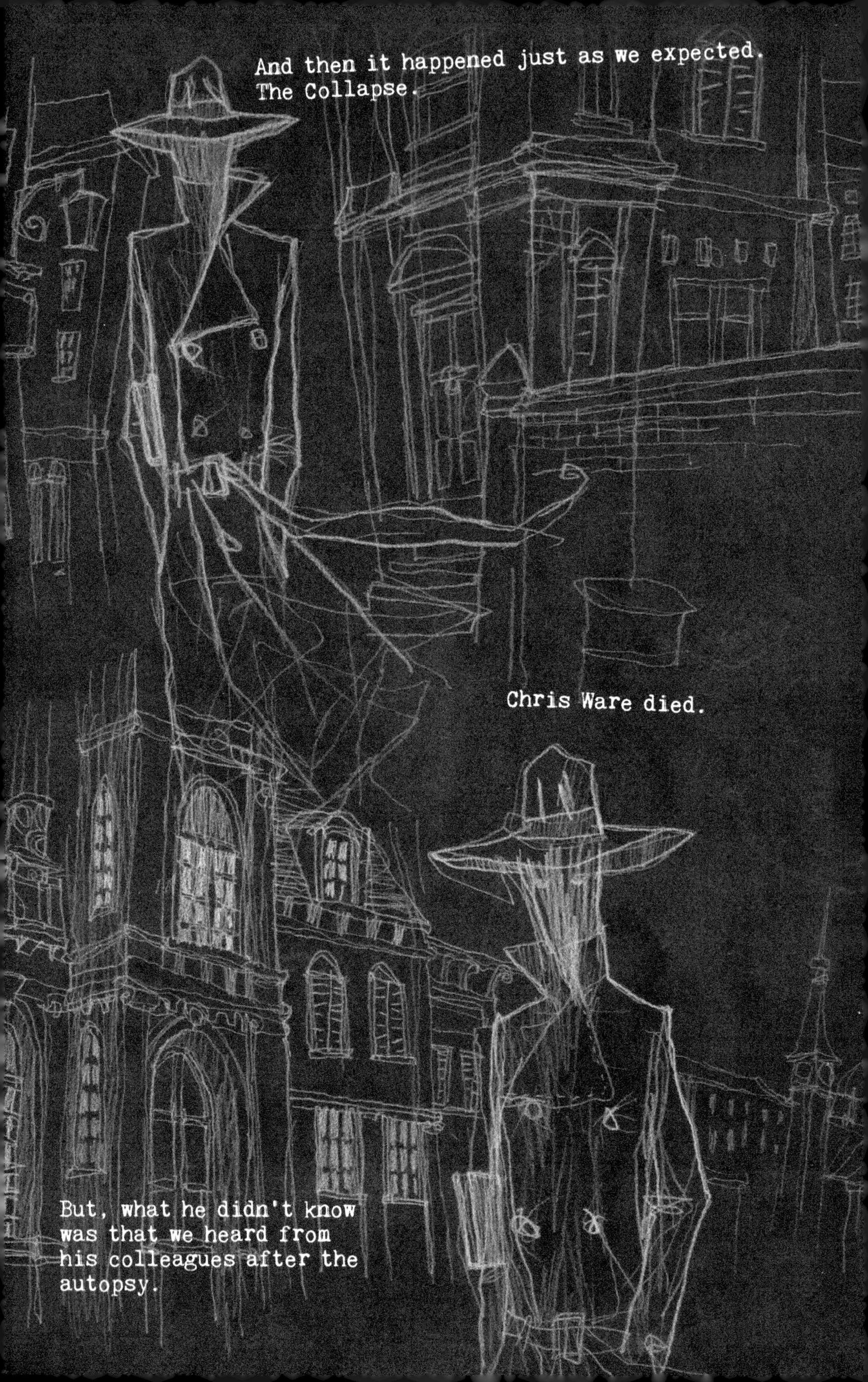
And then it happened just as we expected.
The Collapse.
Chris Ware died.
But, what he didn't know was that we heard from his colleagues after the autopsy.

Chris died of Fatal Familial Insomnia. The disease is a result of a mutation of a normal protein associated with brain tissue. This is the prion protein. In the case of Fatal Familial Insomnia, the affected area of the brain is the thalamus, the area responsible for sleep. The first stage is progressive insomnia, the trademark of FFI. This stage includes a collection of psychiatric problems such as panic attacks and bizarre phobias.

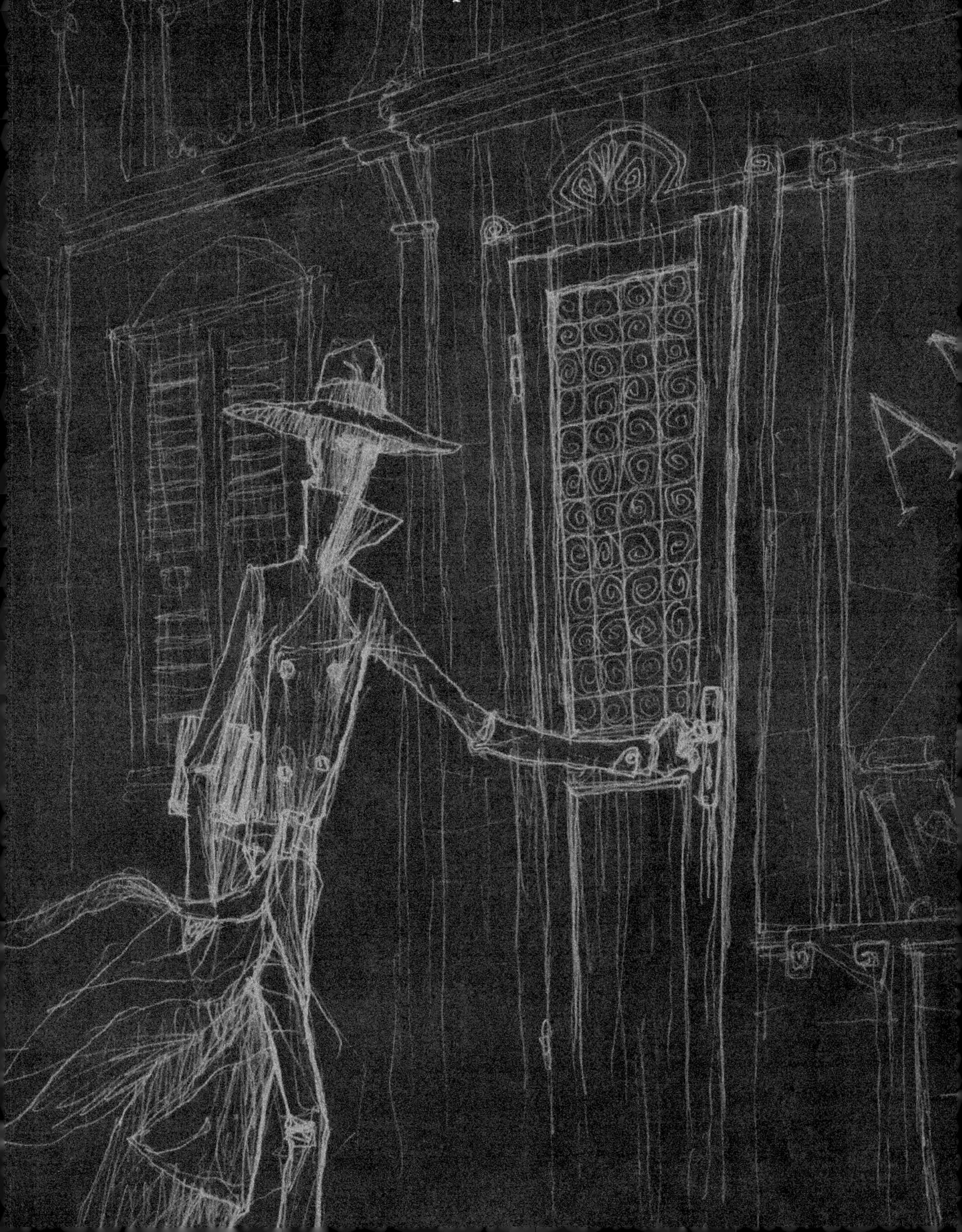

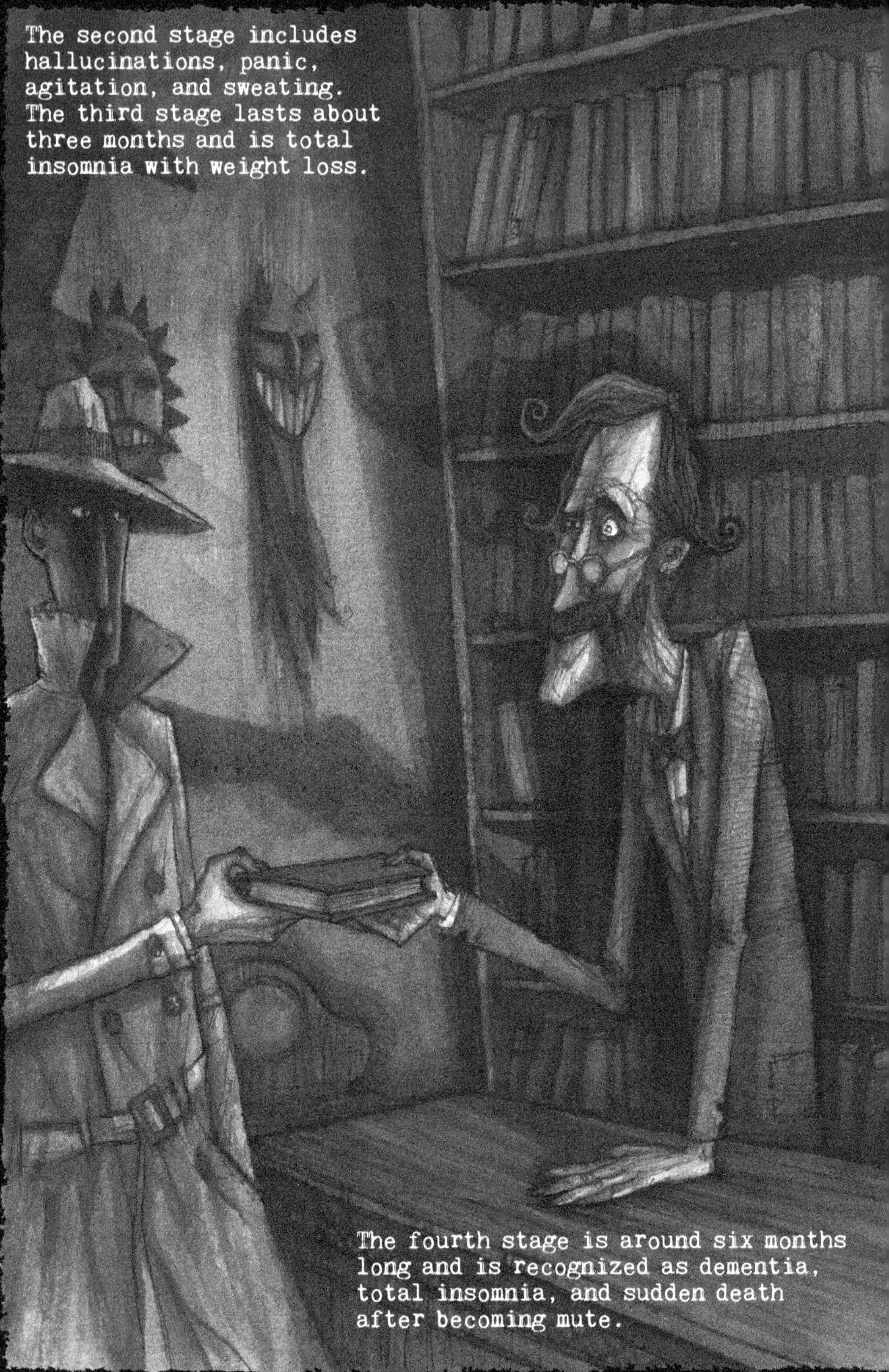
The second stage includes hallucinations, panic, agitation, and sweating. The third stage lasts about three months and is total insomnia with weight loss.
The fourth stage is around six months long and is recognized as dementia, total insomnia, and sudden death after becoming mute.

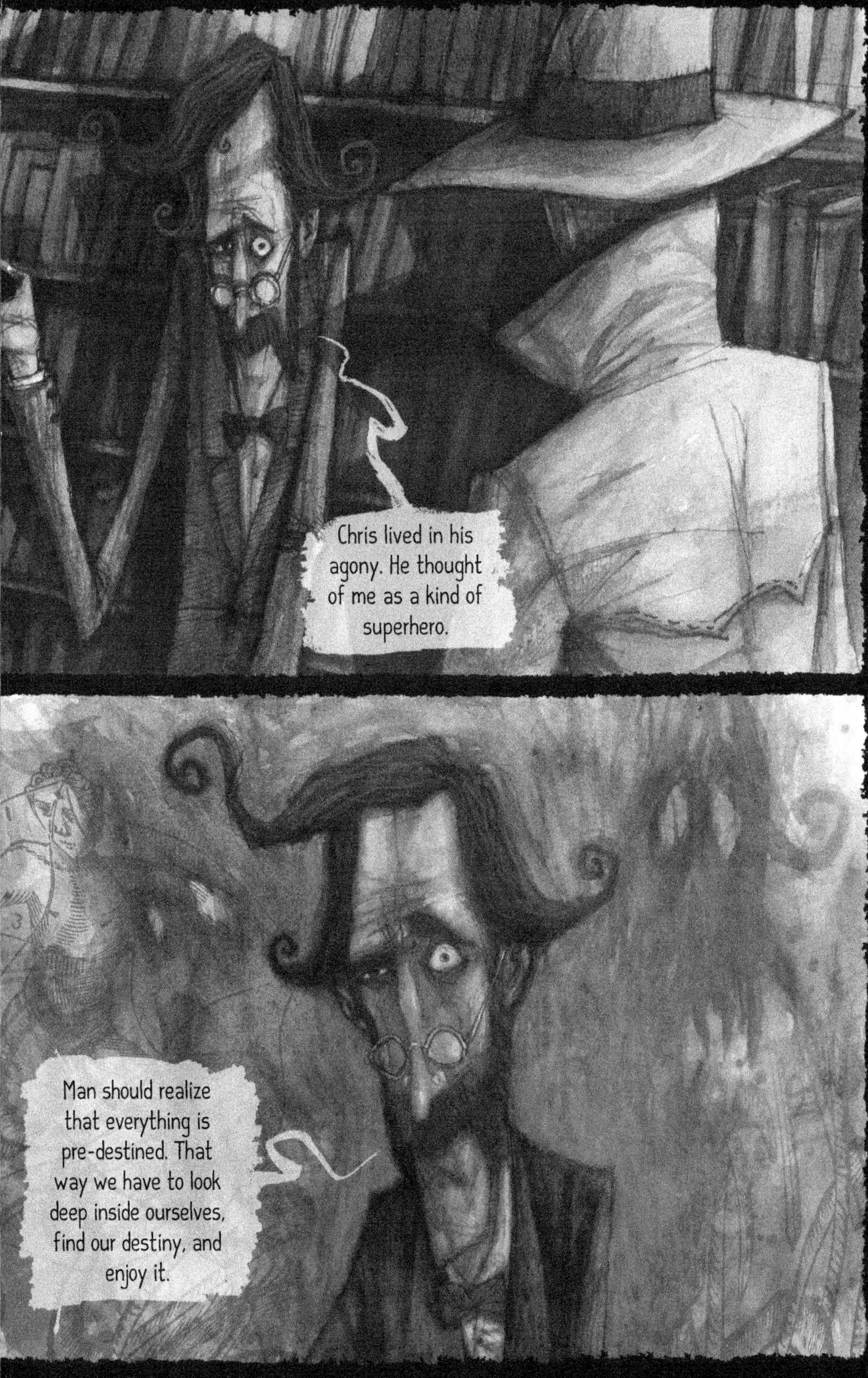

Chris lived in his agony. He thought of me as a kind of superhero.
Man should realize that everything is pre-destined. That way we have to look deep inside ourselves, find our destiny, and enjoy it.

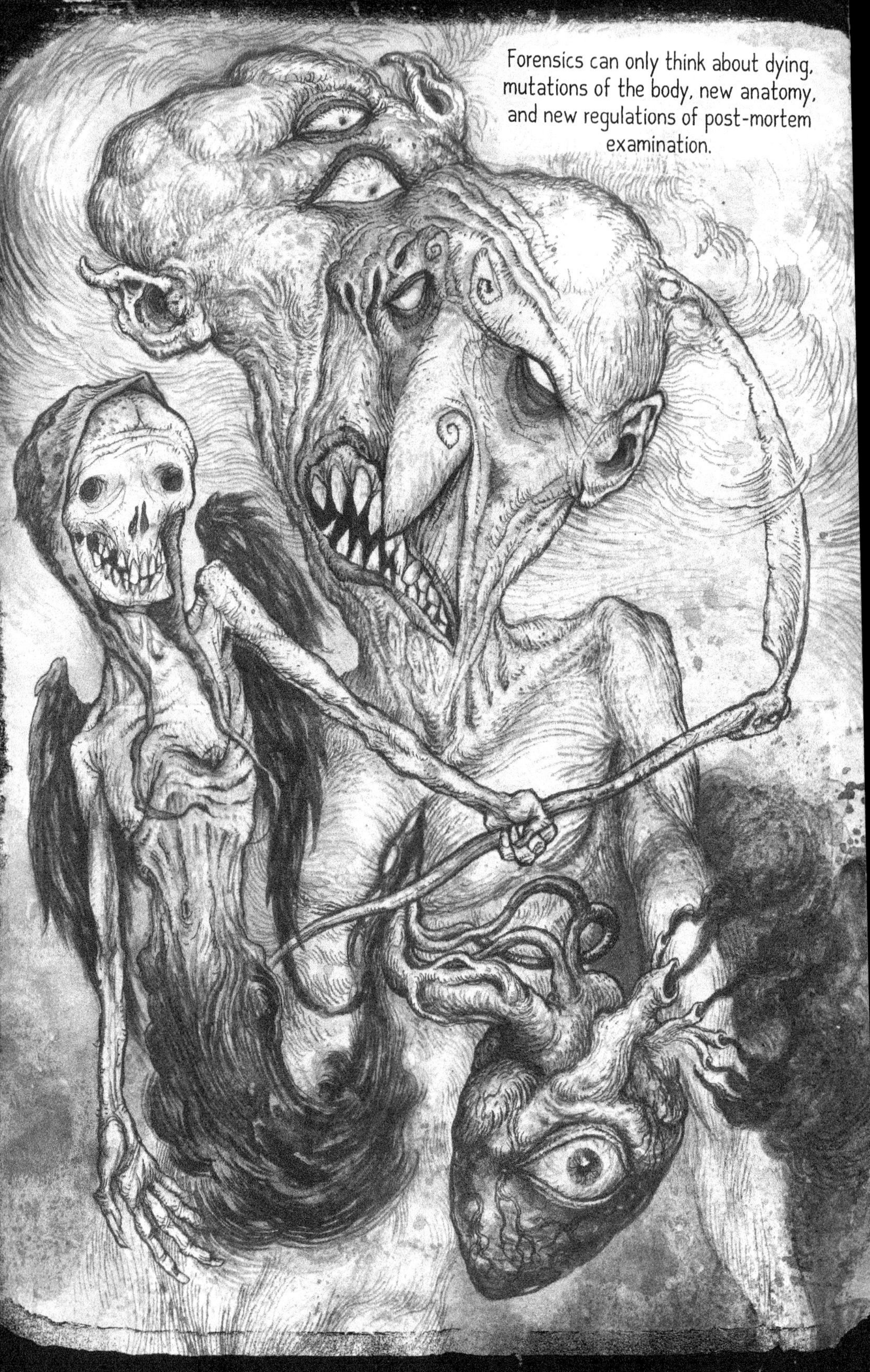
Forensics can only think about dying, mutations of the body, new anatomy, and new regulations of post-mortem examination.

That's the whole story.
Very interesting. Do you know any similar cases that could be of value to the CIA?

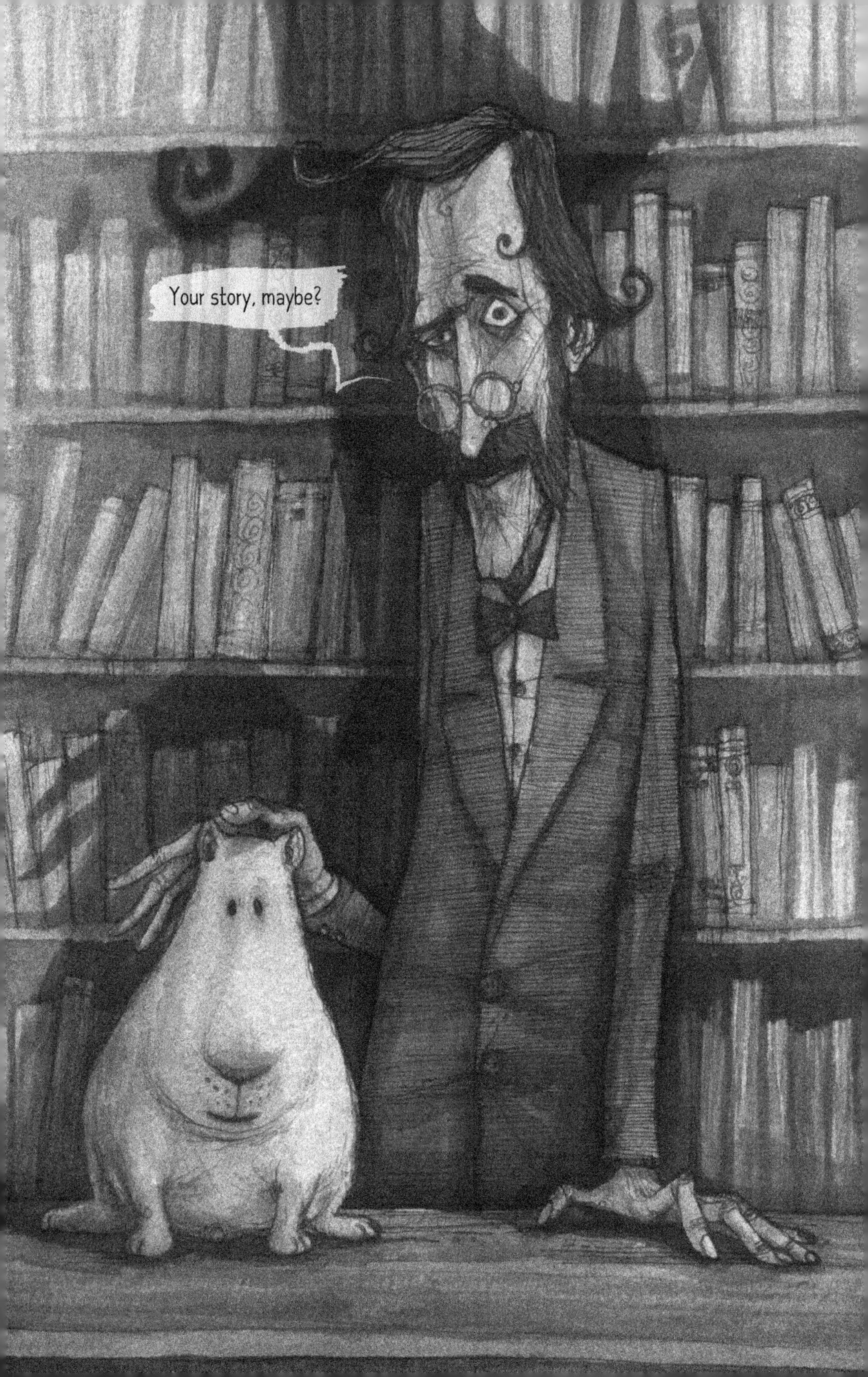
Your story, maybe?

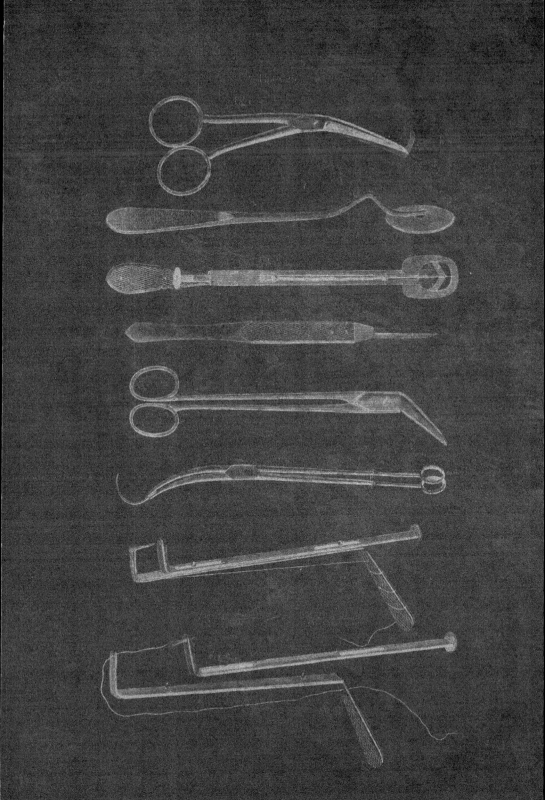

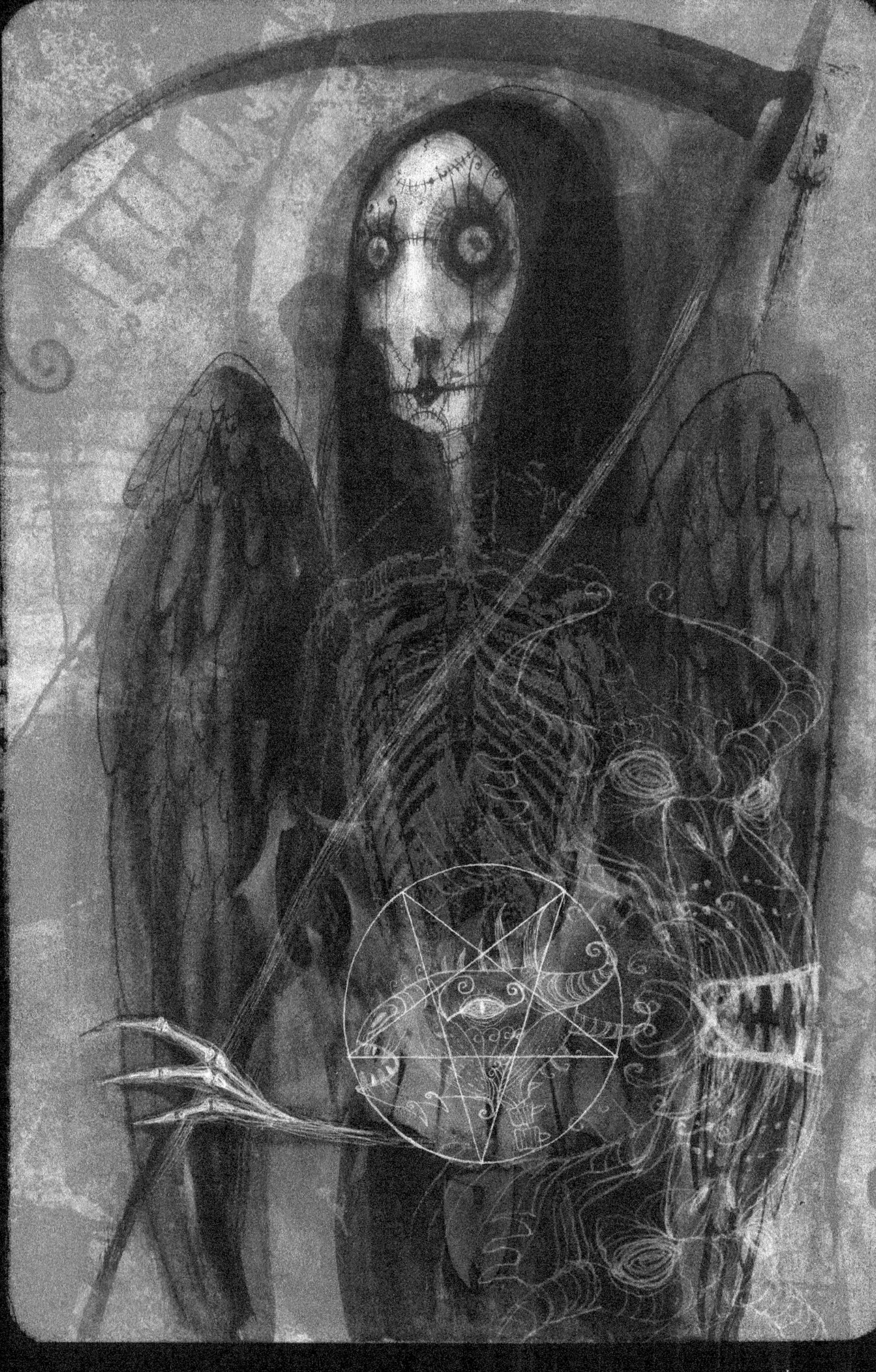

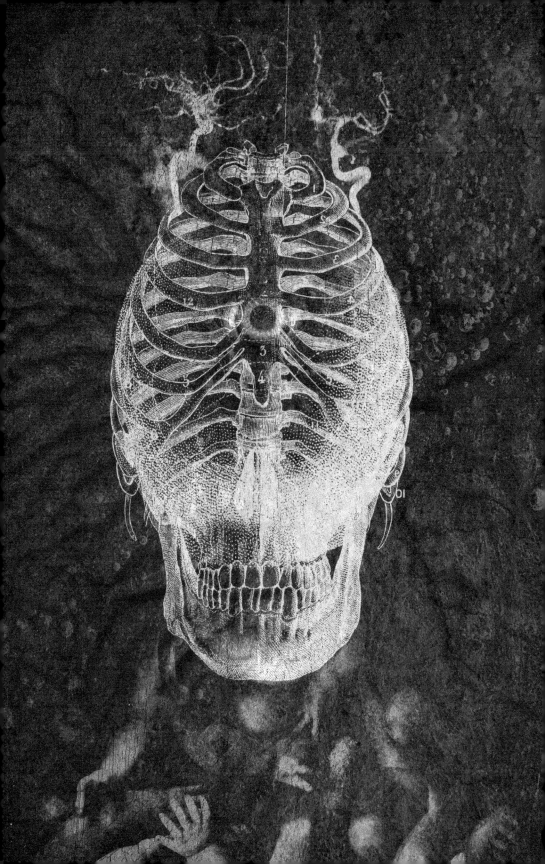

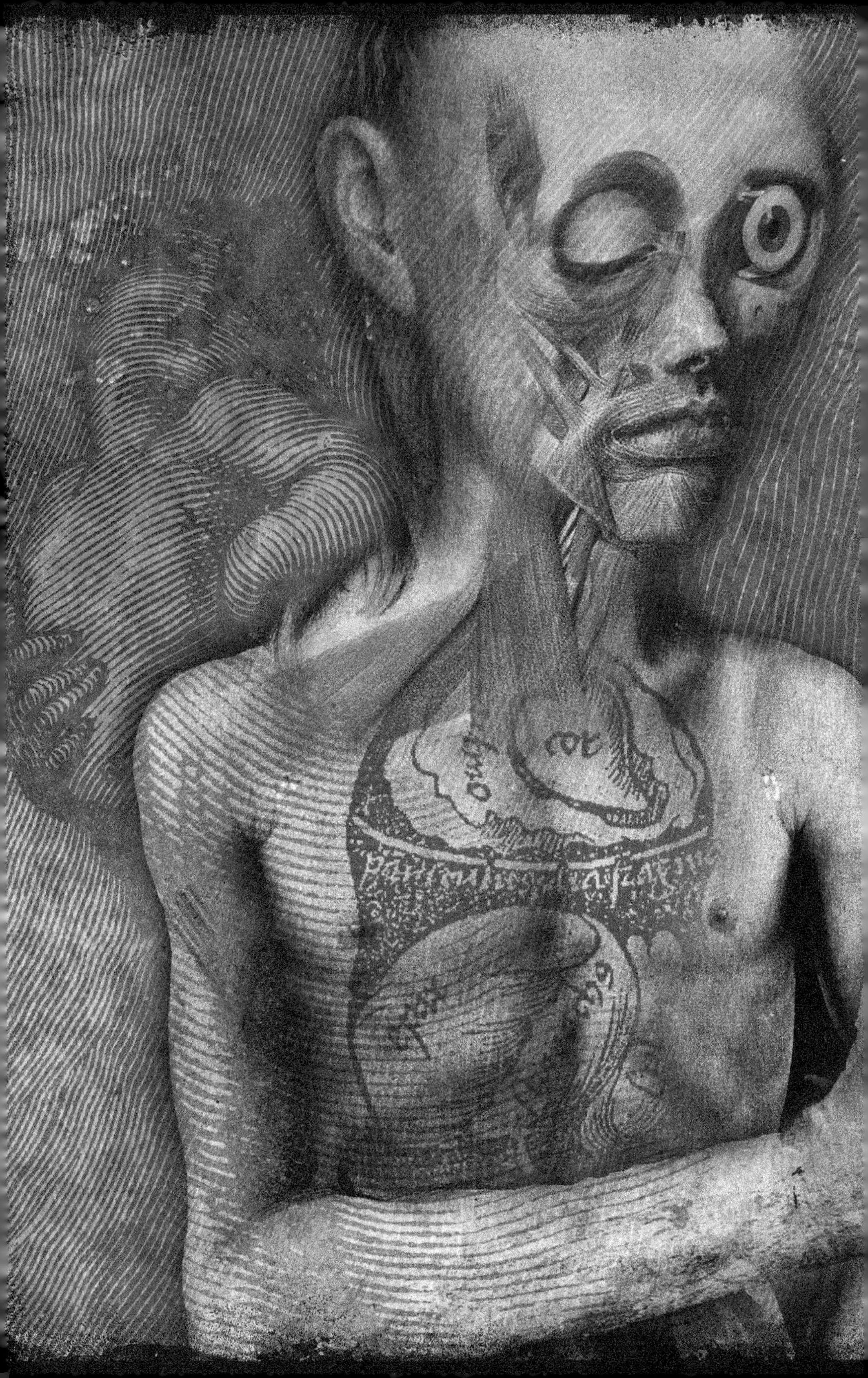

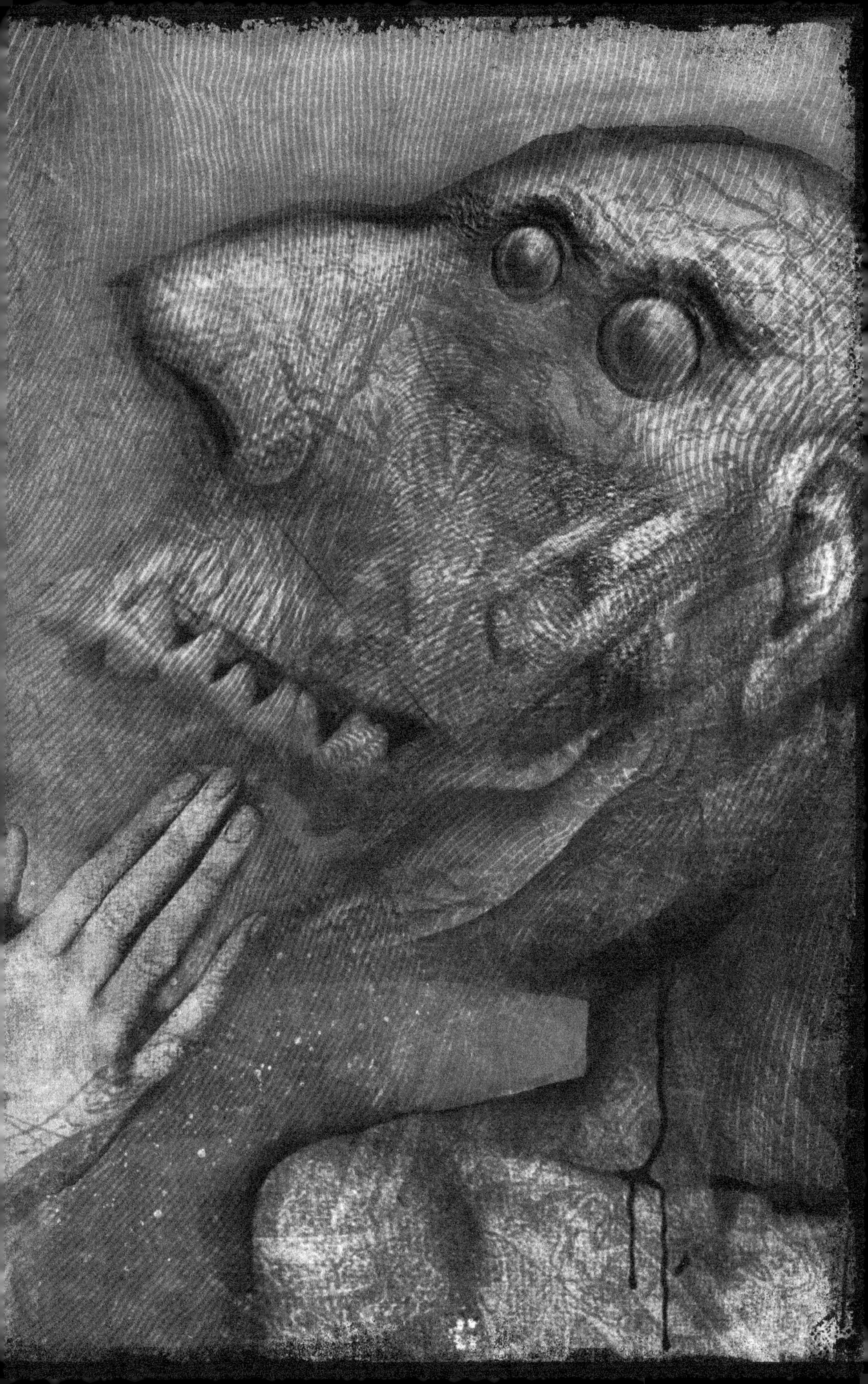

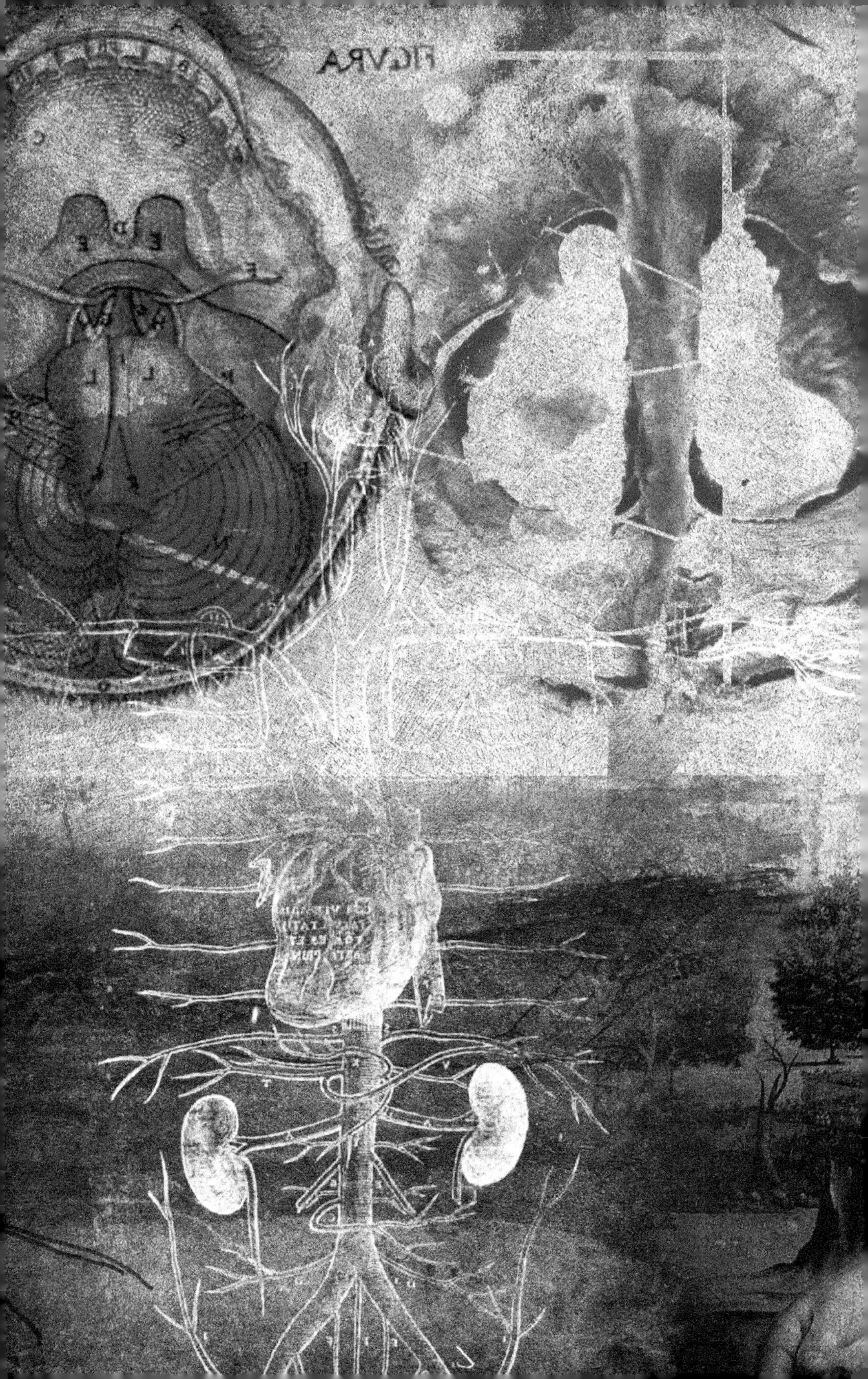

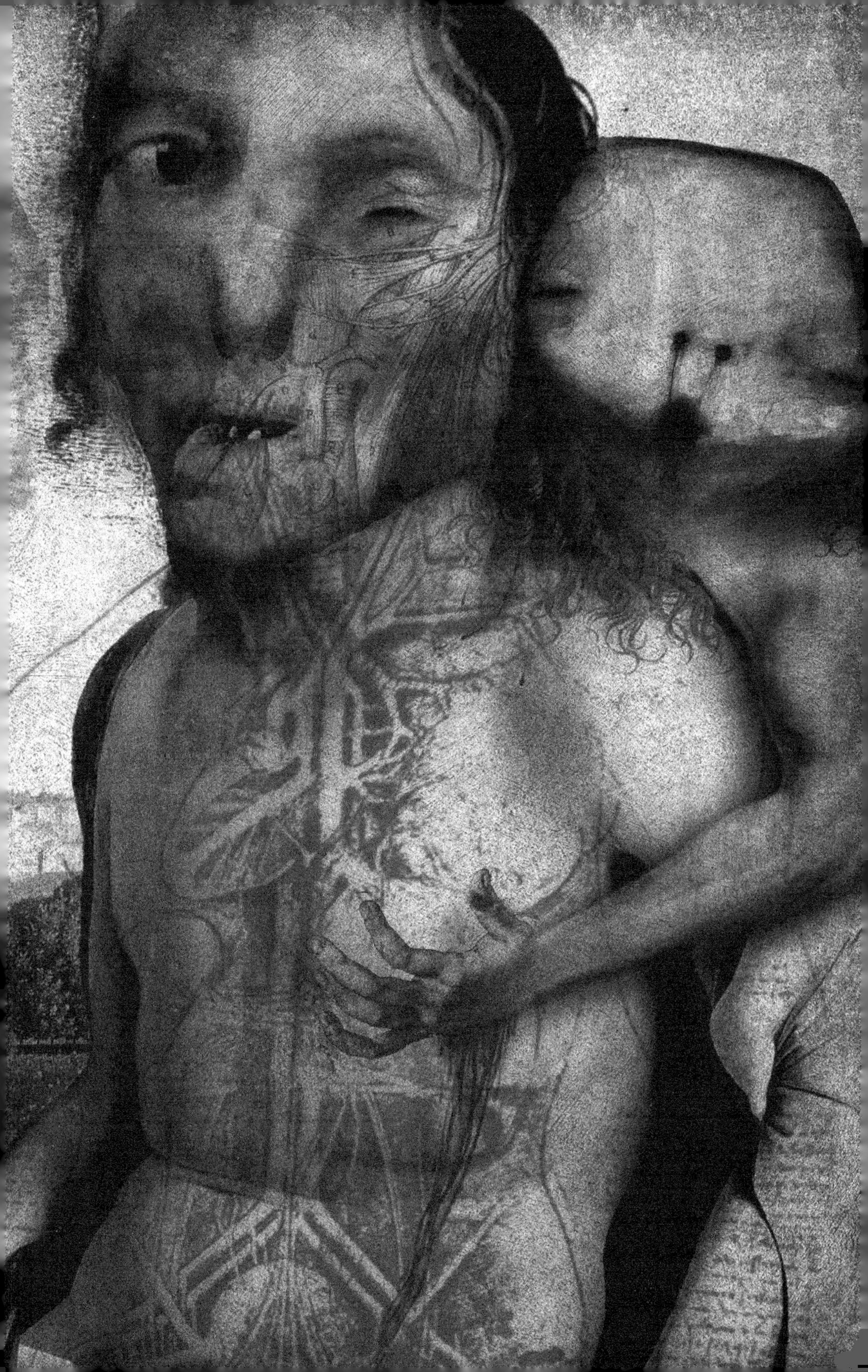

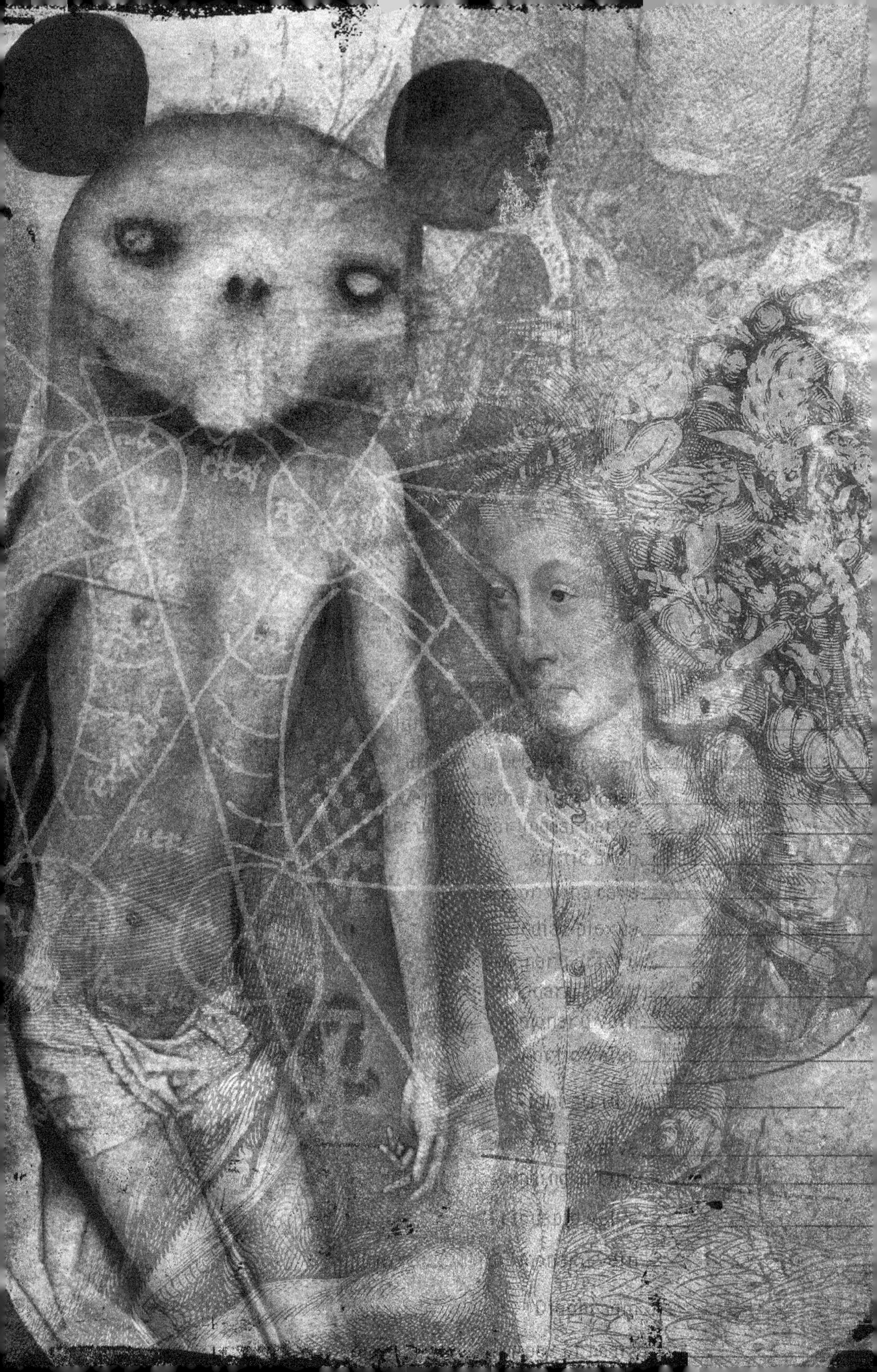

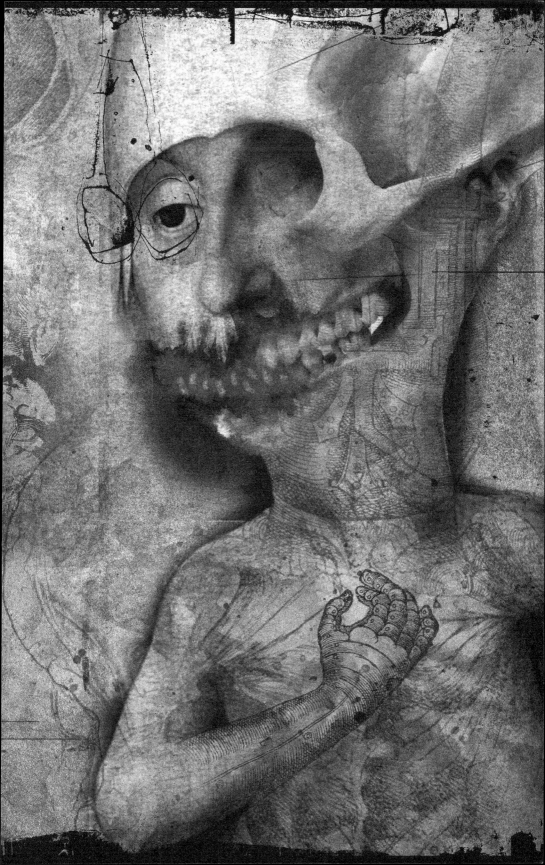

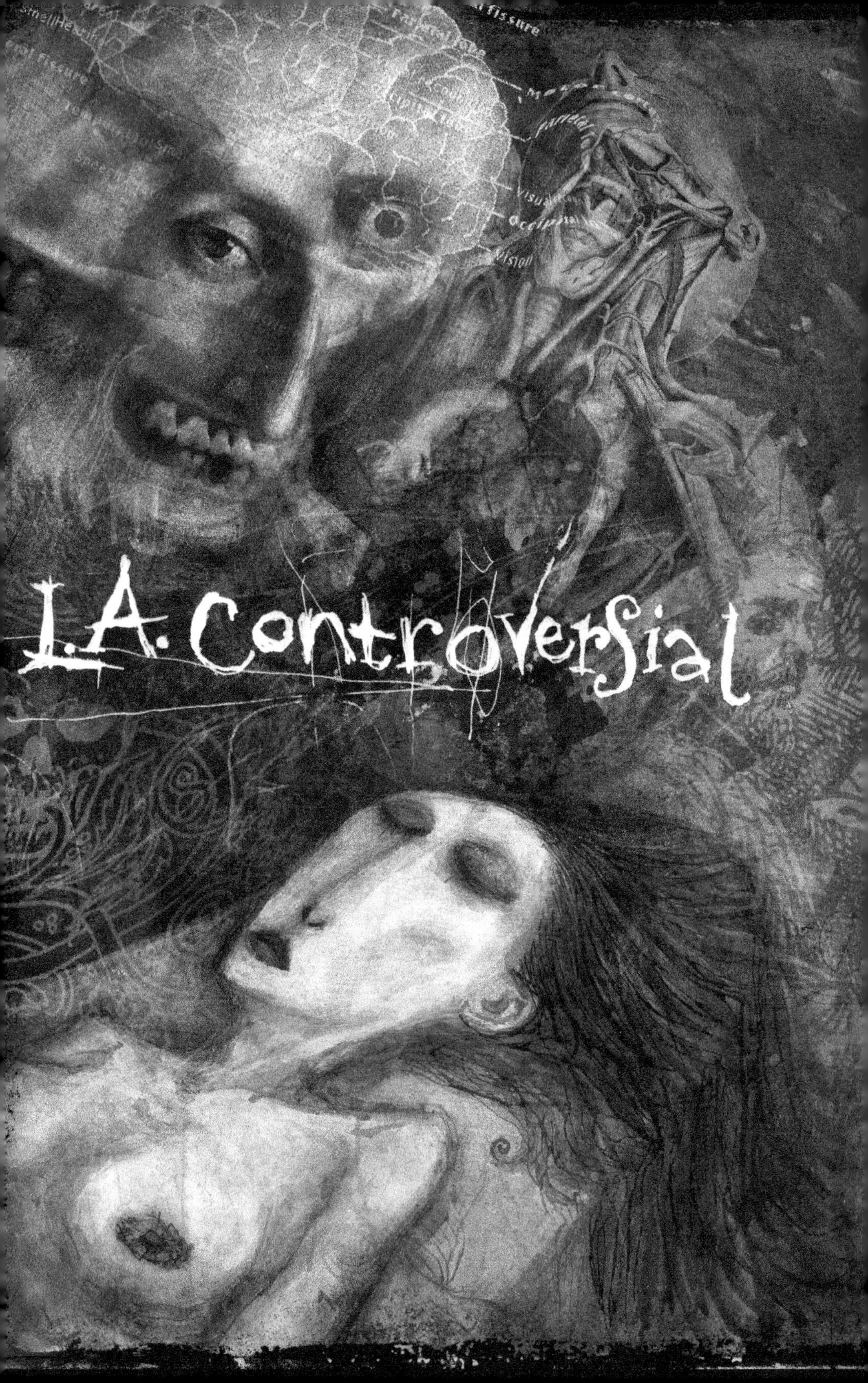
L.A. Controversial

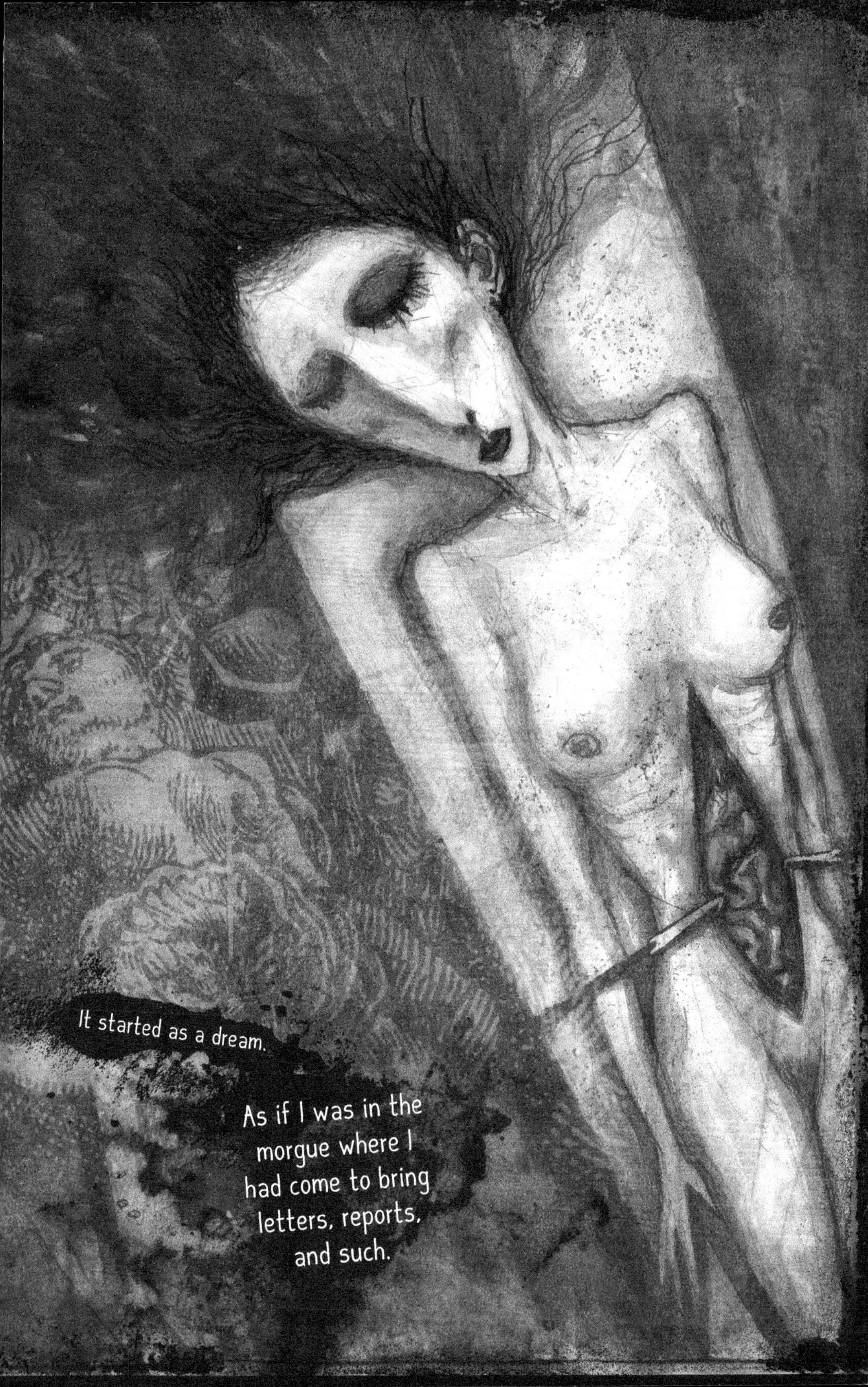
It started as a dream.
As if I was in the morgue where I had come to bring letters, reports, and such.

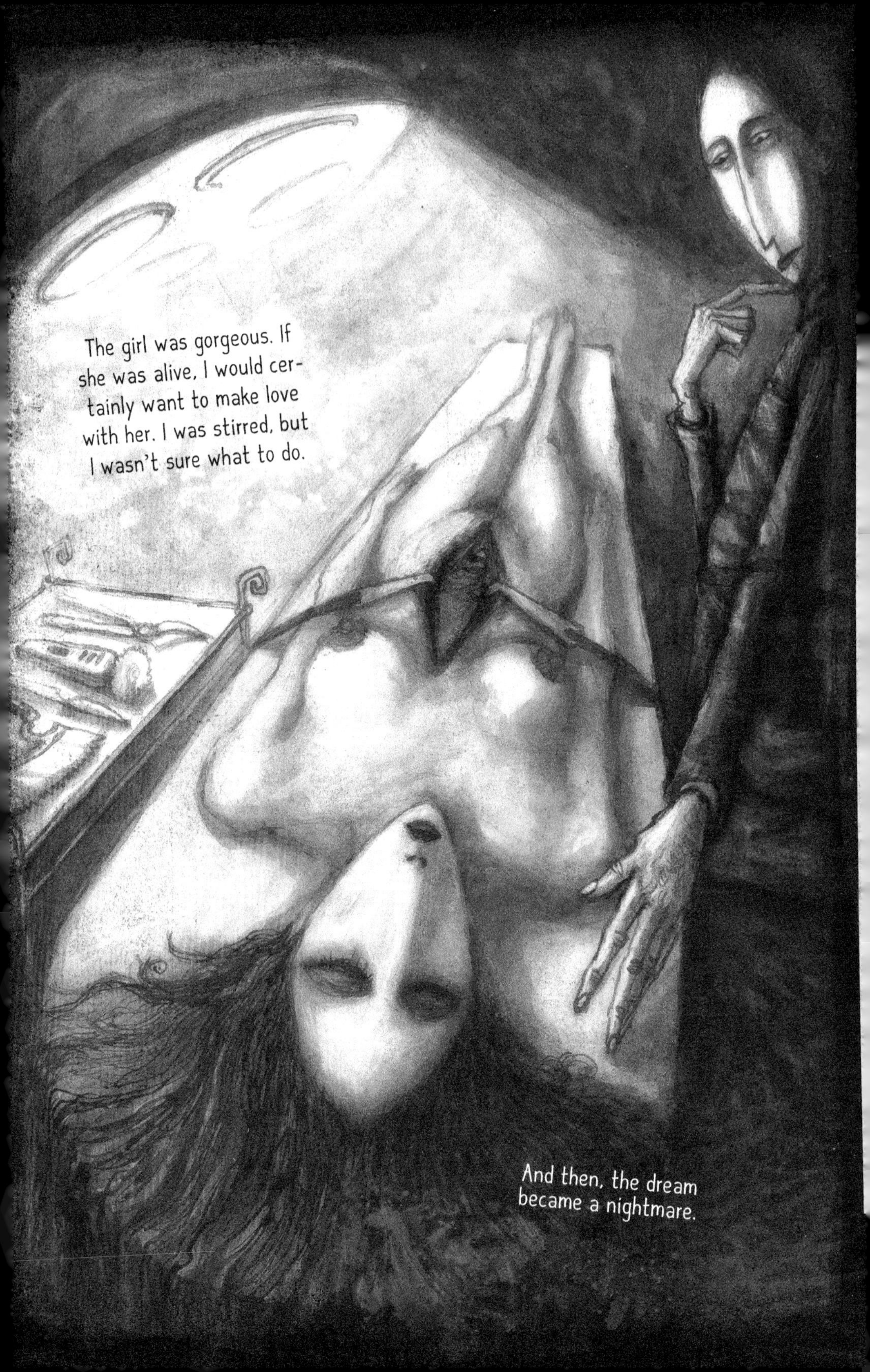
The girl was gorgeous. If she was alive, I would certainly want to make love with her. I was stirred, but I wasn't sure what to do.
And then, the dream became a nightmare.

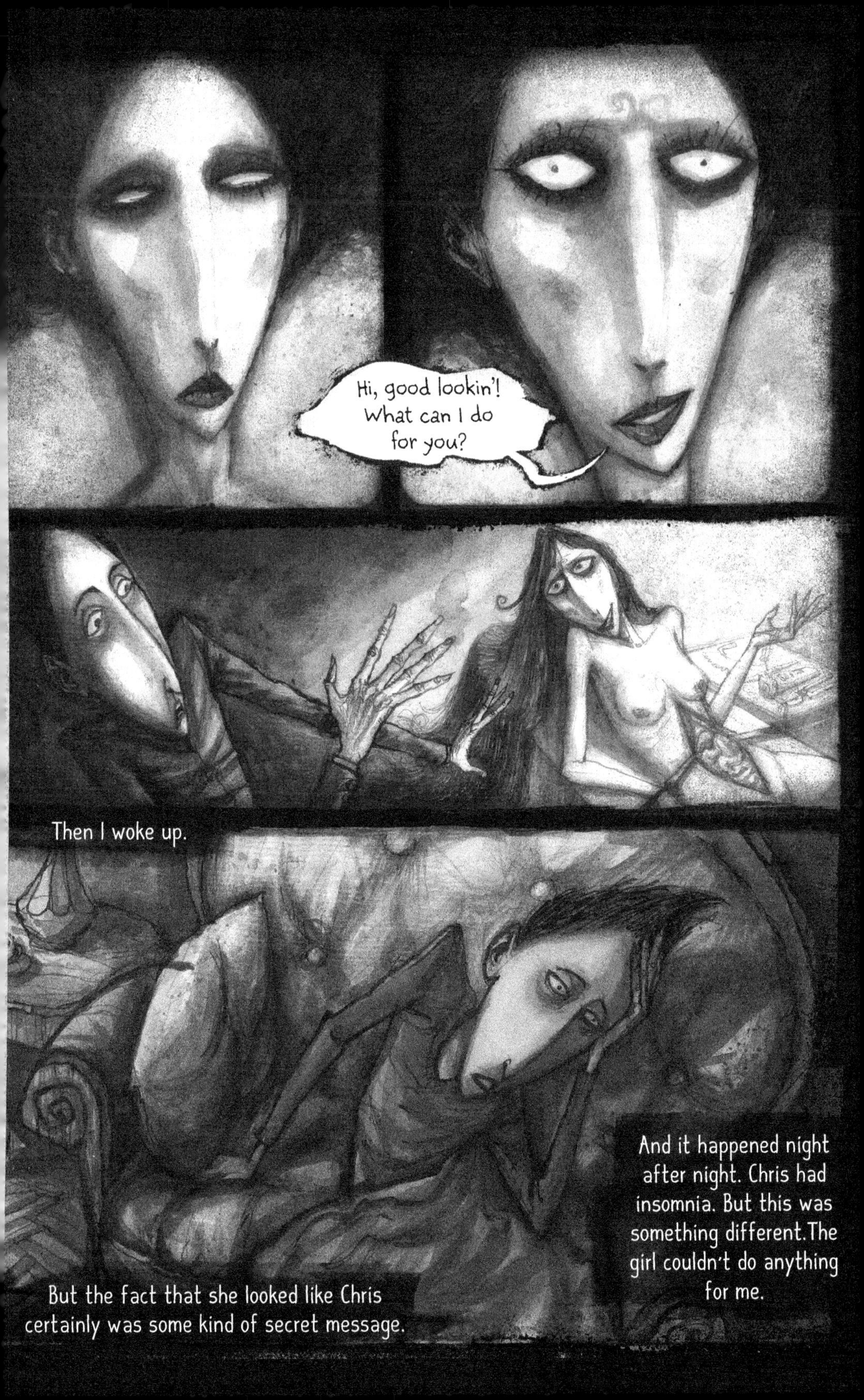
Hi, good lookin'! What can I do for you?
Then I woke up.
But the fact that she looked like Chris certainly was some kind of secret message.
And it happened night after night. Chris had insomnia. But this was something different. The girl couldn't do anything for me.

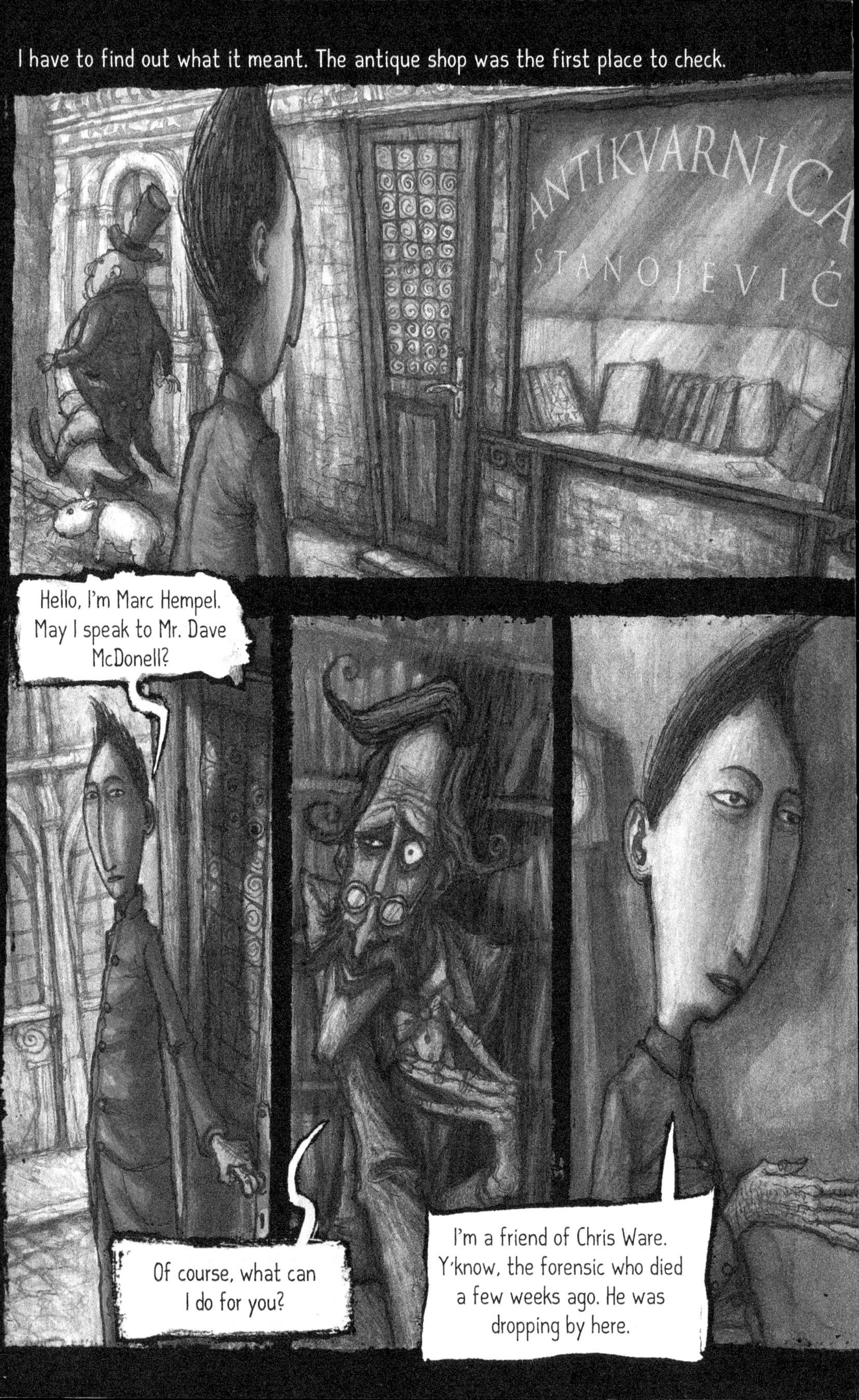
I have to find out what it meant. The antique shop was the first place to check.
ANTIKVARNICA
STANOJEVIĆ
Hello, I'm Marc Hempel. May I speak to Mr. Dave McDonell?
Of course, what can I do for you?
I'm a friend of Chris Ware. Y'know, the forensic who died a few weeks ago. He was dropping by here.

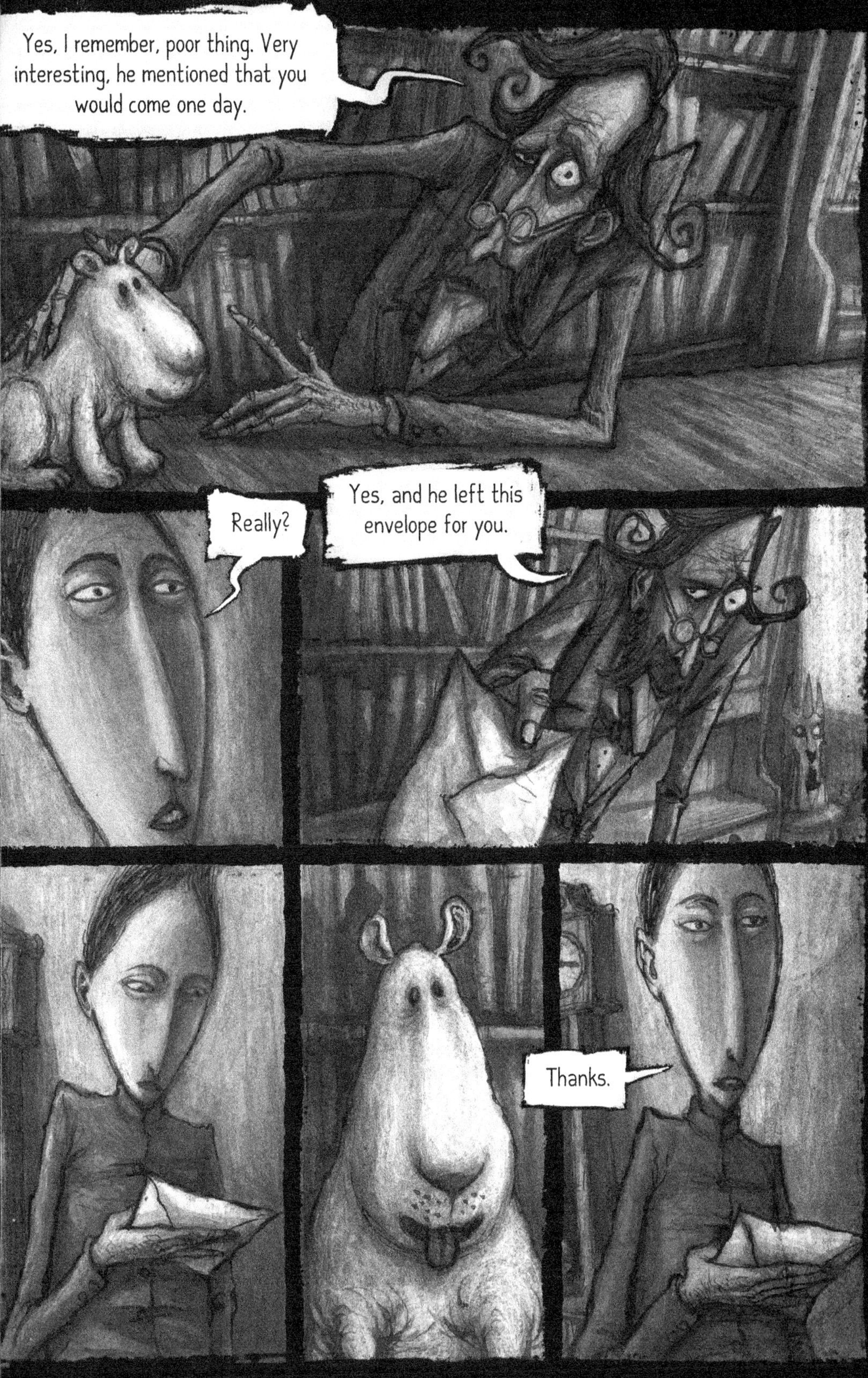
Yes, I remember, poor thing. Very interesting, he mentioned that you would come one day.
Really?
Yes, and he left this envelope for you.
Thanks.

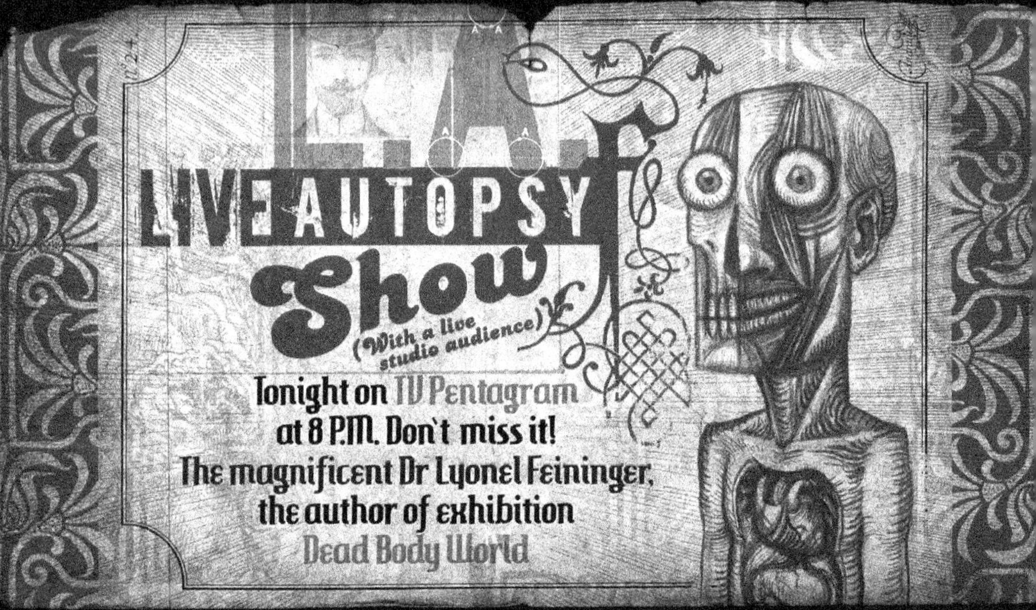
L.A.
LIVE AUTOPSY
Show
(With a live studio audience)
Tonight on TV Pentagram
at 8 P.M. Don't miss it!
The magnificent Dr Lyonel Feininger,
the author of exhibition
Dead Body World

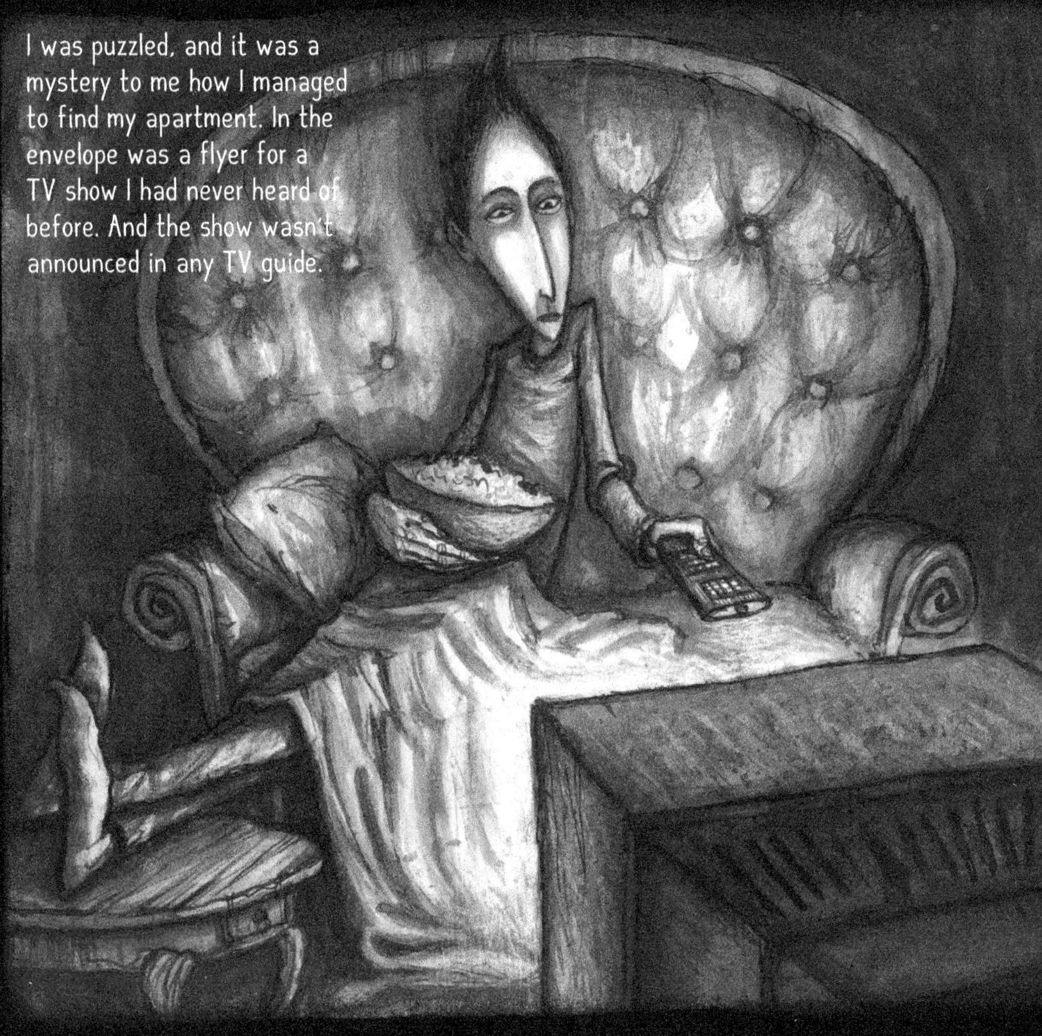
I was puzzled, and it was a mystery to me how I managed to find my apartment. In the envelope was a flyer for a TV show I had never heard of before. And the show wasn't announced in any TV guide.

Anyway, I had to watch it. I waited eagerly all evening.

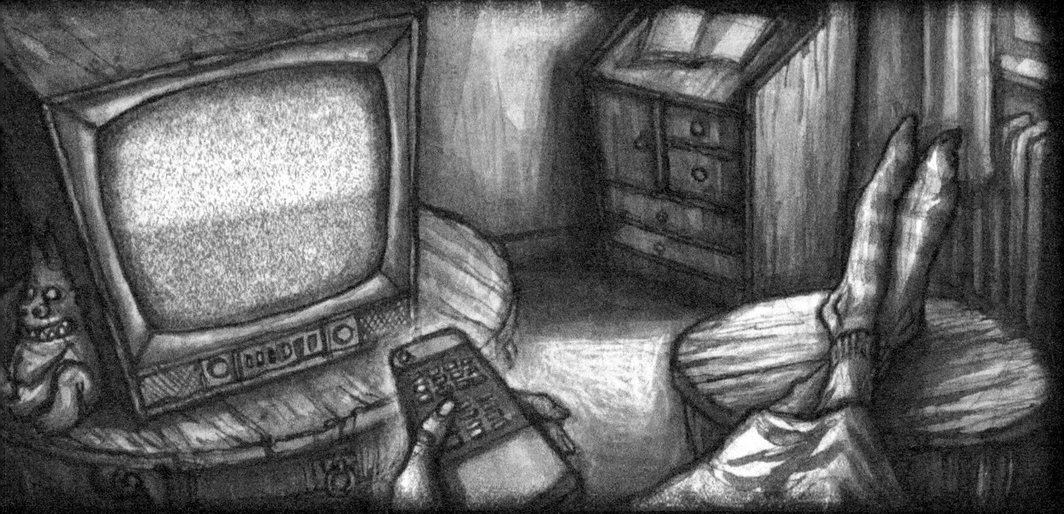

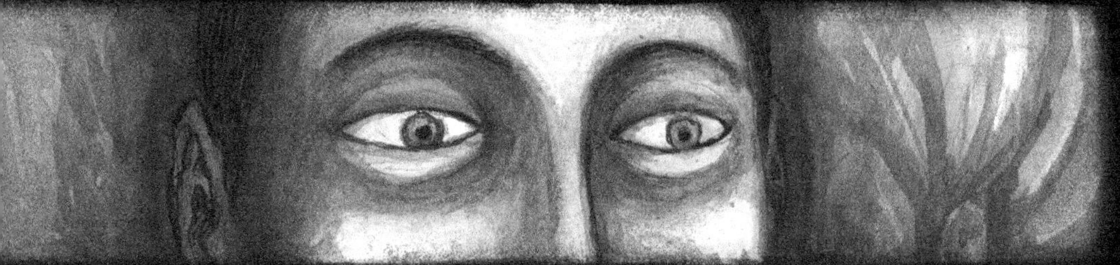

And then the dream and the nightmare...

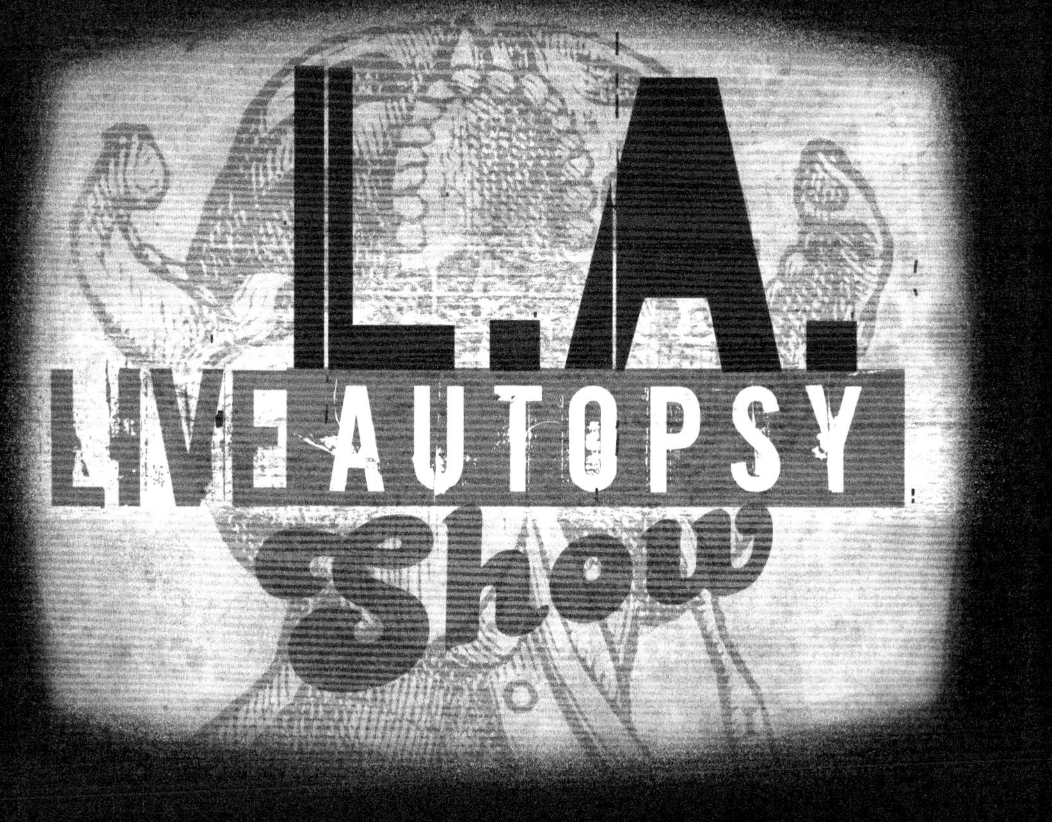
L.A.
LIVE AUTOPSY
Show

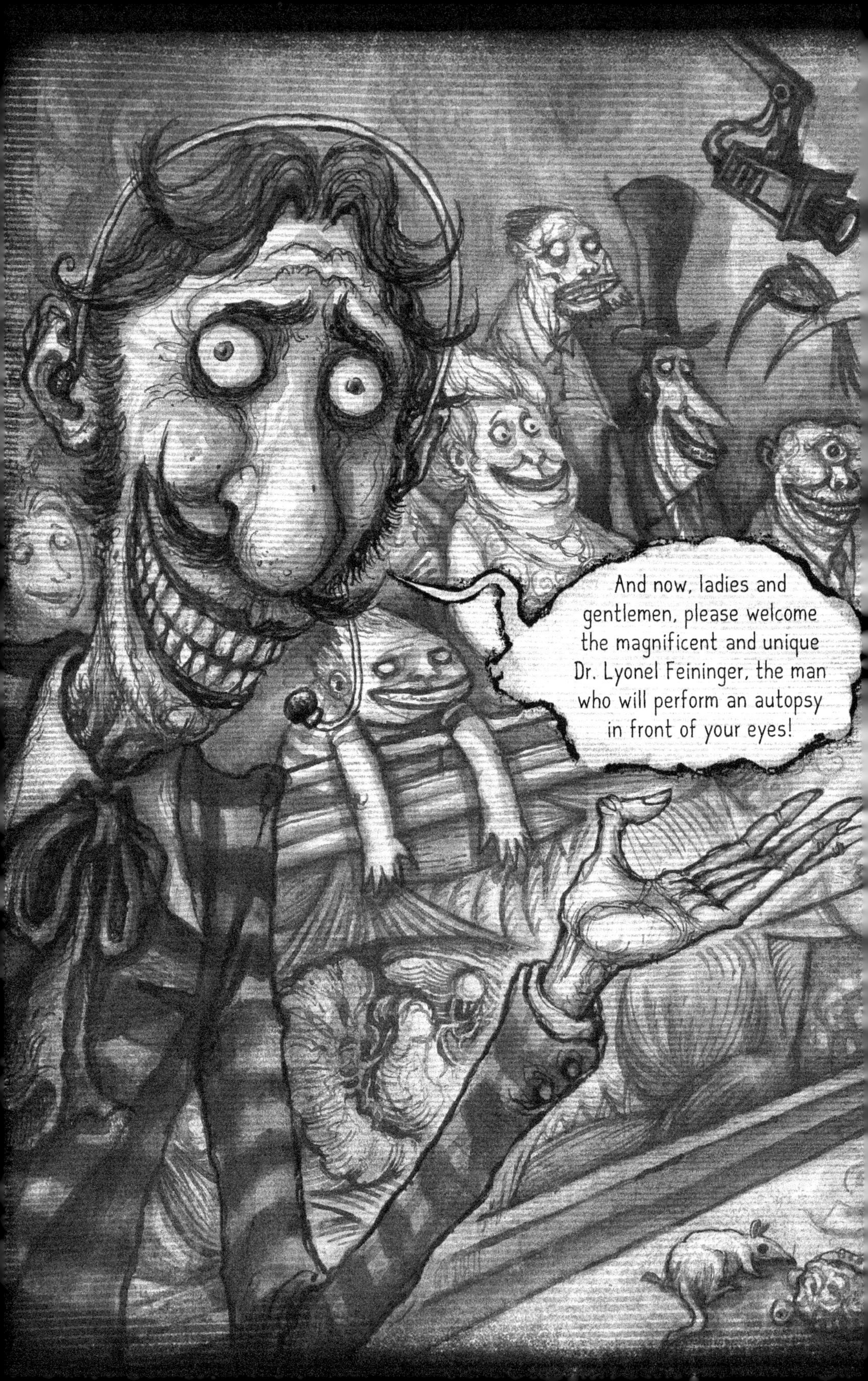
And now, ladies and gentlemen, please welcome the magnificent and unique Dr. Lyonel Feininger, the man who will perform an autopsy in front of your eyes!

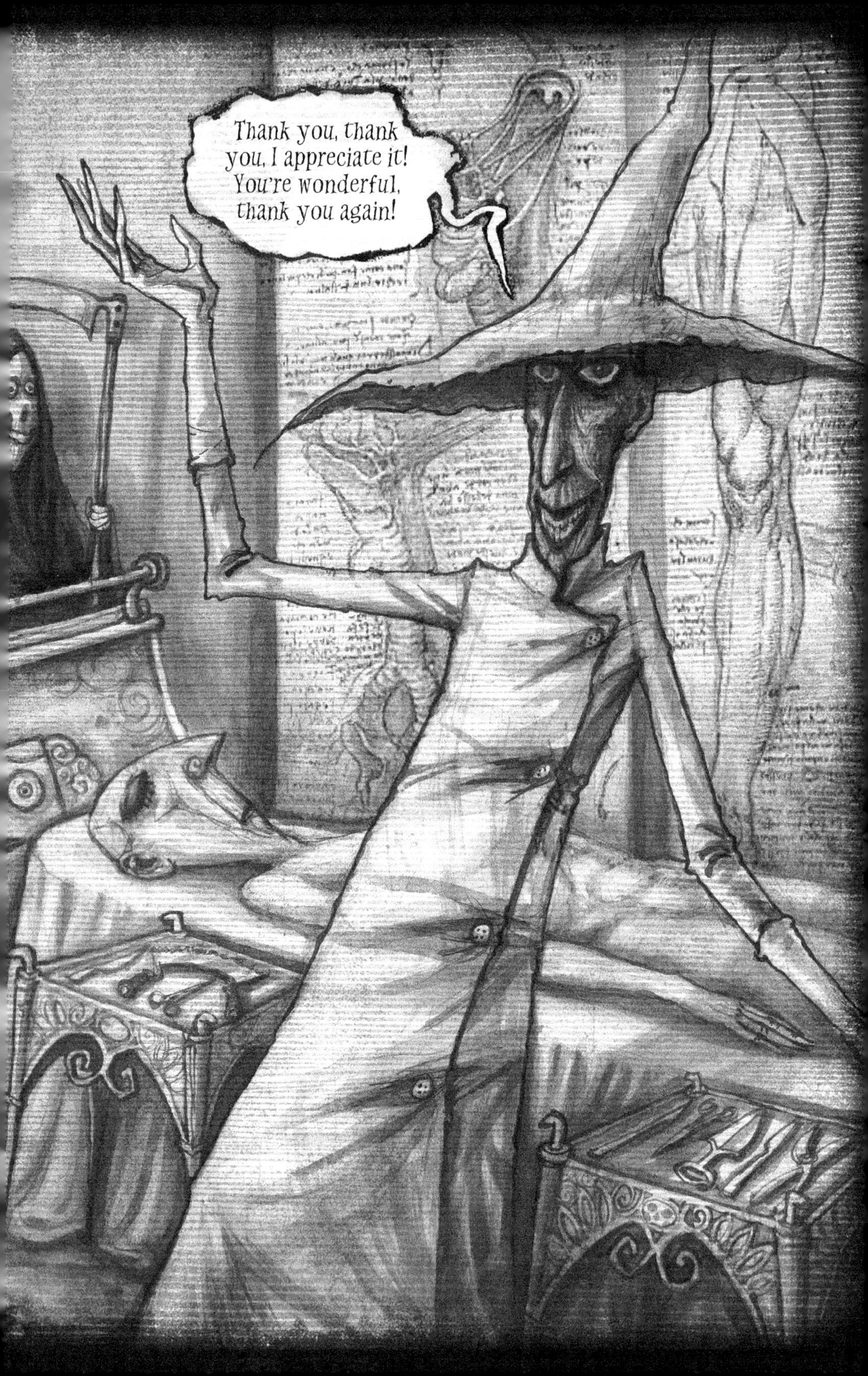
Thank you, thank you, I appreciate it! You're wonderful, thank you again!

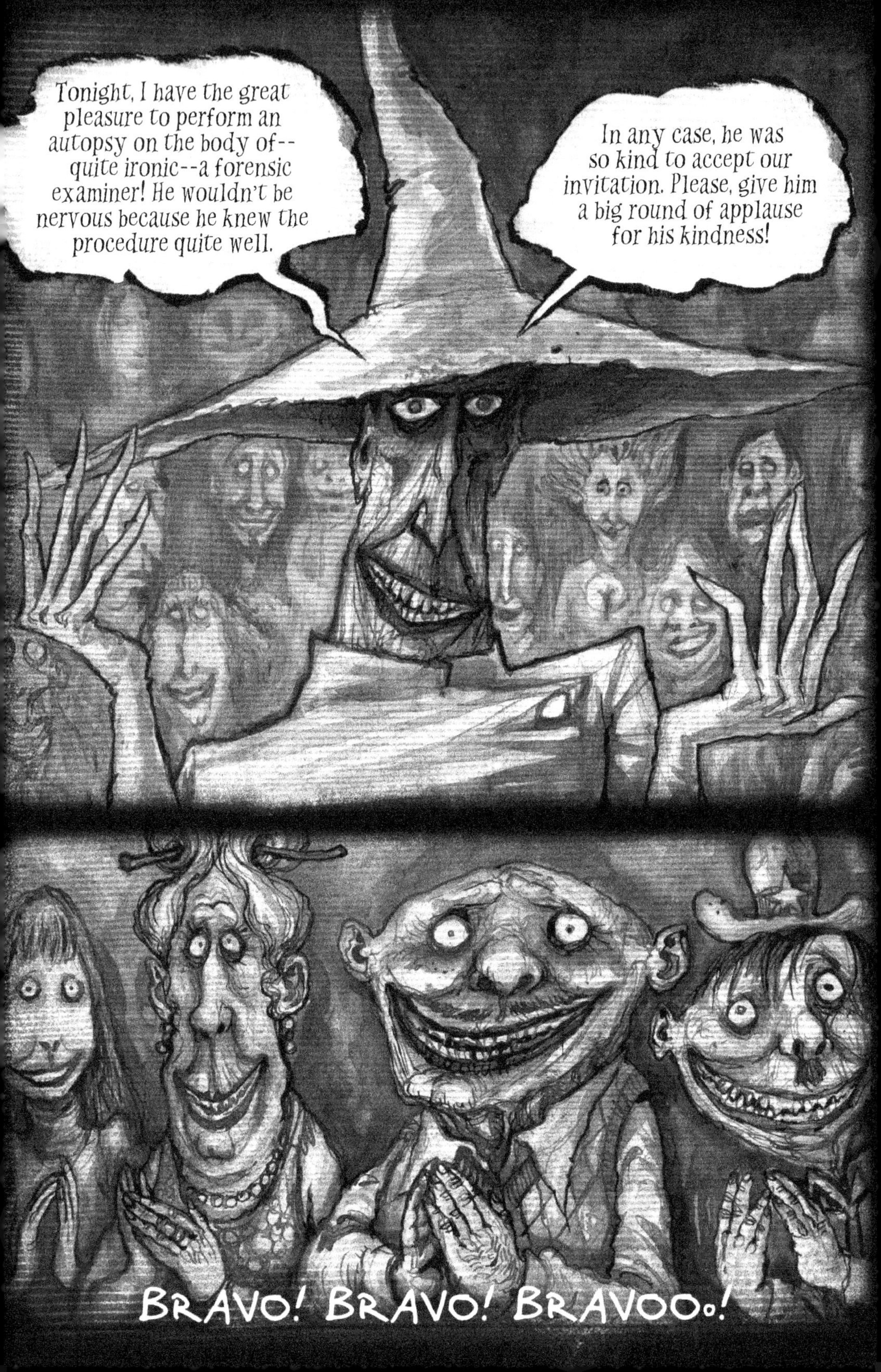
Tonight, I have the great pleasure to perform an autopsy on the body of--quite ironic--a forensic examiner! He wouldn't be nervous because he knew the procedure quite well.
In any case, he was so kind to accept our invitation. Please, give him a big round of applause for his kindness!
BRAVO! BRAVO! BRAVOOo!

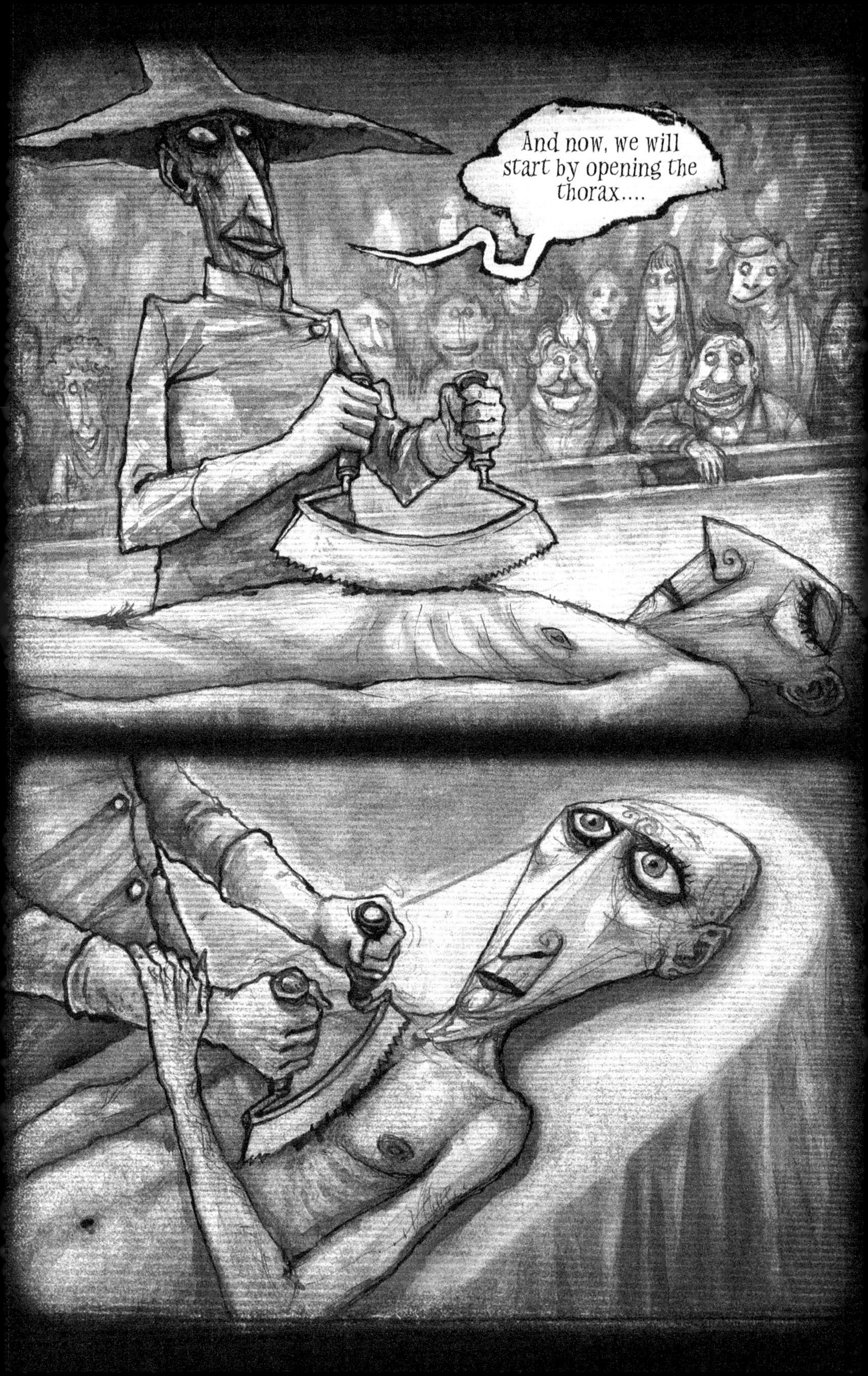
And now, we will start by opening the thorax....

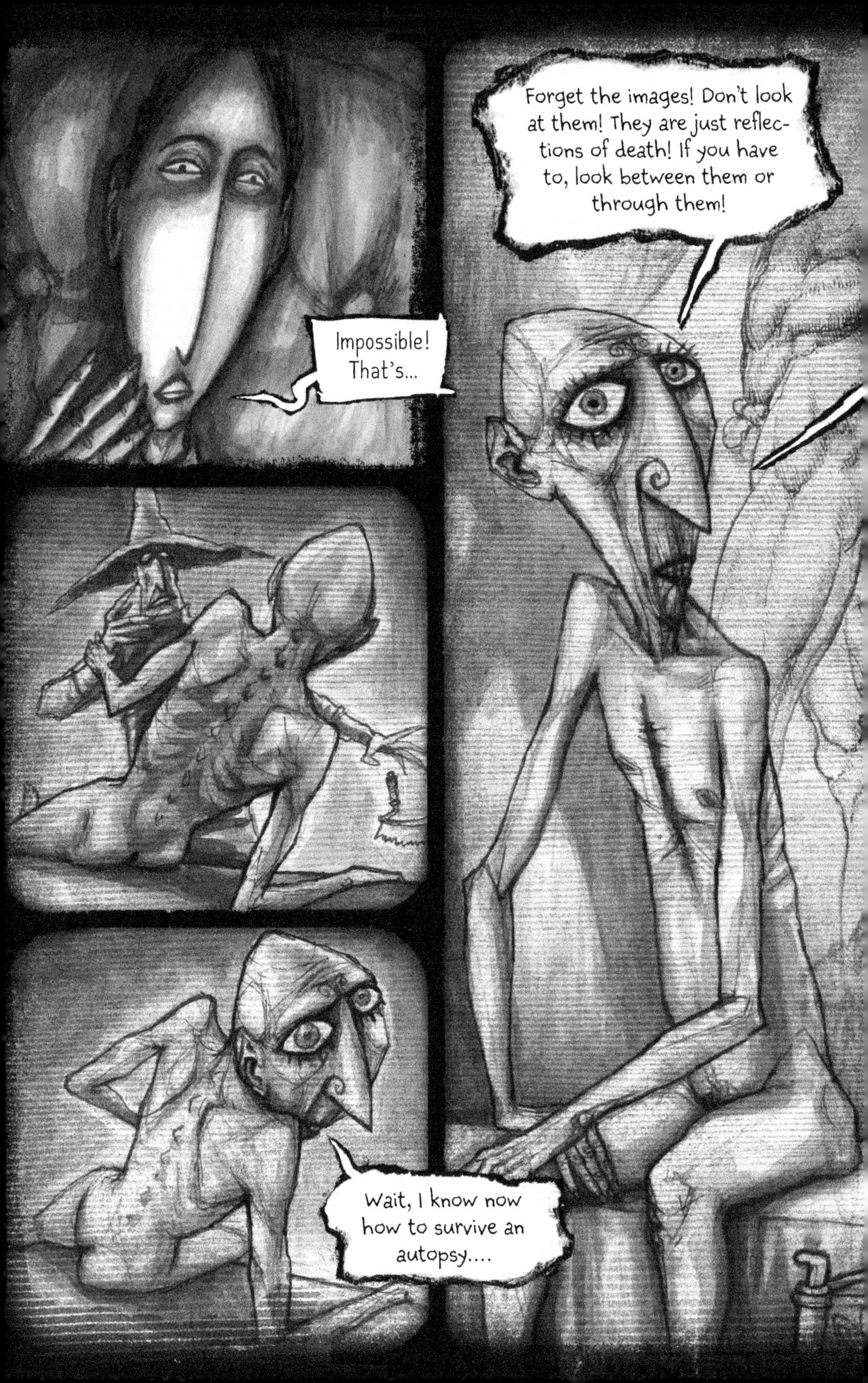
Impossible! That's...
Forget the images! Don't look at them! They are just reflections of death! If you have to, look between them or through them!
Wait, I know now how to survive an autopsy....

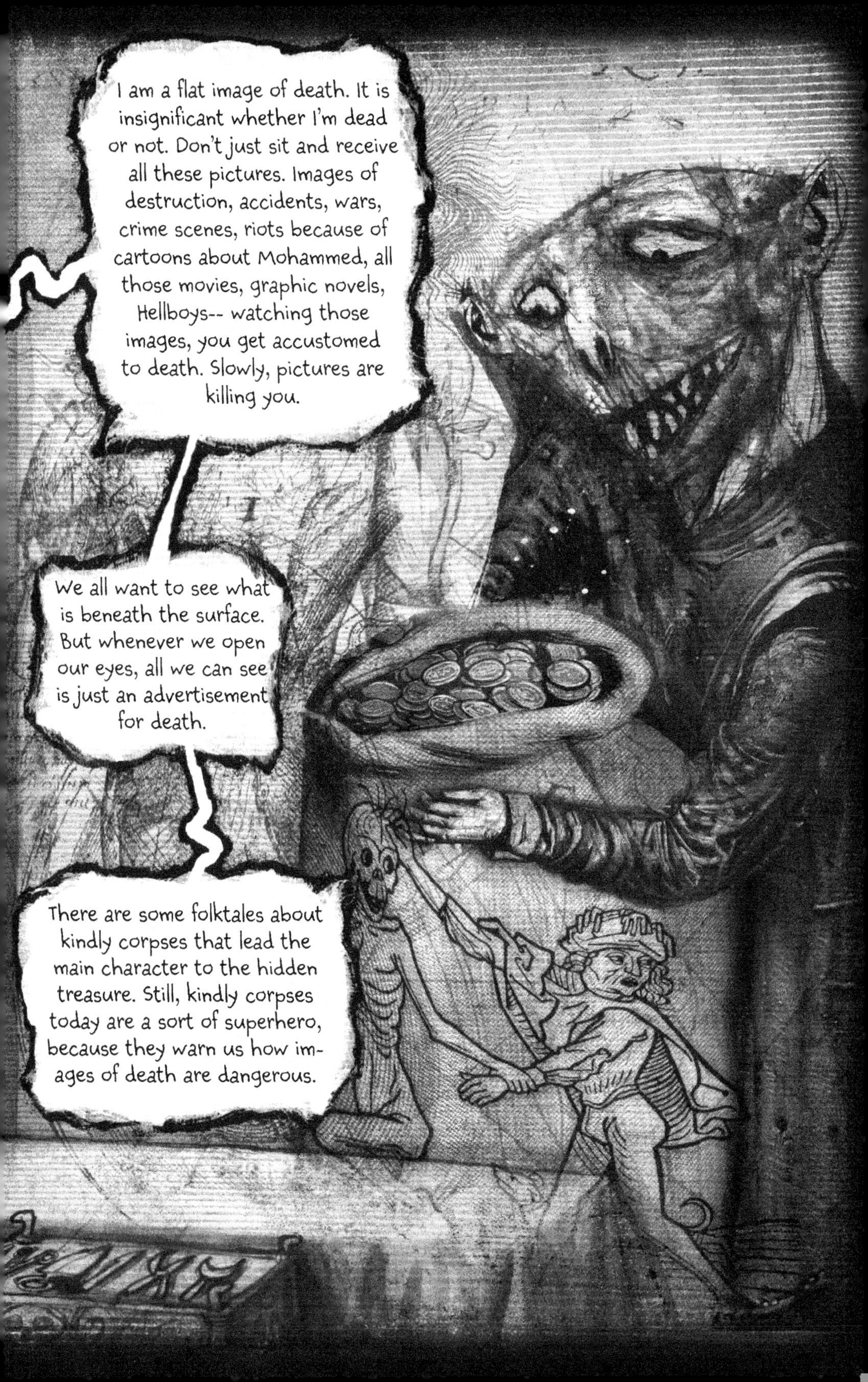
I am a flat image of death. It is insignificant whether I'm dead or not. Don't just sit and receive all these pictures. Images of destruction, accidents, wars, crime scenes, riots because of cartoons about Mohammed, all those movies, graphic novels, Hellboys-- watching those images, you get accustomed to death. Slowly, pictures are killing you.
We all want to see what is beneath the surface. But whenever we open our eyes, all we can see is just an advertisement for death.
There are some folktales about kindly corpses that lead the main character to the hidden treasure. Still, kindly corpses today are a sort of superhero, because they warn us how images of death are dangerous.

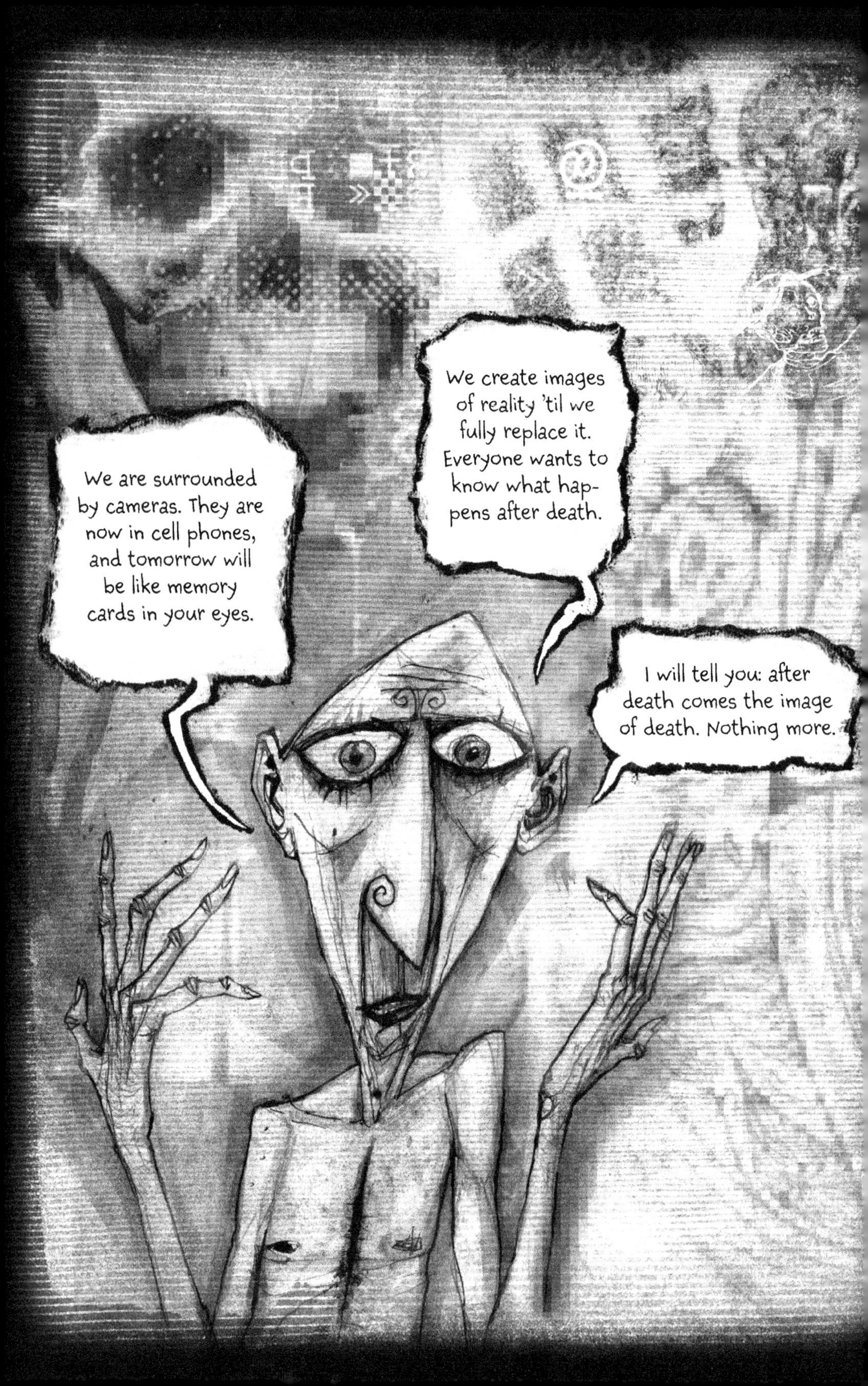
We are surrounded by cameras. They are now in cell phones, and tomorrow will be like memory cards in your eyes.
We create images of reality 'til we fully replace it. Everyone wants to know what happens after death.
I will tell you: after death comes the image of death. Nothing more.

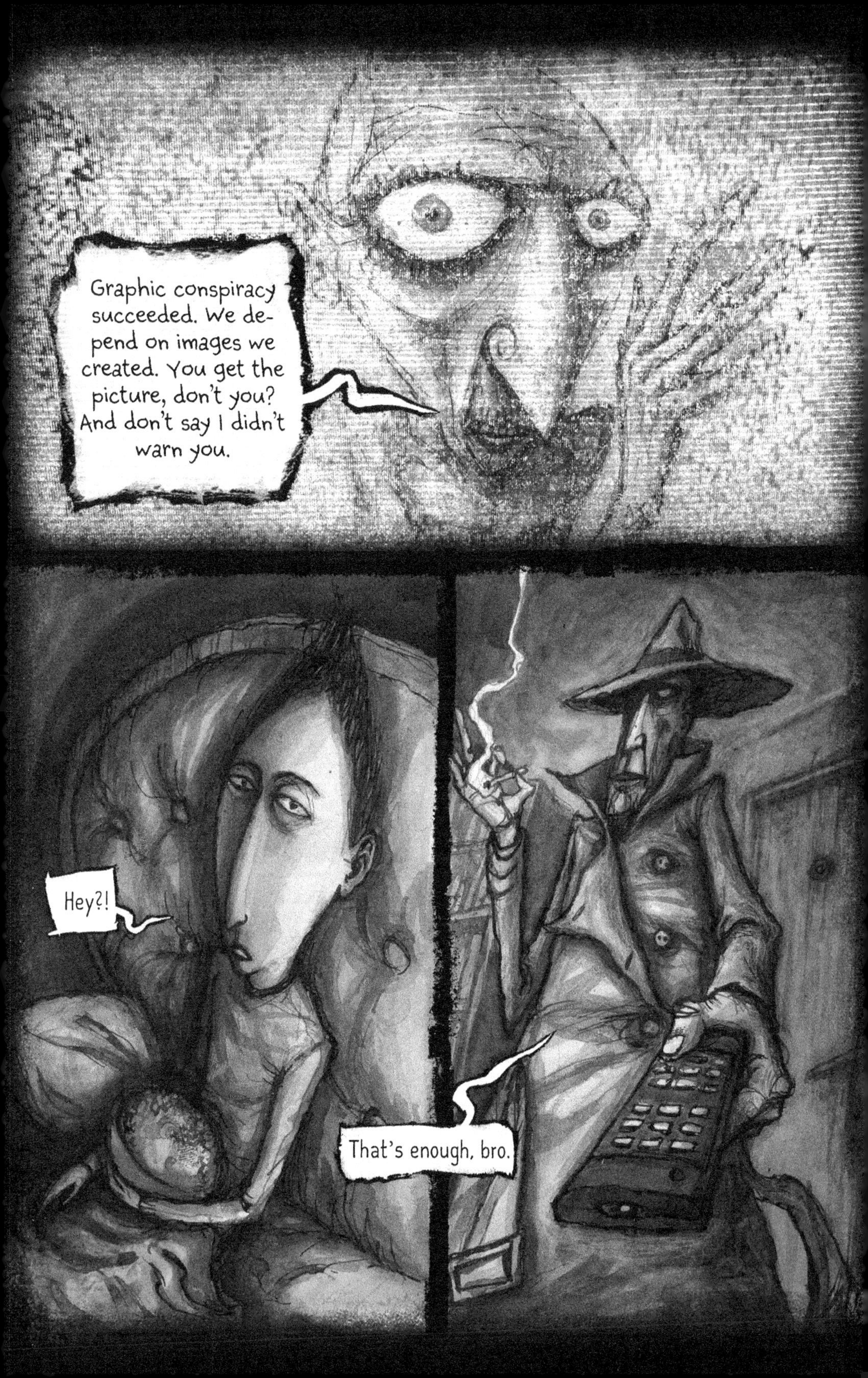
Graphic conspiracy succeeded. We depend on images we created. You get the picture, don't you? And don't say I didn't warn you.
Hey?!
That's enough, bro.

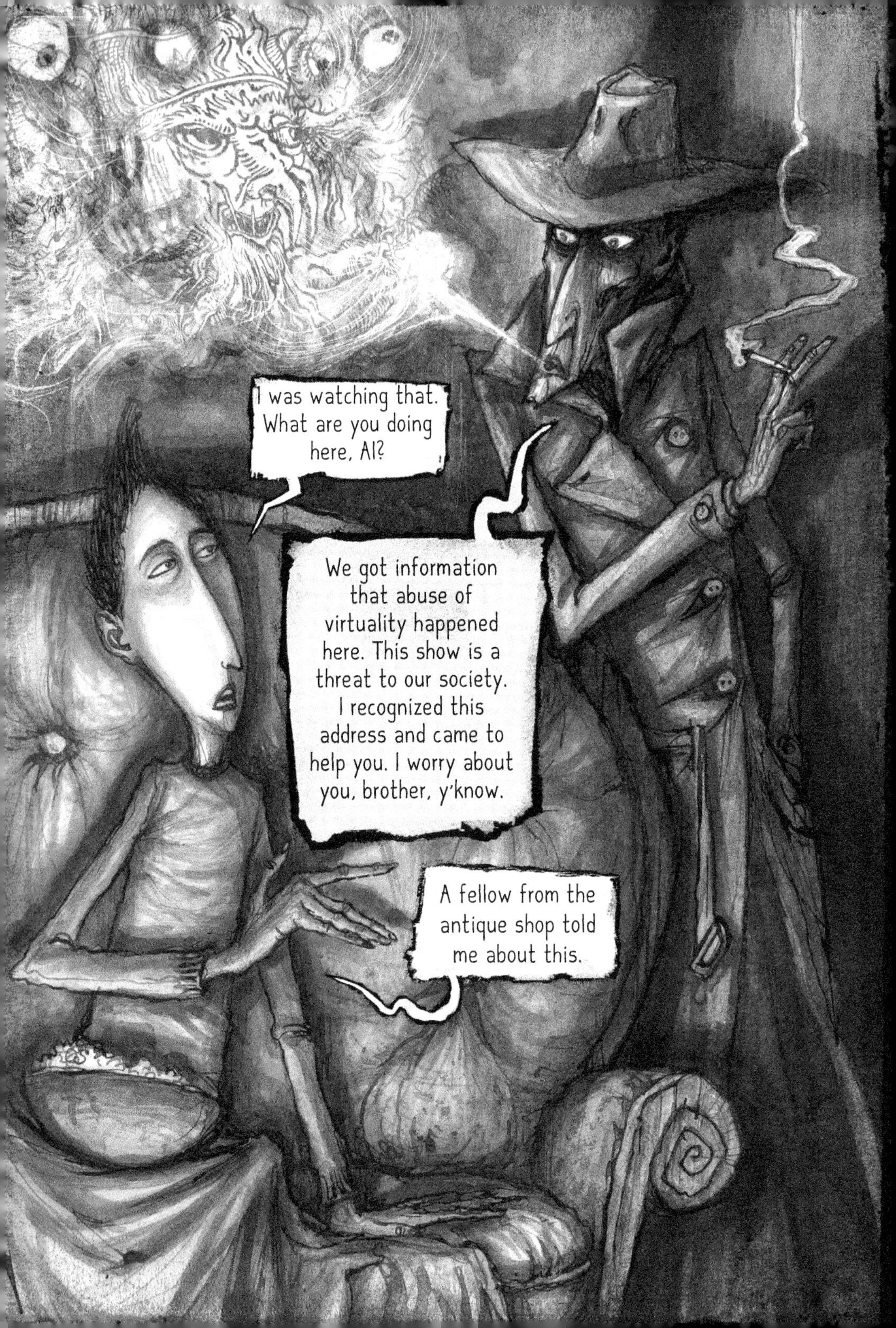
I was watching that. What are you doing here, Al?
We got information that abuse of virtuality happened here. This show is a threat to our society. I recognized this address and came to help you. I worry about you, brother, y'know.
A fellow from the antique shop told me about this.

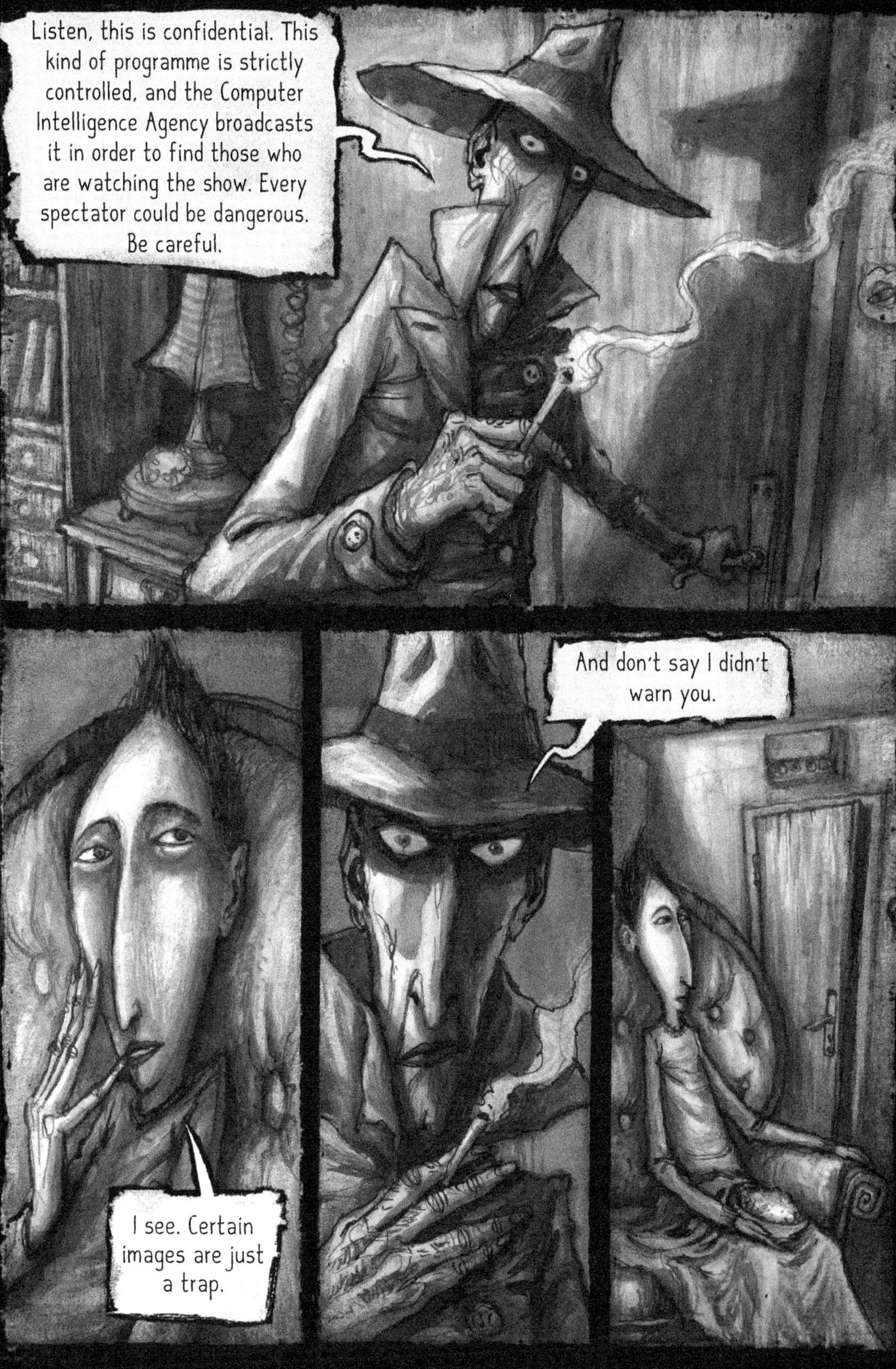
Listen, this is confidential. This kind of programme is strictly controlled, and the Computer Intelligence Agency broadcasts it in order to find those who are watching the show. Every spectator could be dangerous. Be careful.
I see. Certain images are just a trap.
And don't say I didn't warn you.

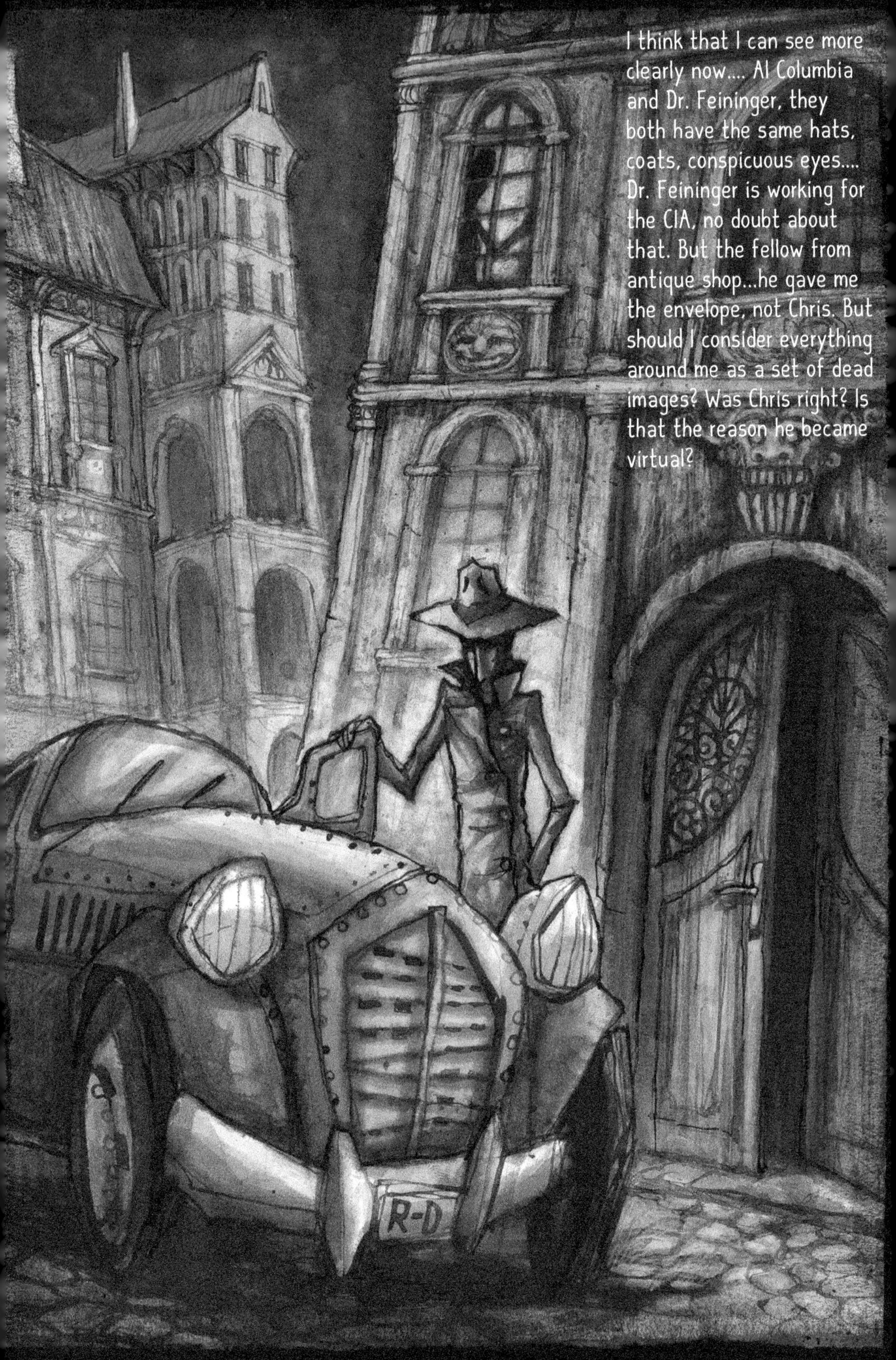
I think that I can see more clearly now.... Al Columbia and Dr. Feininger, they both have the same hats, coats, conspicuous eyes.... Dr. Feininger is working for the CIA, no doubt about that. But the fellow from antique shop...he gave me the envelope, not Chris. But should I consider everything around me as a set of dead images? Was Chris right? Is that the reason he became virtual?
R-D

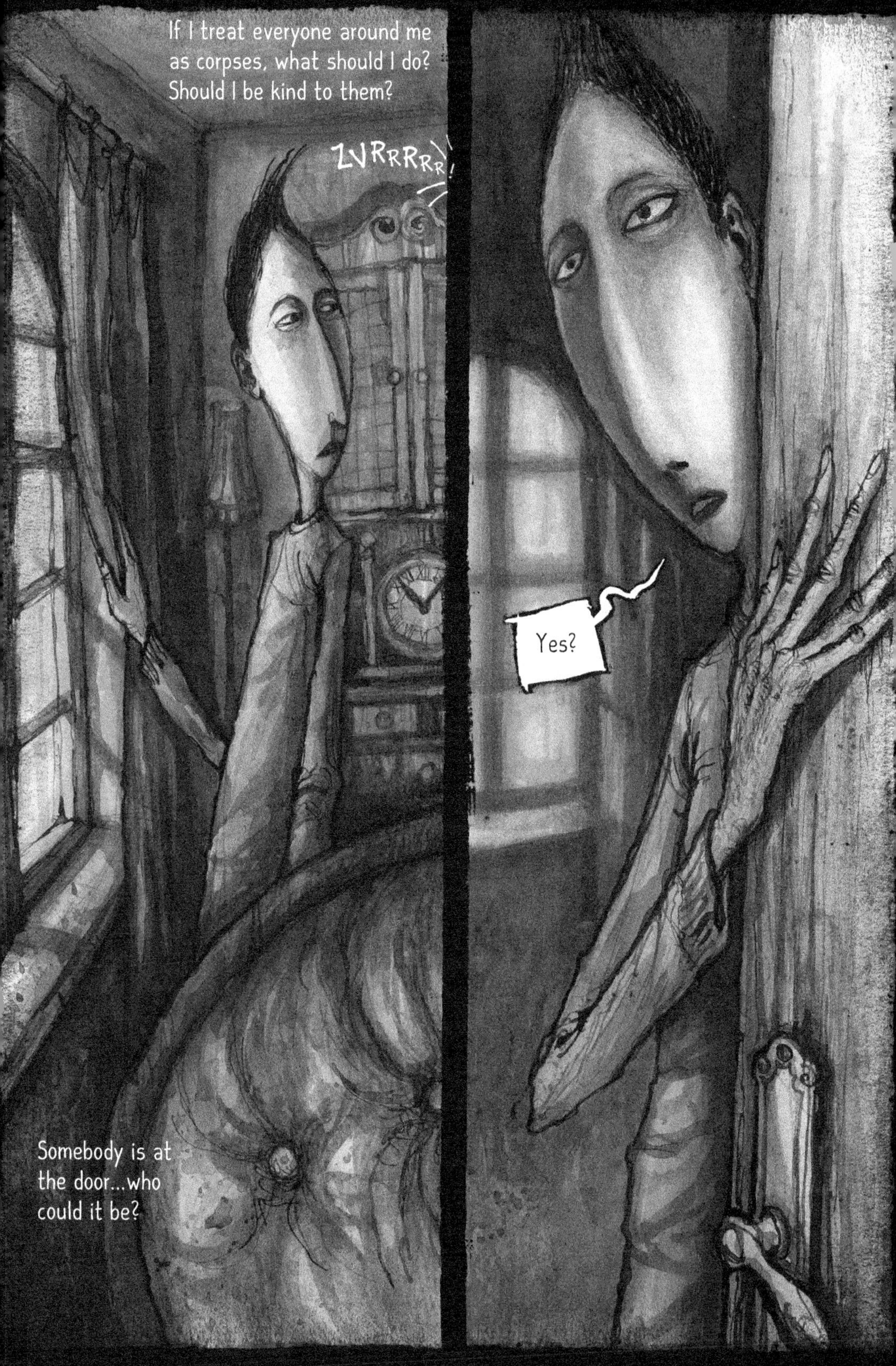
If I treat everyone around me as corpses, what should I do? Should I be kind to them?
ZVRRRRR!
Somebody is at the door...who could it be?
Yes?

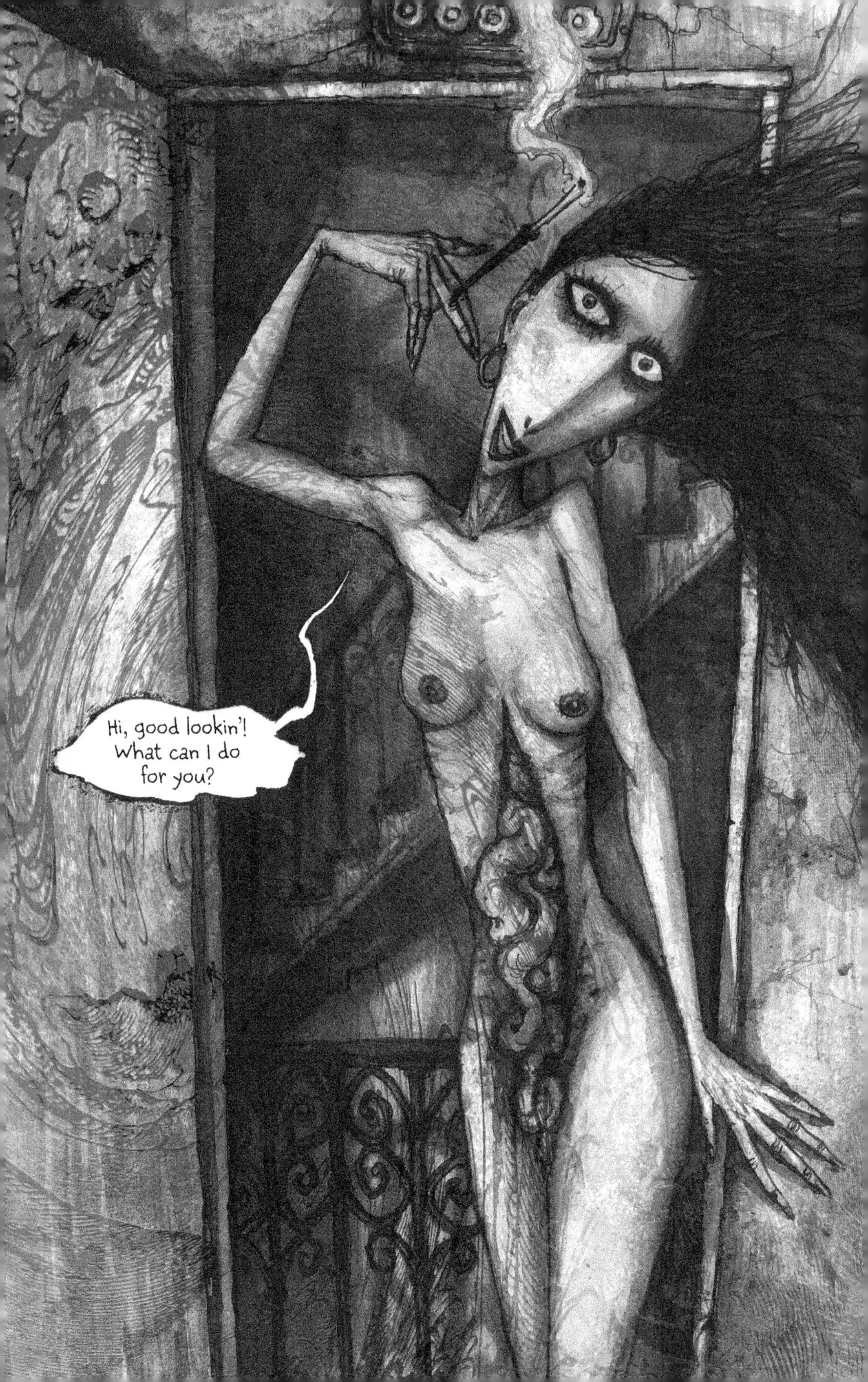
Hi, good lookin'! What can I do for you?

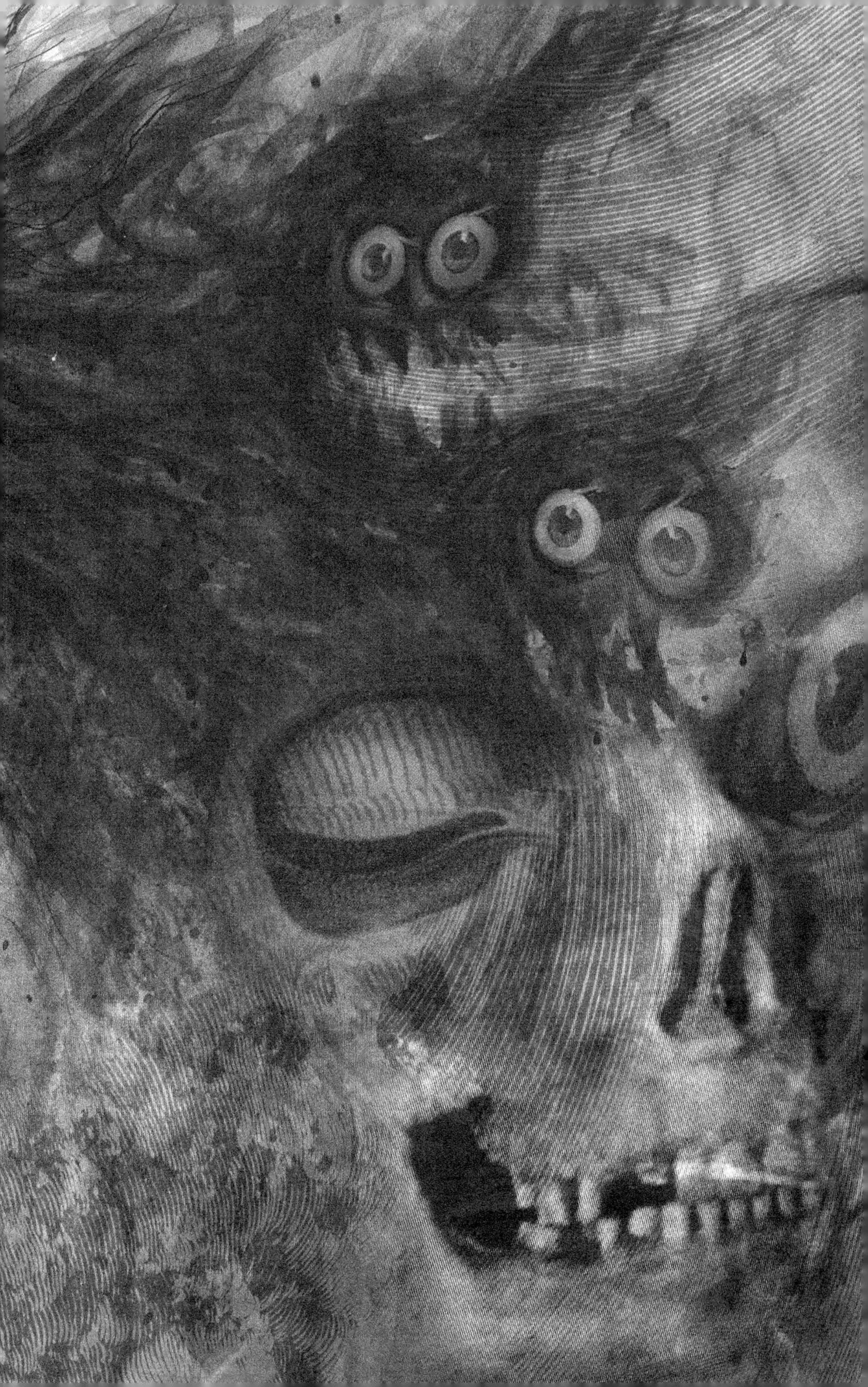

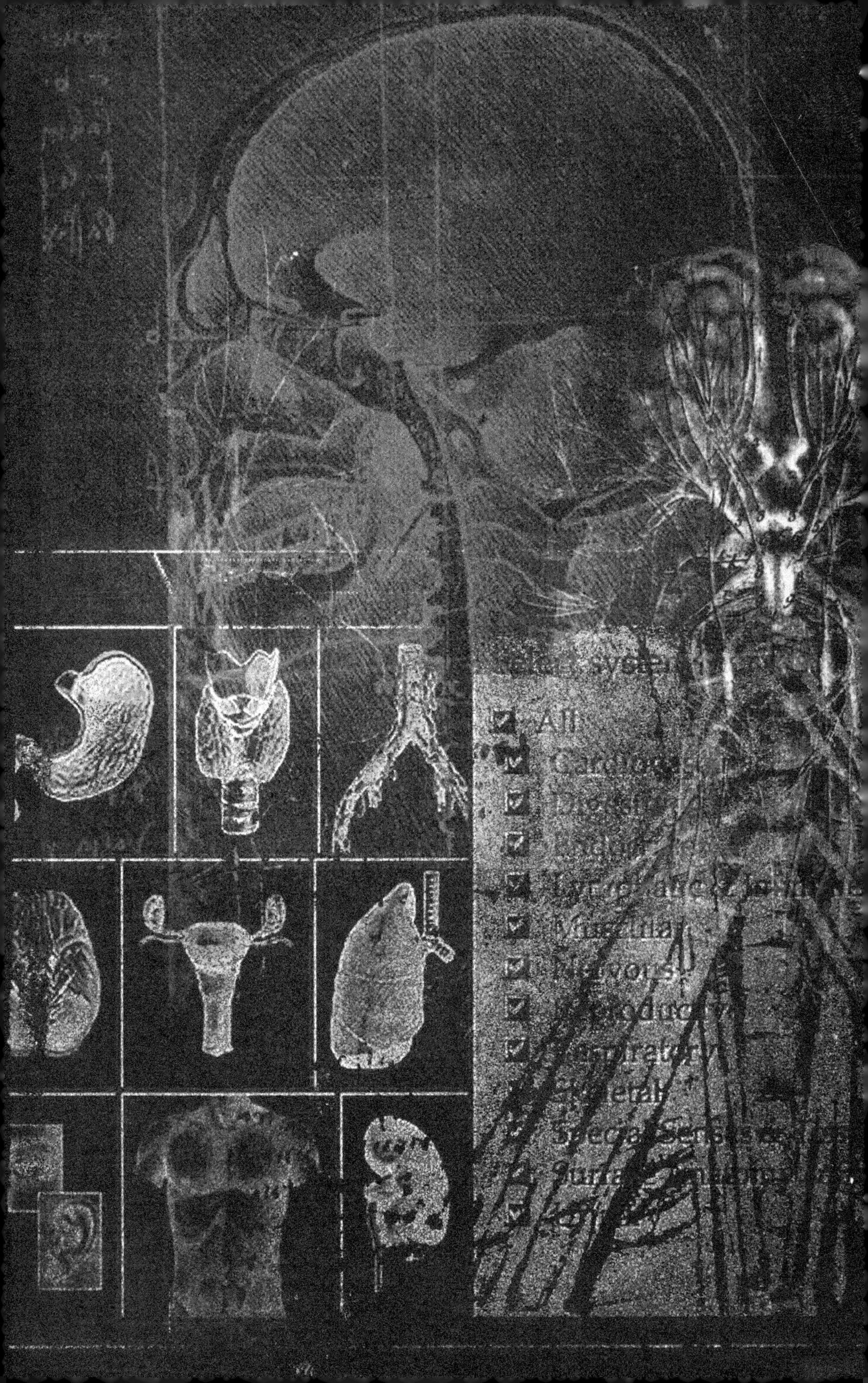
All

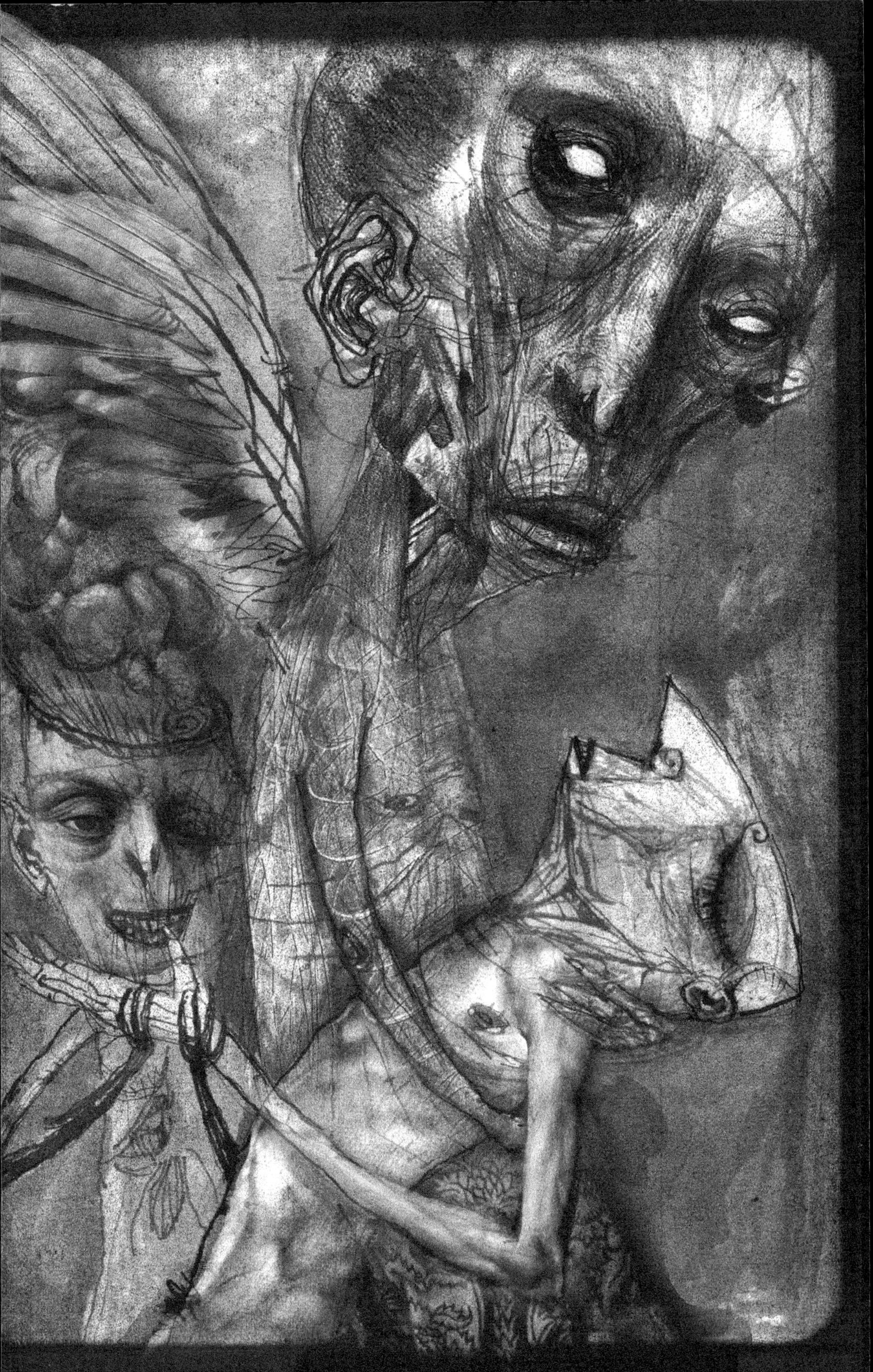

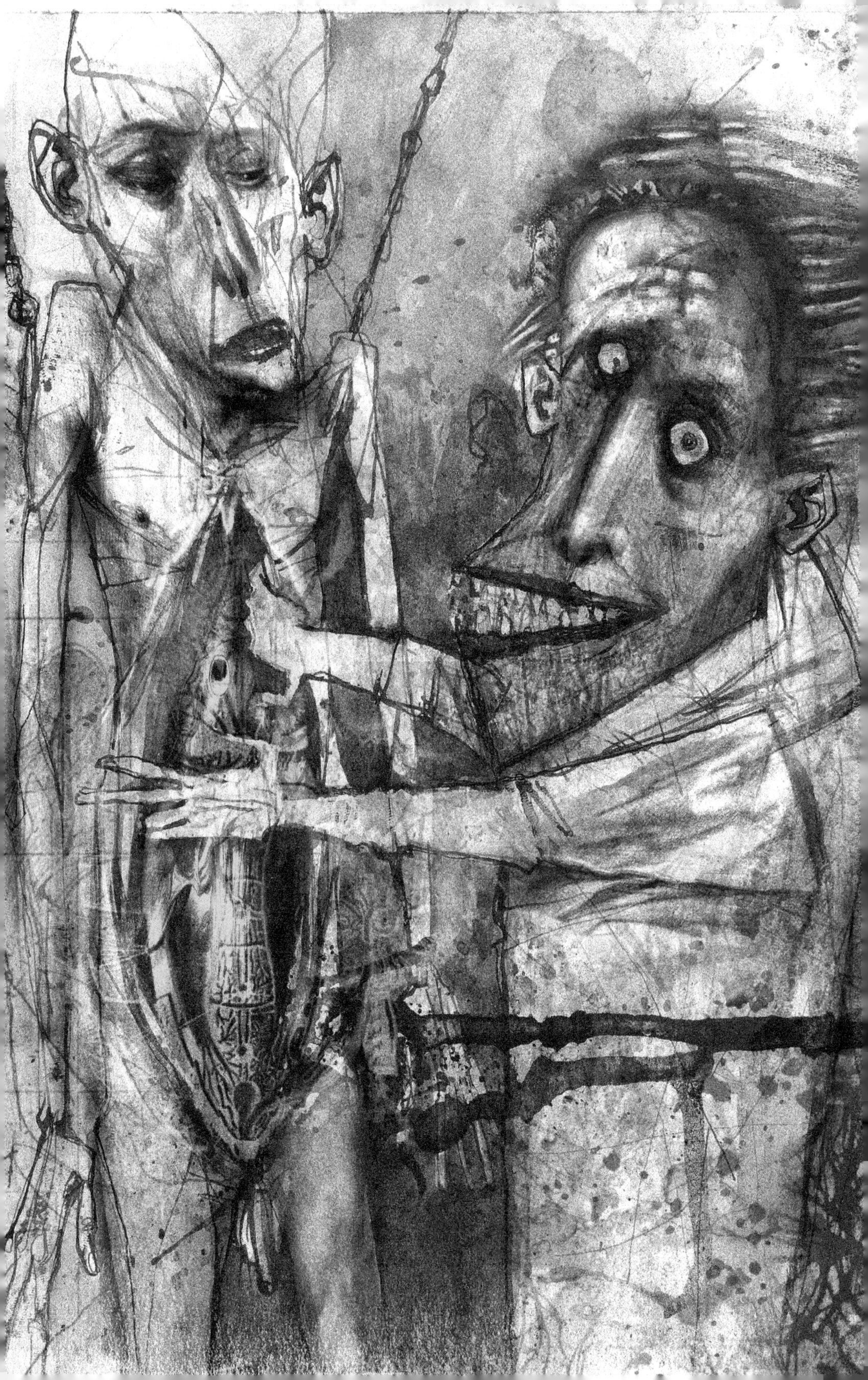

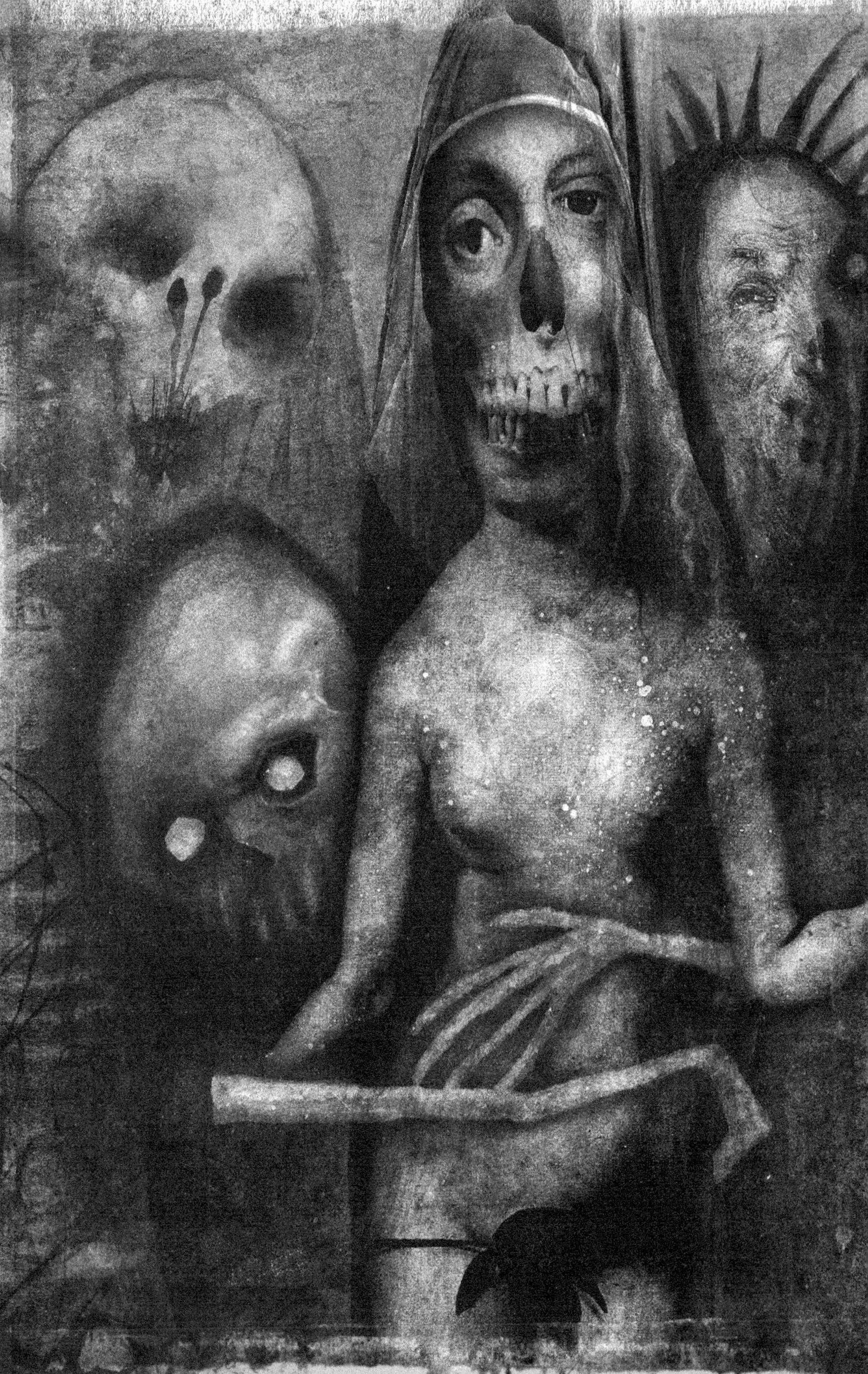

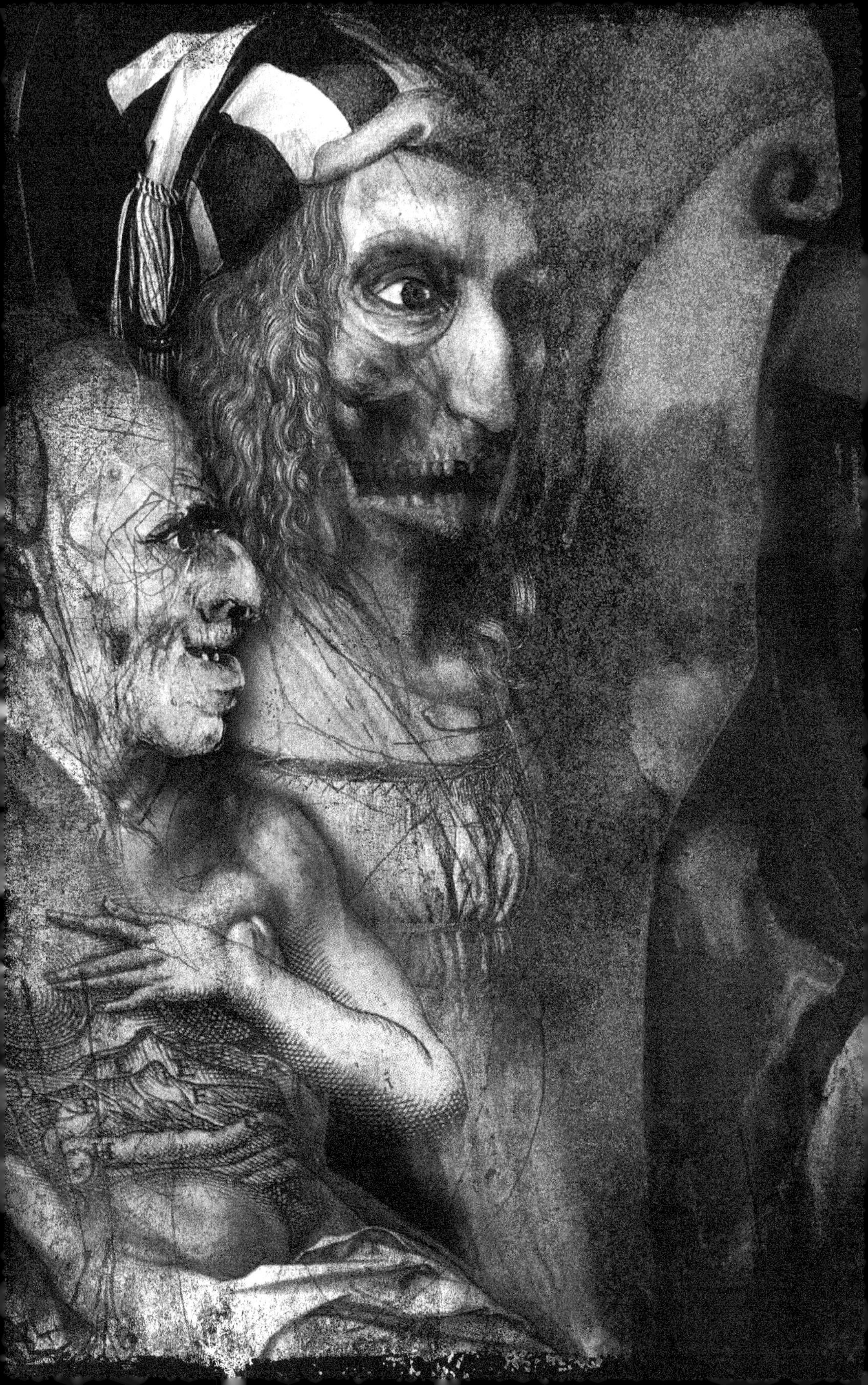

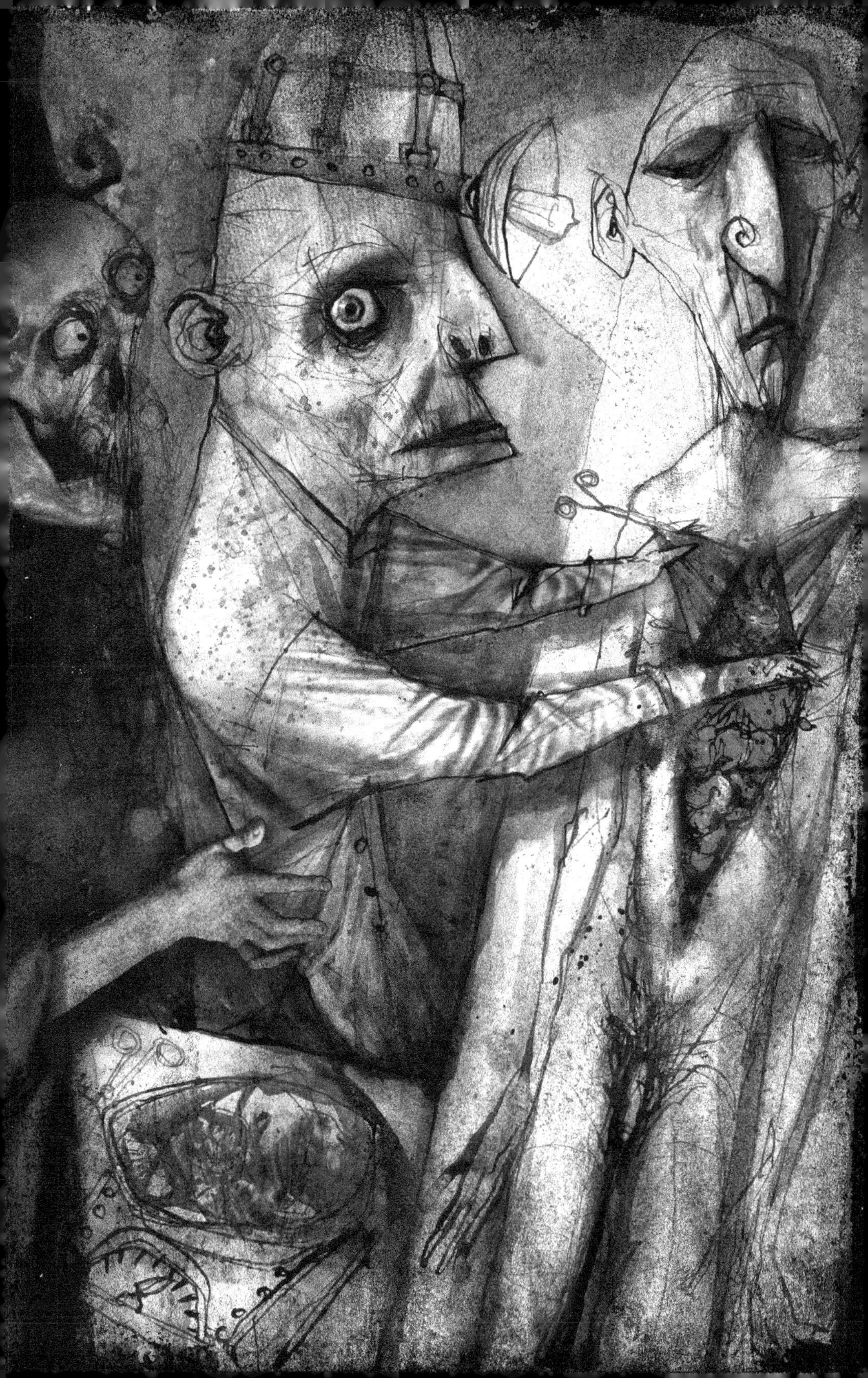

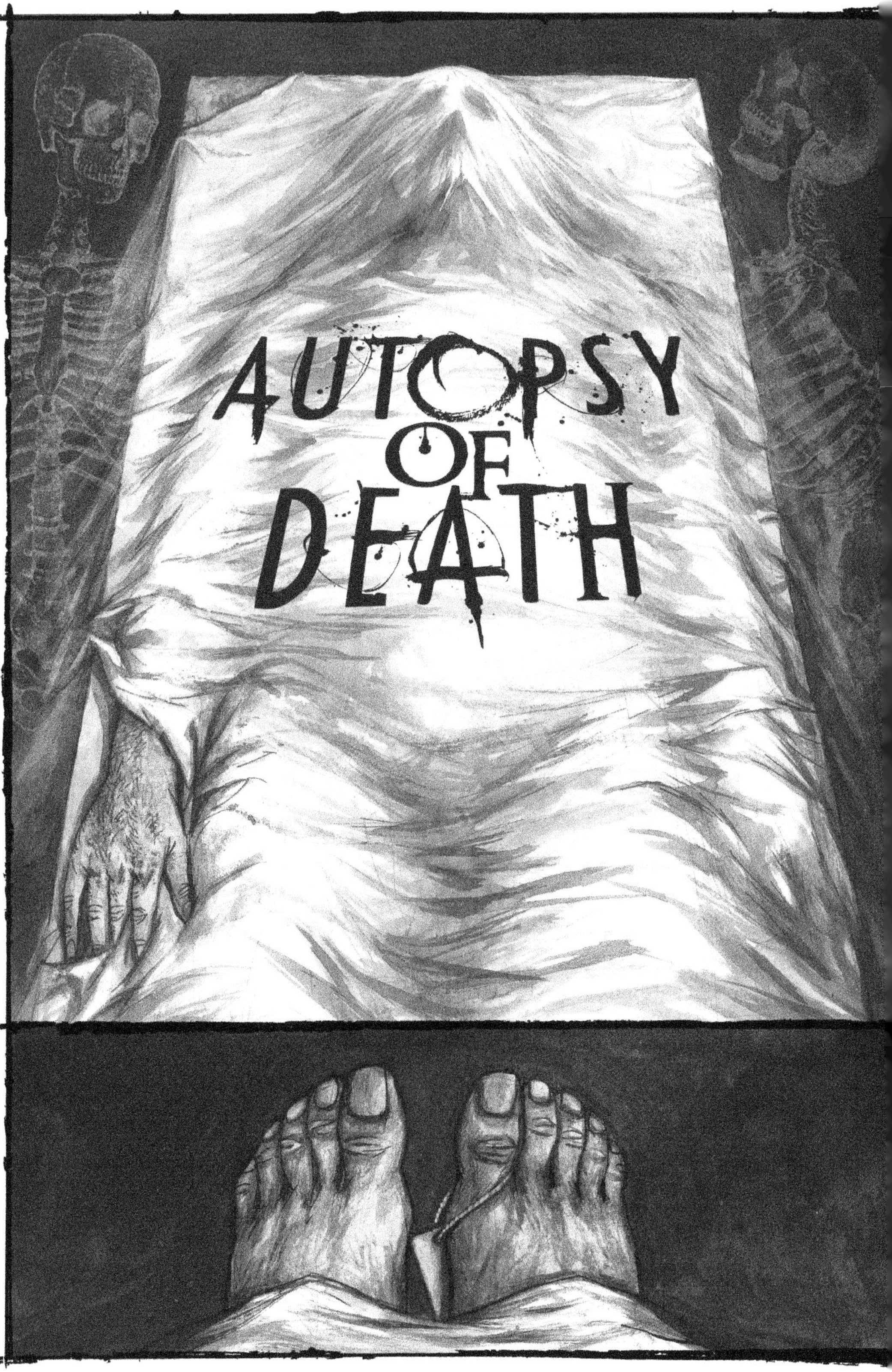
AUTOPSY
OF
DEATH

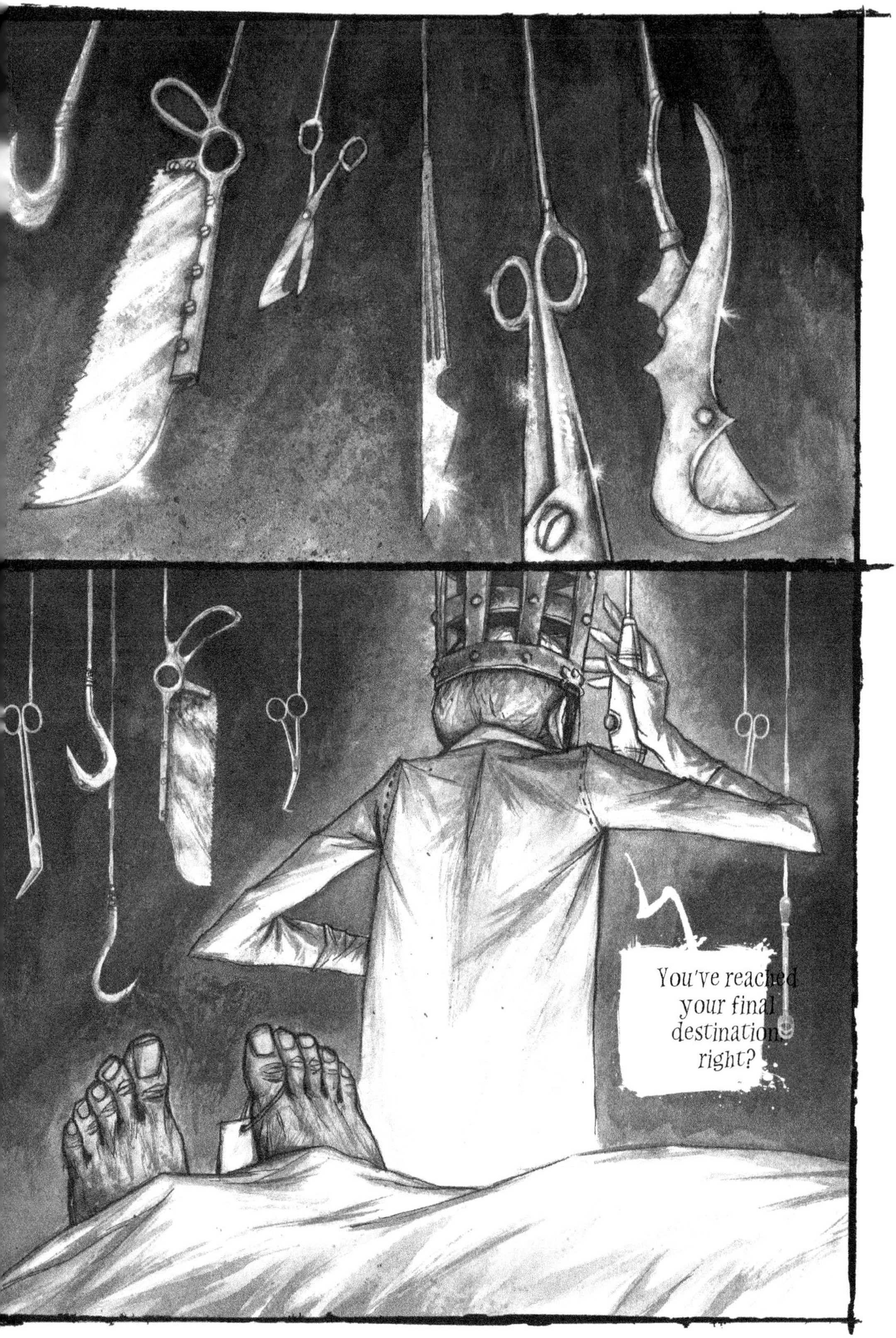
You've reached your final destination, right?

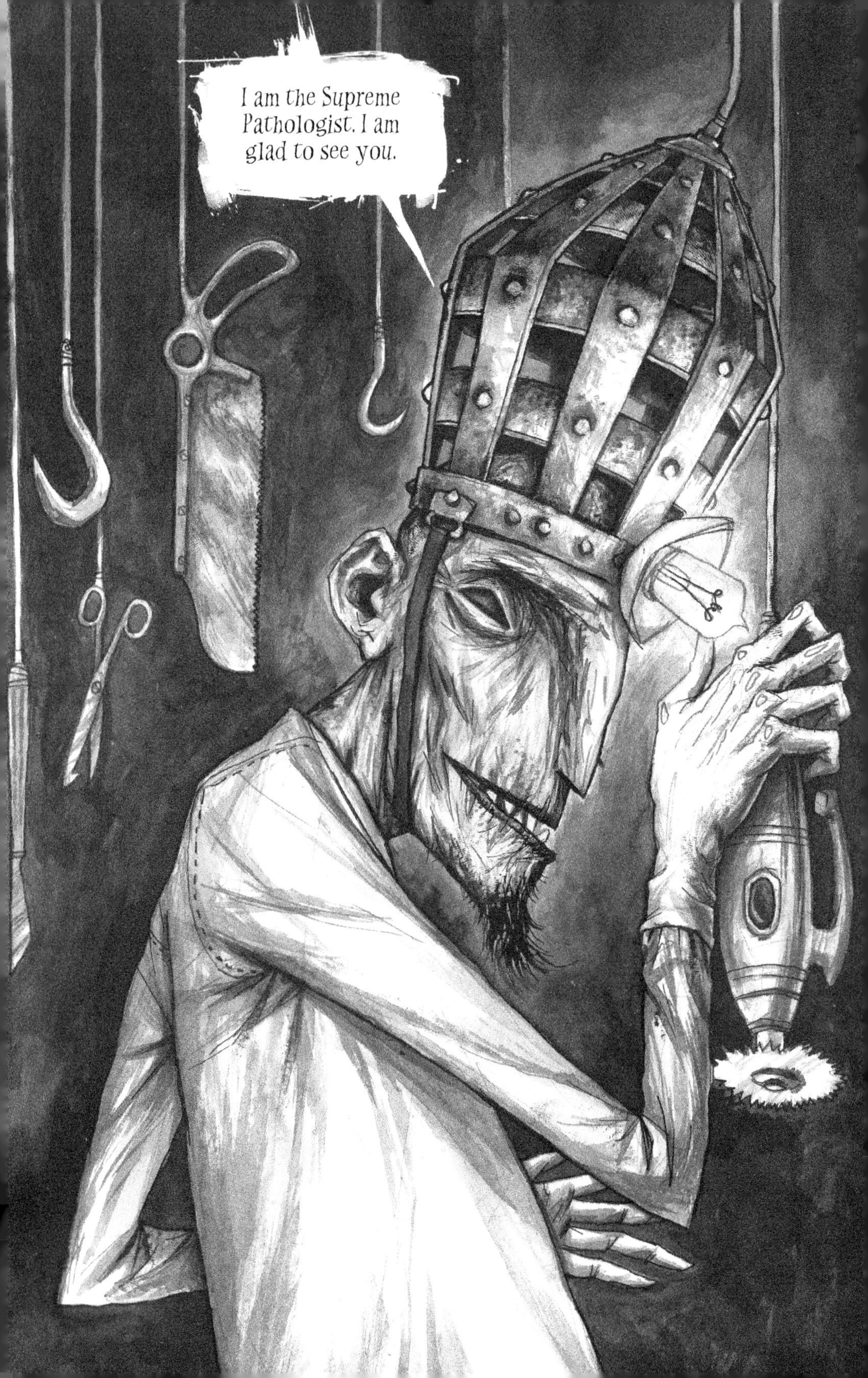
I am the Supreme Pathologist. I am glad to see you.

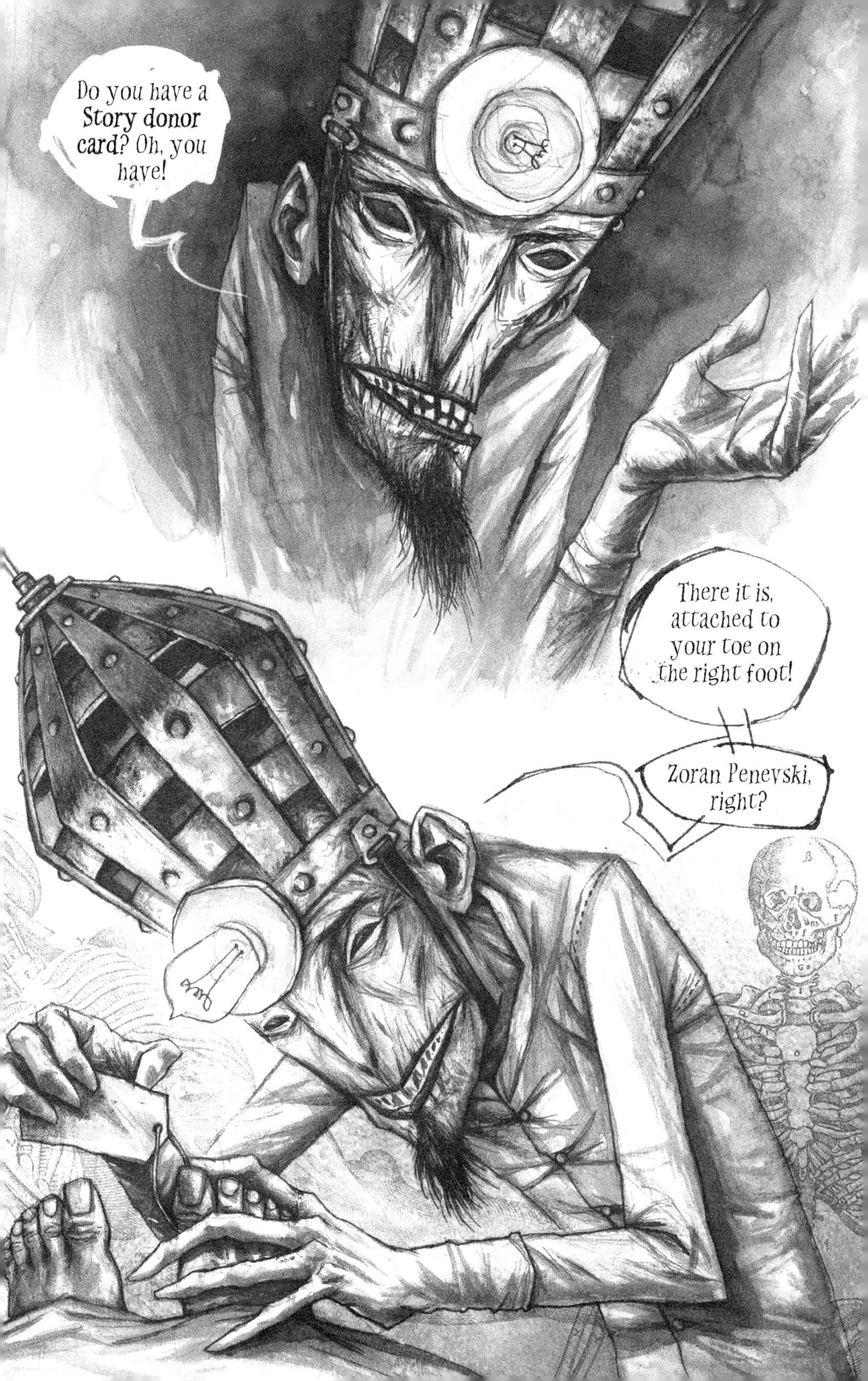
Do you have a **Story donor card**? Oh, you have!
There it is, attached to your toe on the right foot!
Zoran Penevski, right?

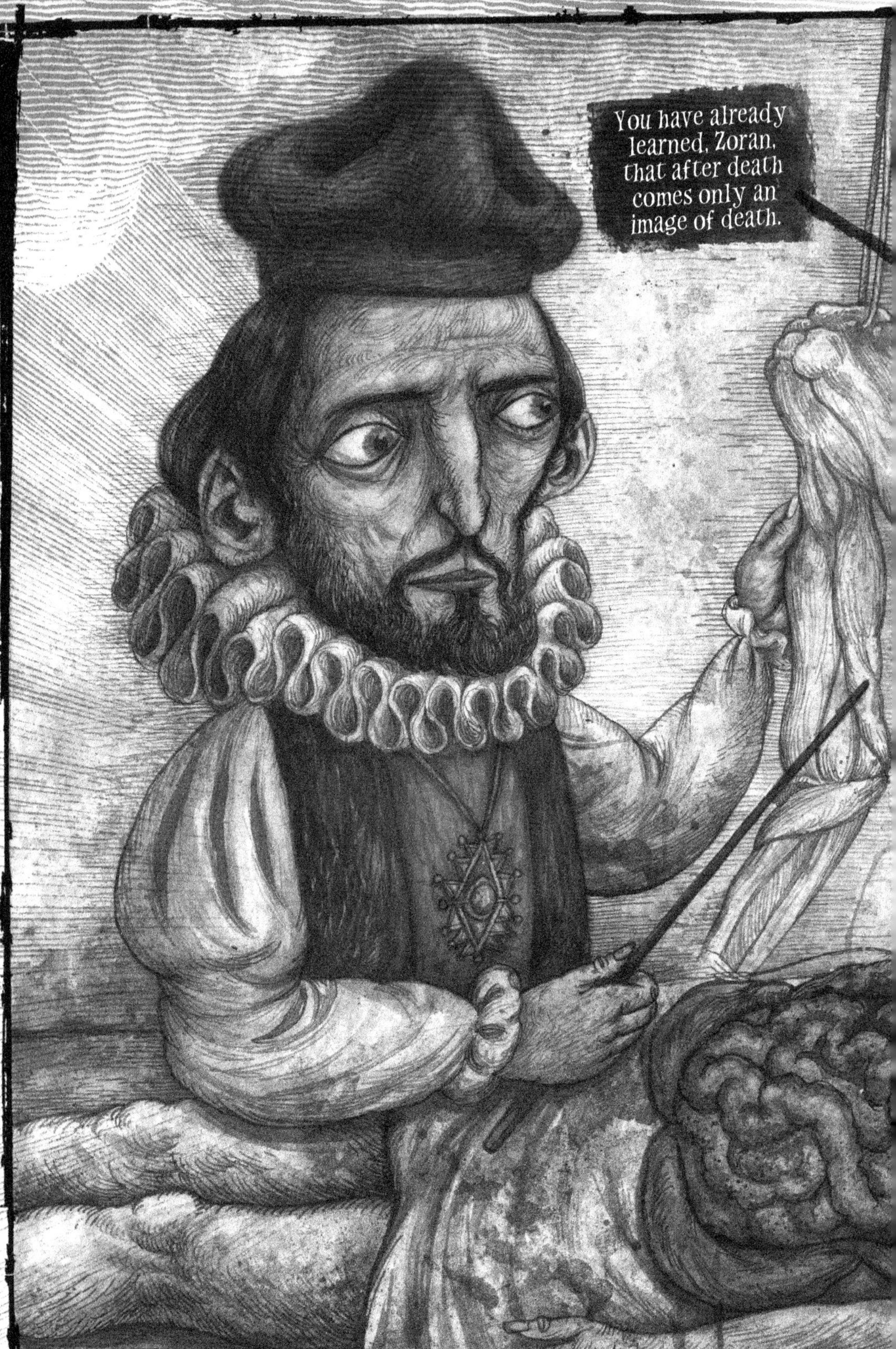
You have already learned, Zoran, that after death comes only an image of death.

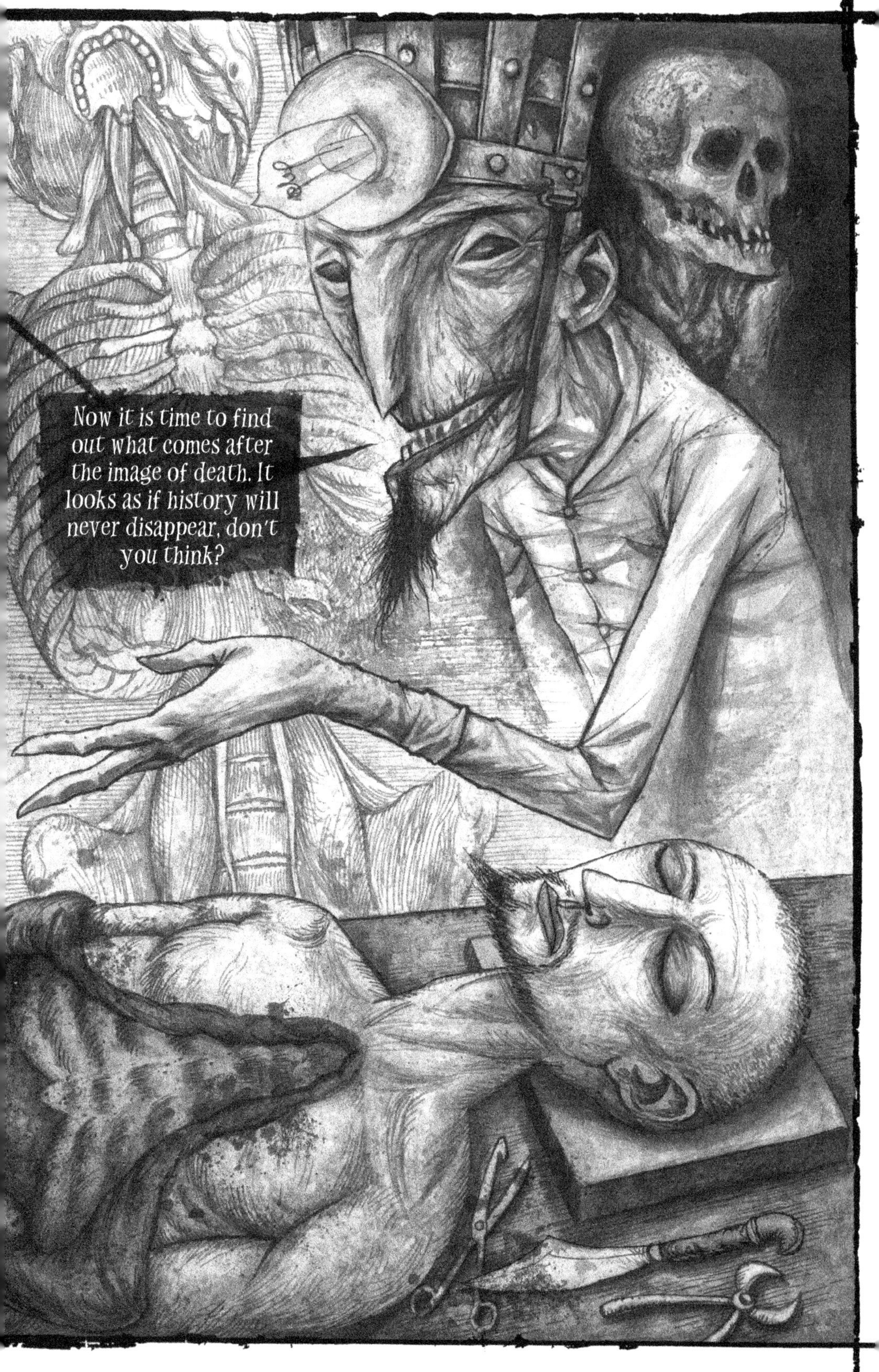
Now it is time to find out what comes after the image of death. It looks as if history will never disappear, don't you think?

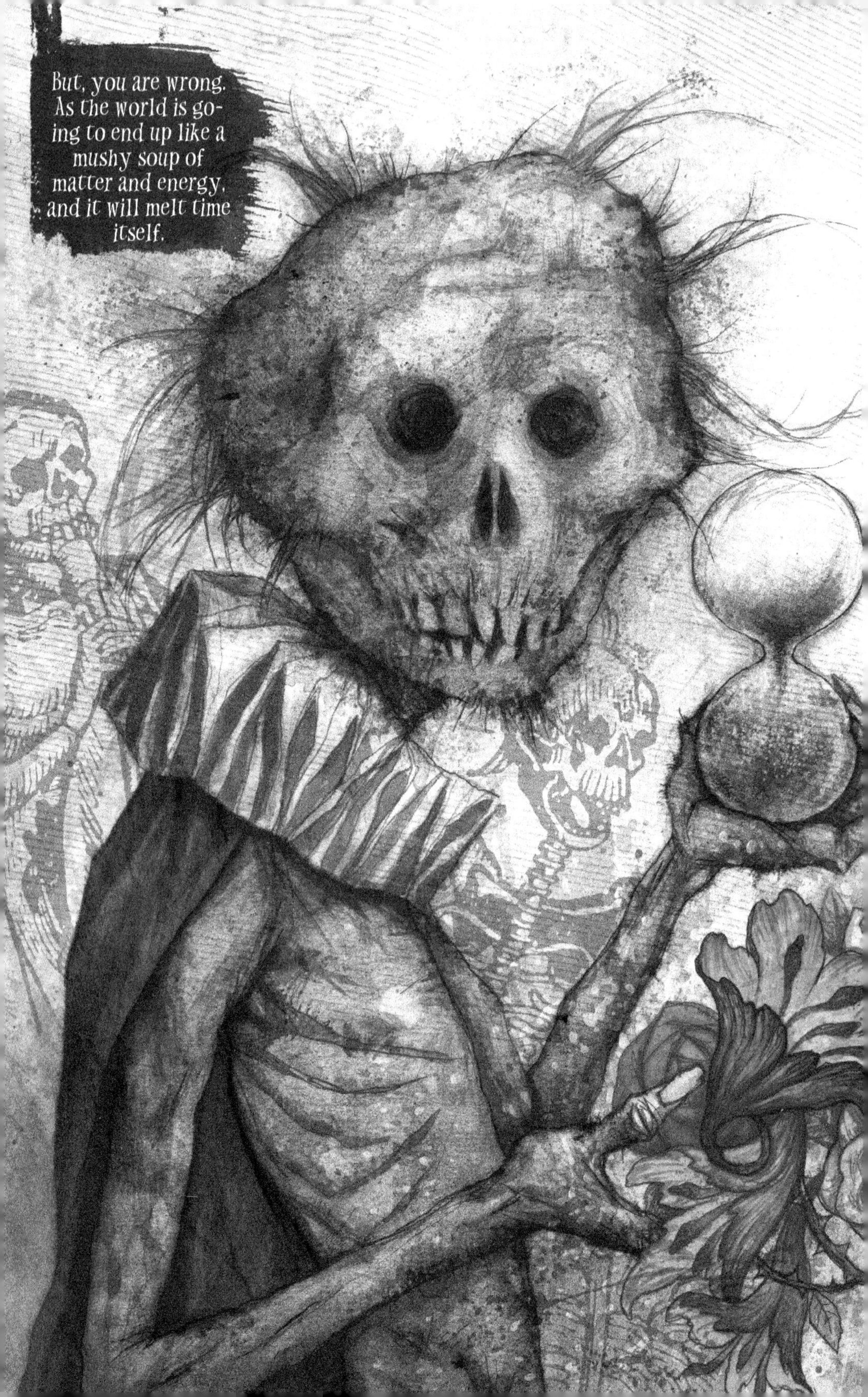
But, you are wrong. As the world is going to end up like a mushy soup of matter and energy, and it will melt time itself.

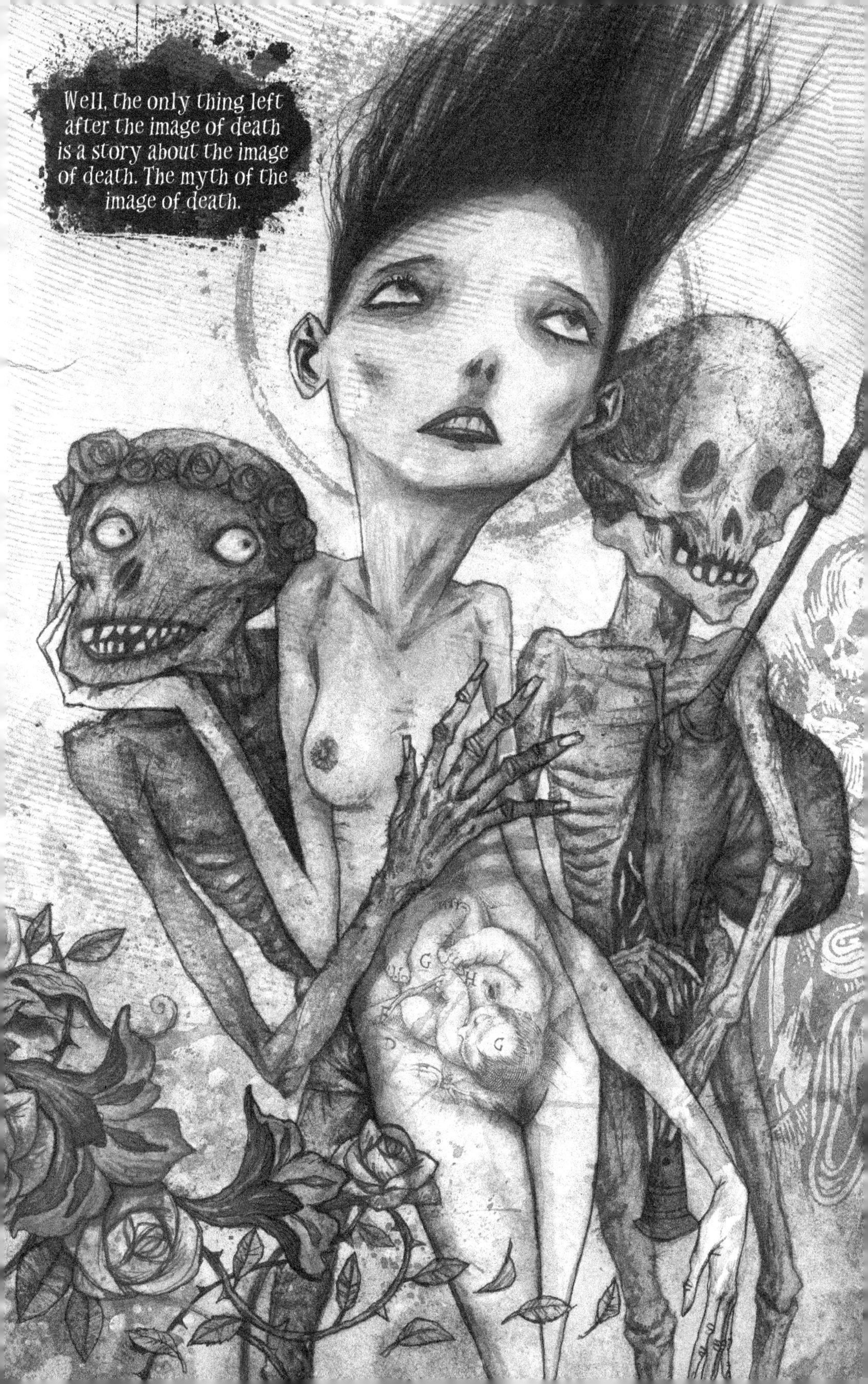
Well, the only thing left after the image of death is a story about the image of death. The myth of the image of death.

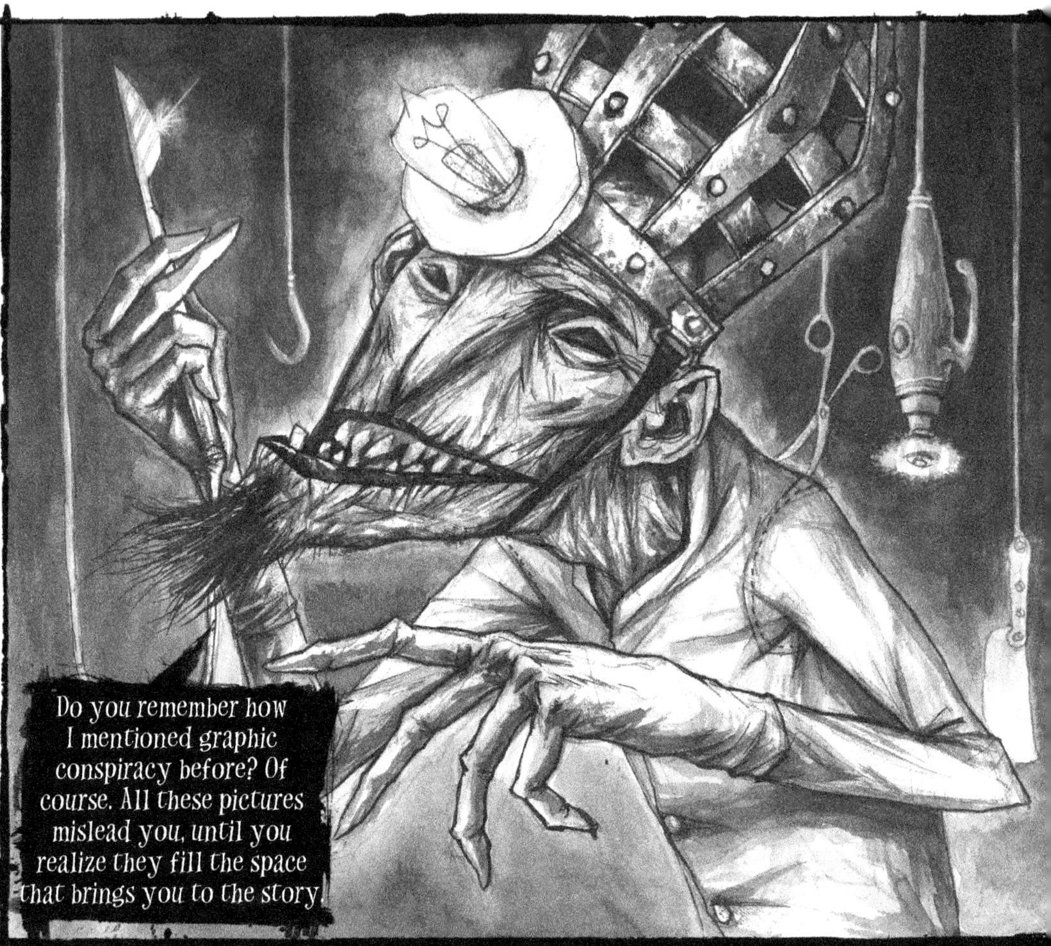
Do you remember how I mentioned graphic conspiracy before? Of course. All these pictures mislead you, until you realize they fill the space that brings you to the story.
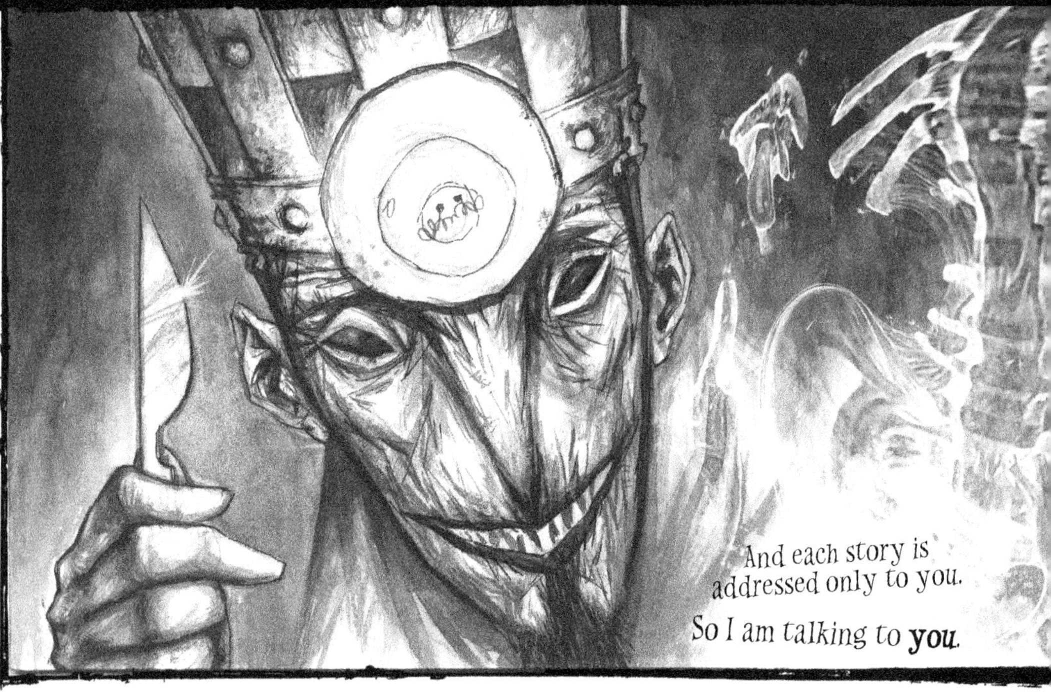
And each story is addressed only to you.
So I am talking to **you**.

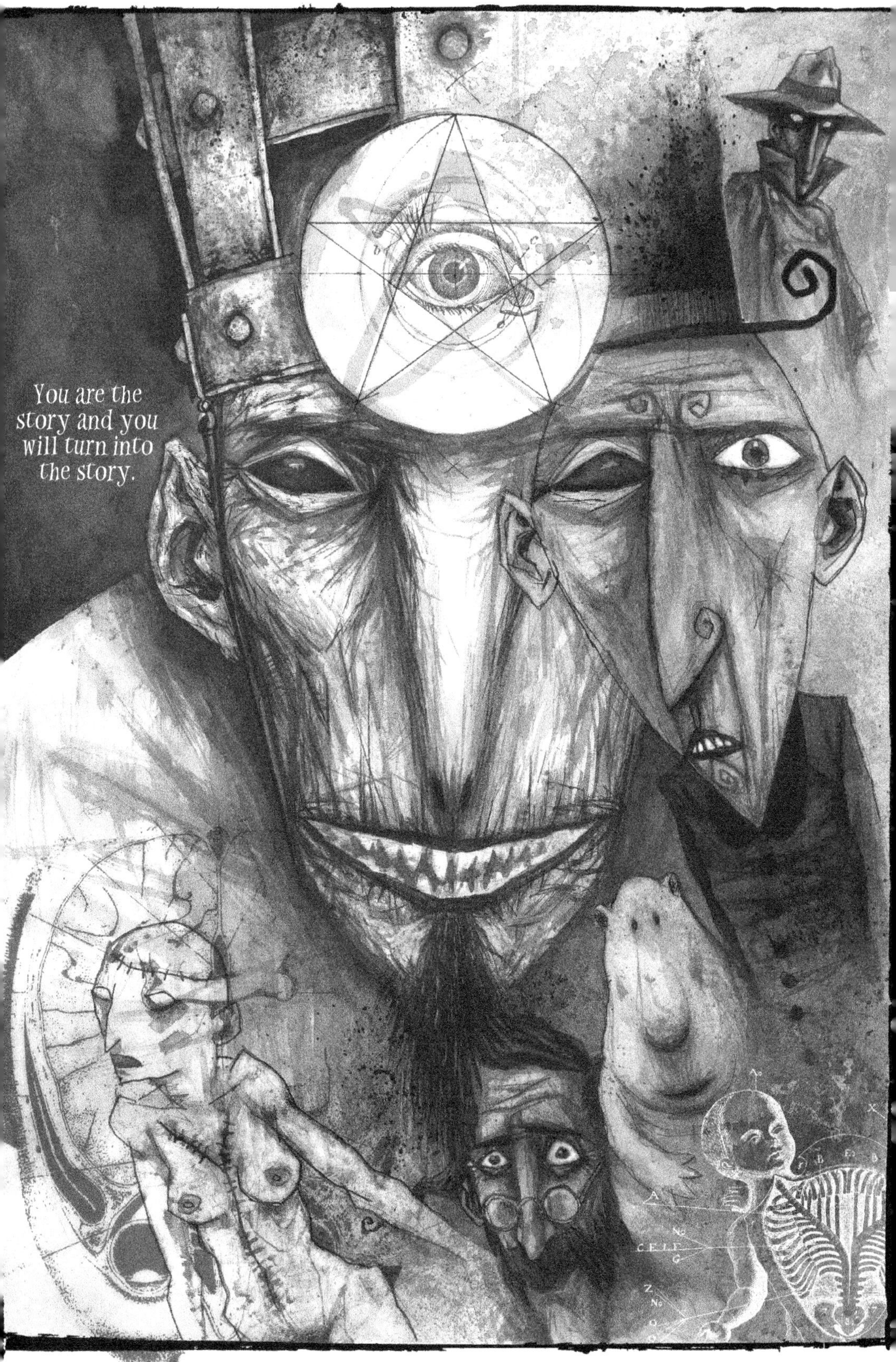
You are the story and you will turn into the story.

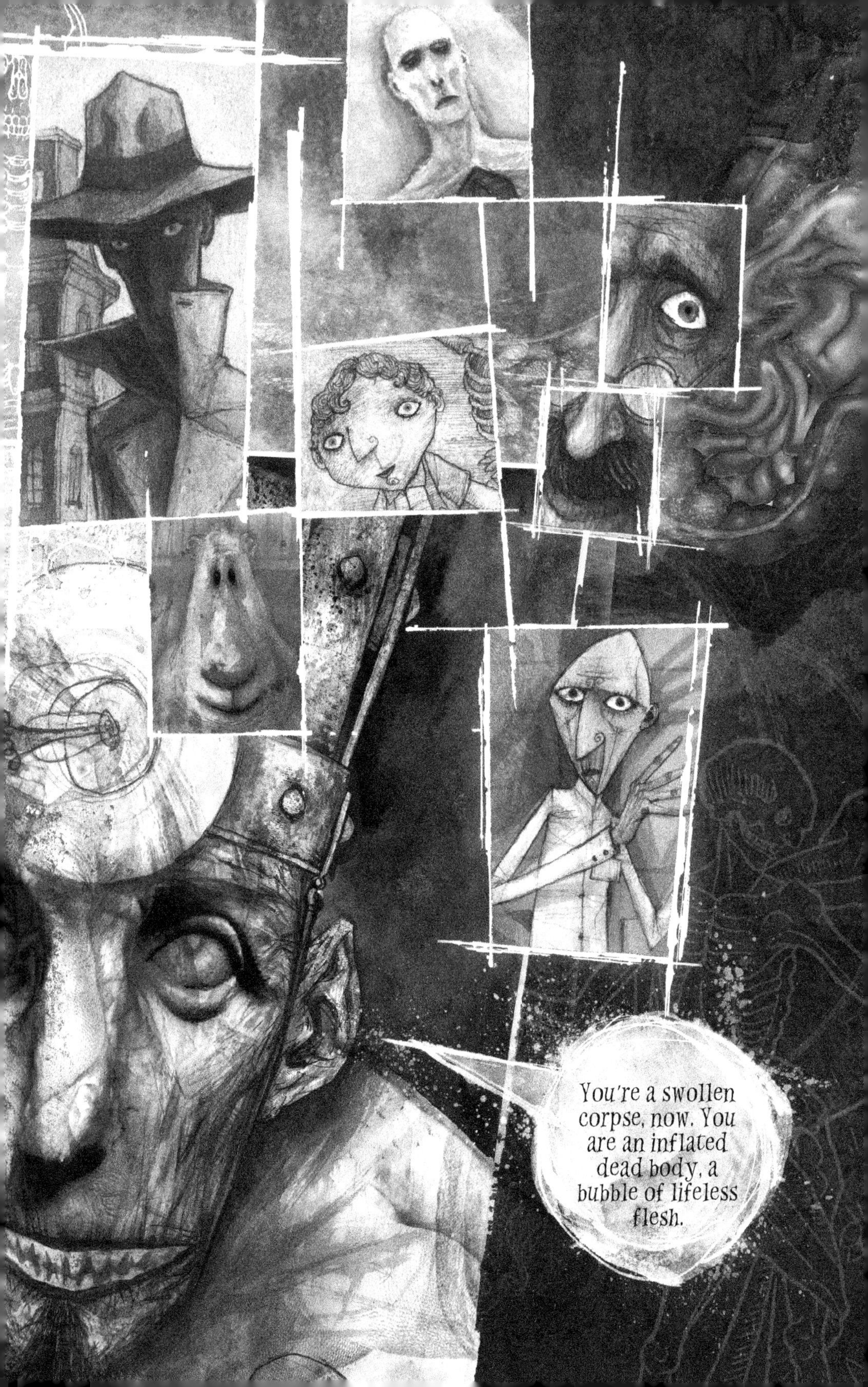
You're a swollen corpse, now. You are an inflated dead body, a bubble of lifeless flesh.

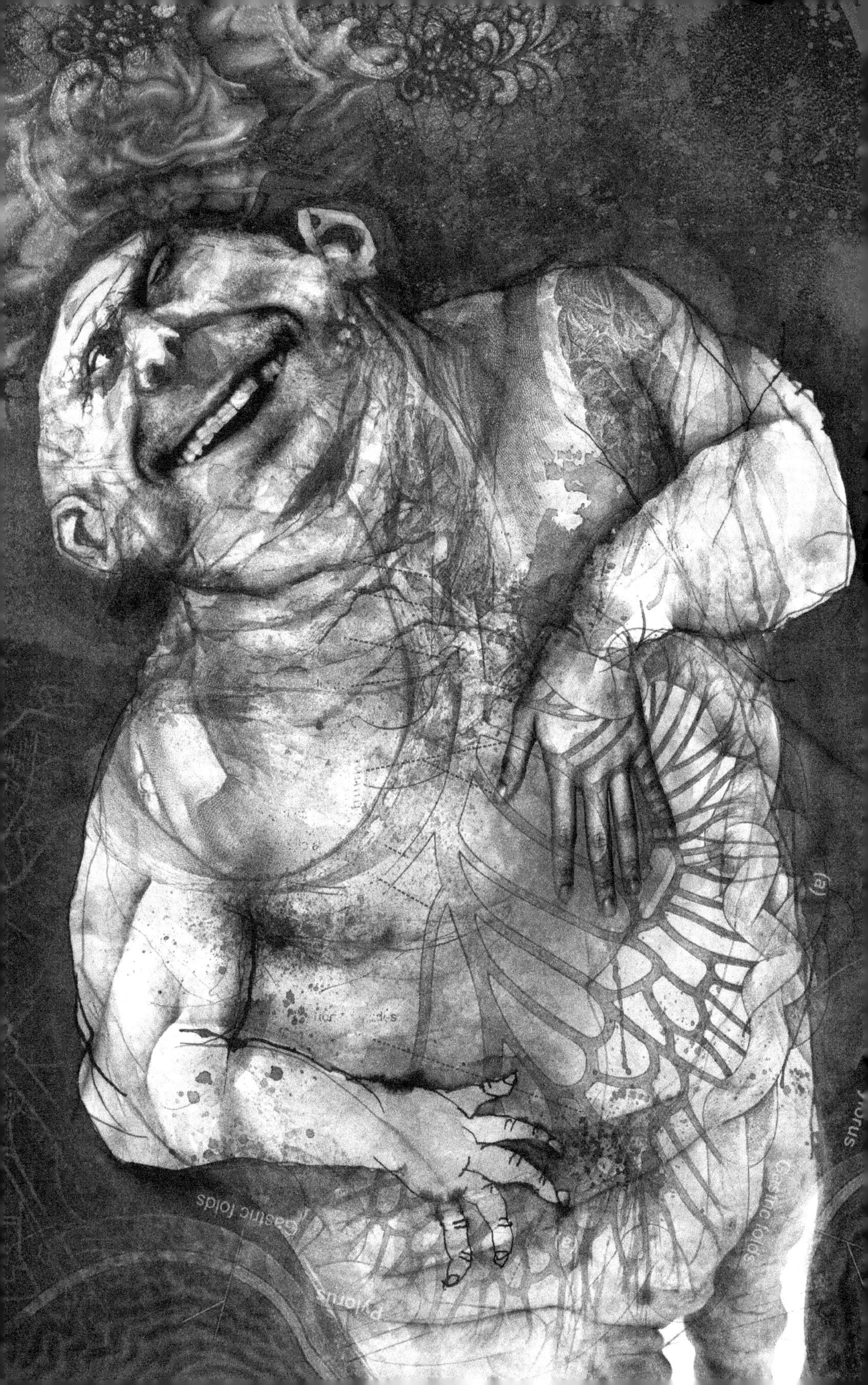
Gastric folds
Pylorus
Gastric folds

I know. I'll set you free.
And open you up.

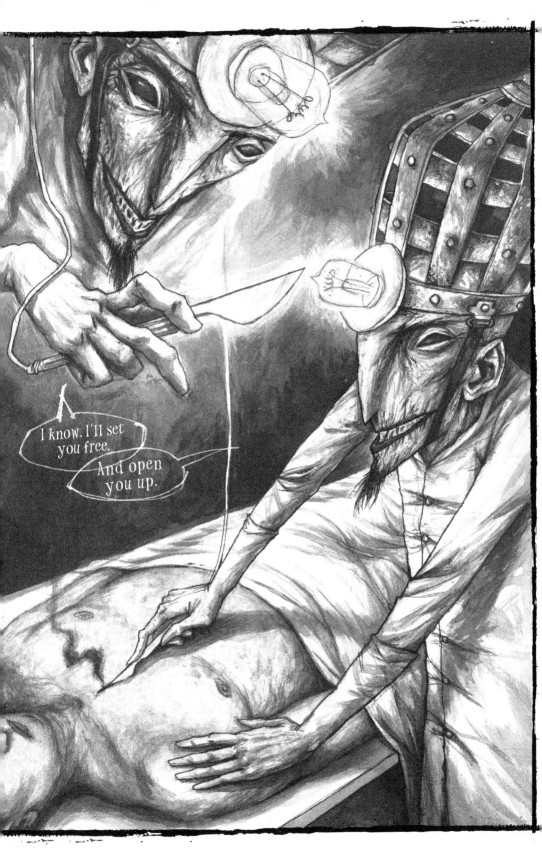

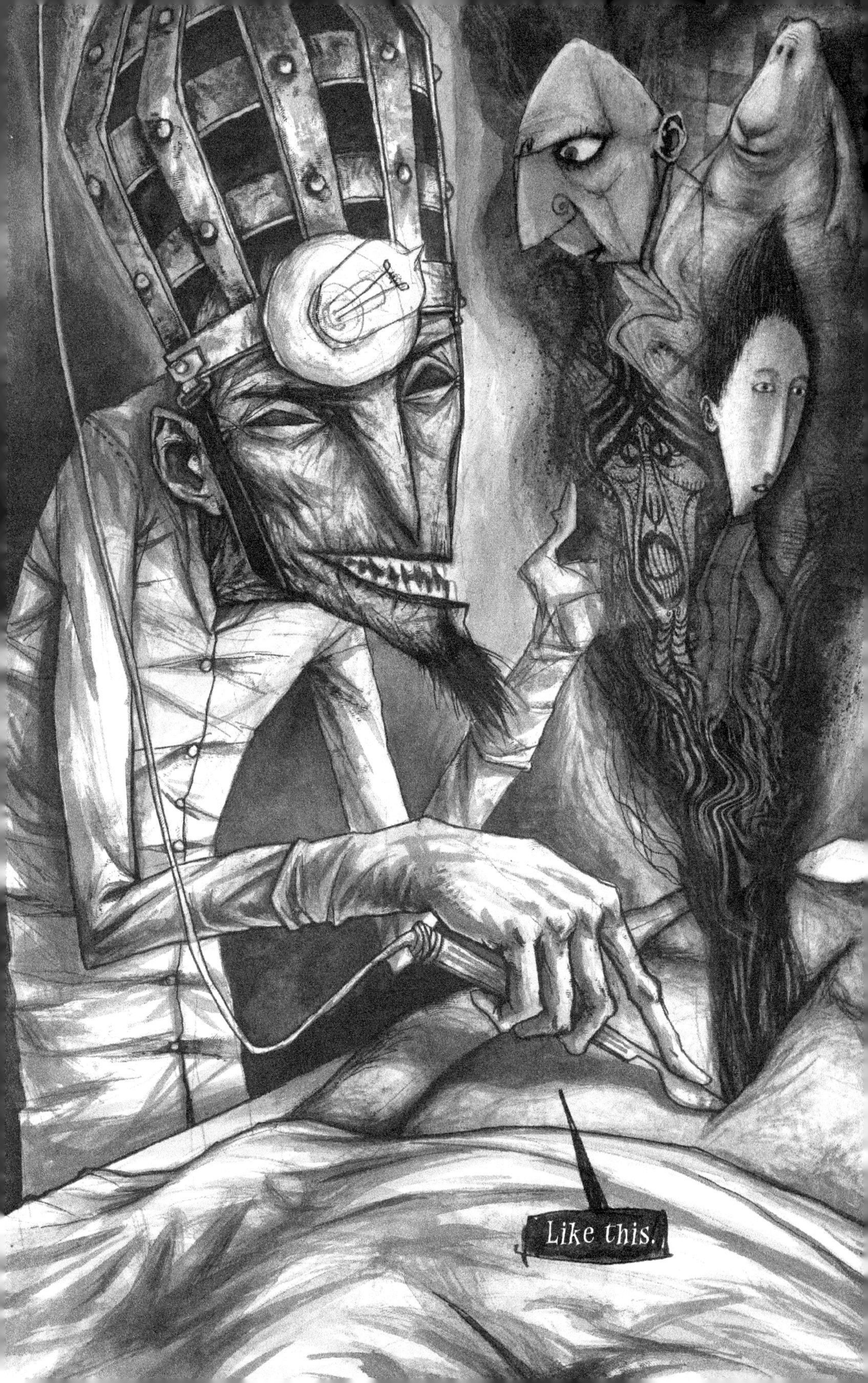
Like this.

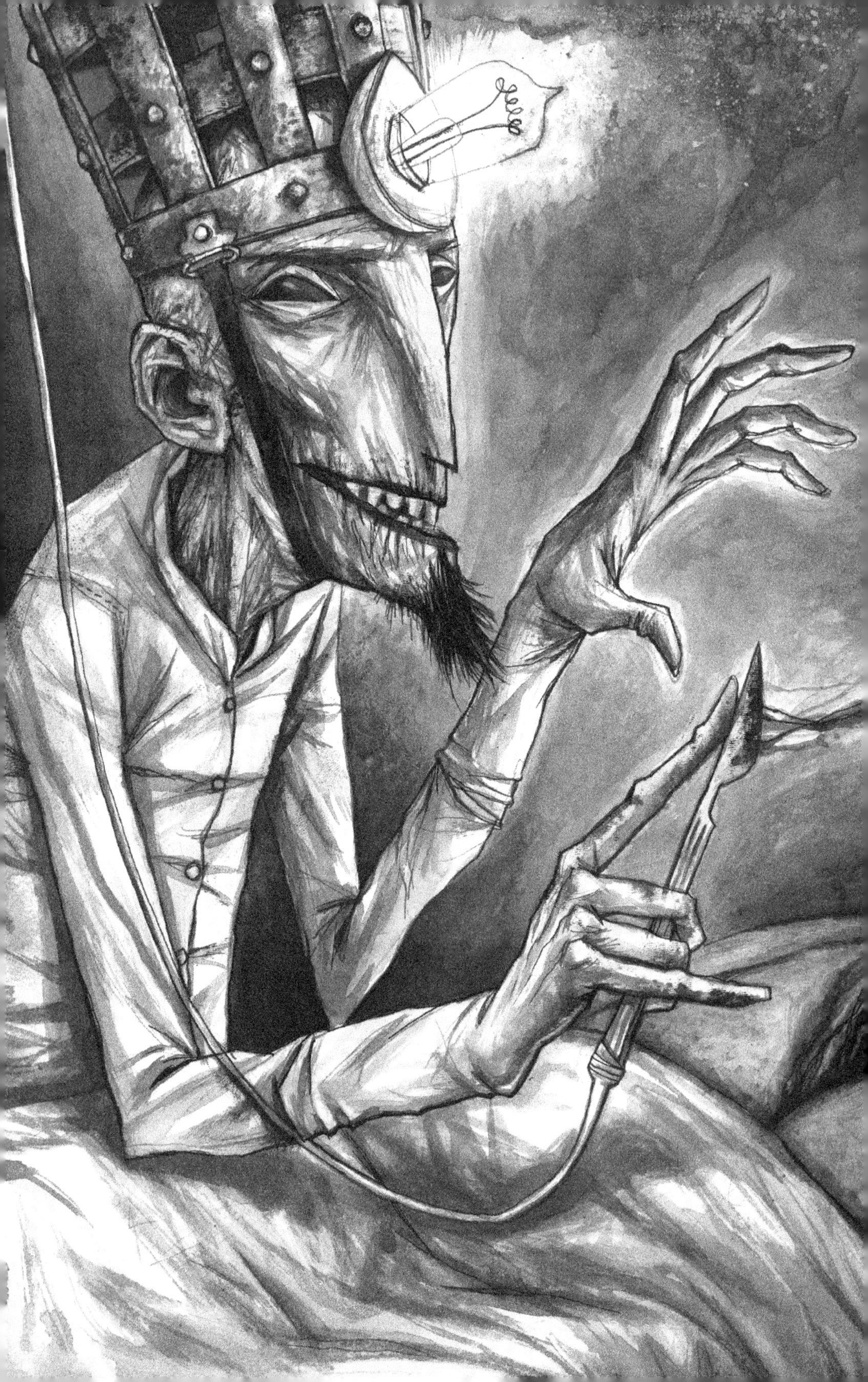

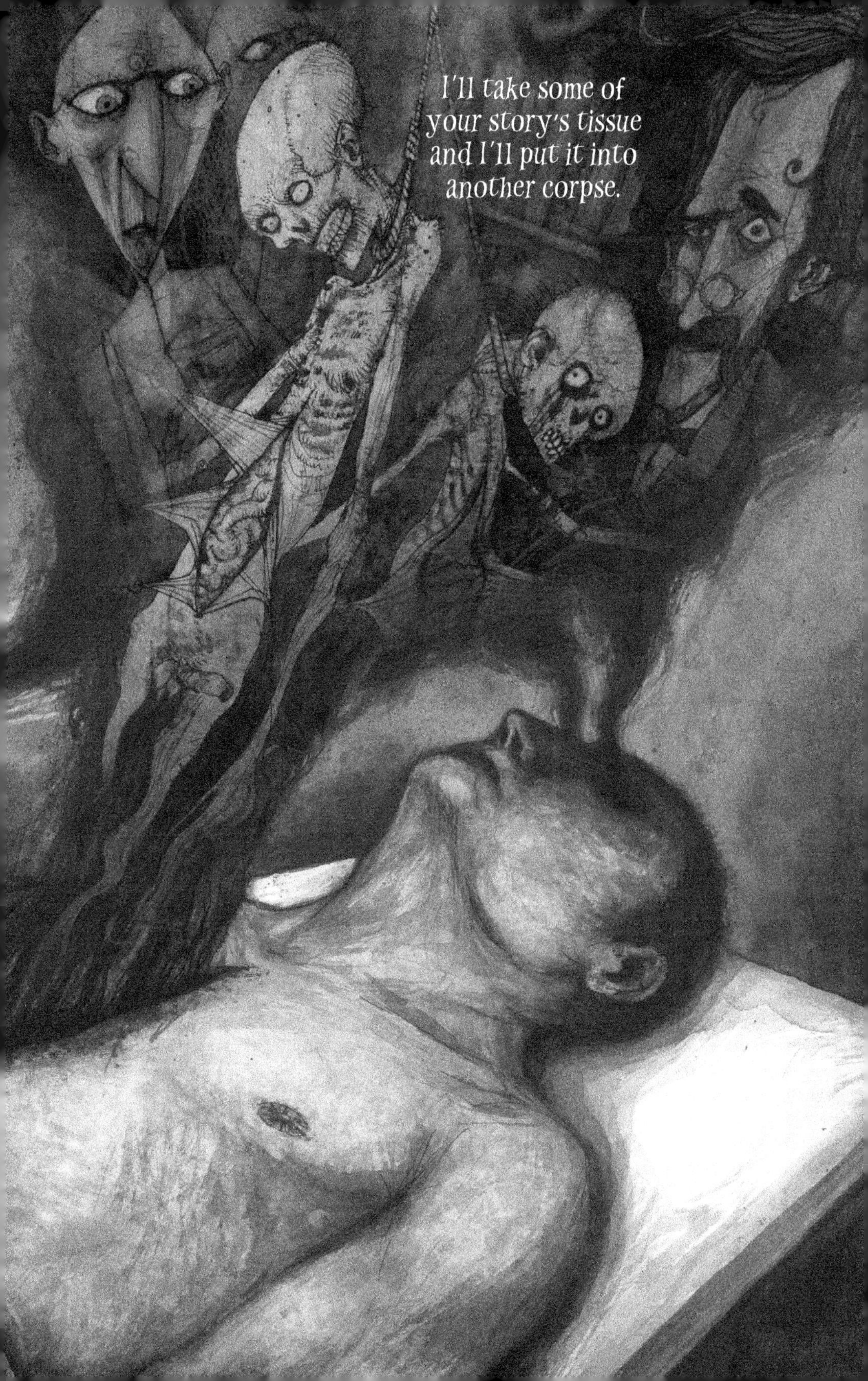
I'll take some of your story's tissue and I'll put it into another corpse.

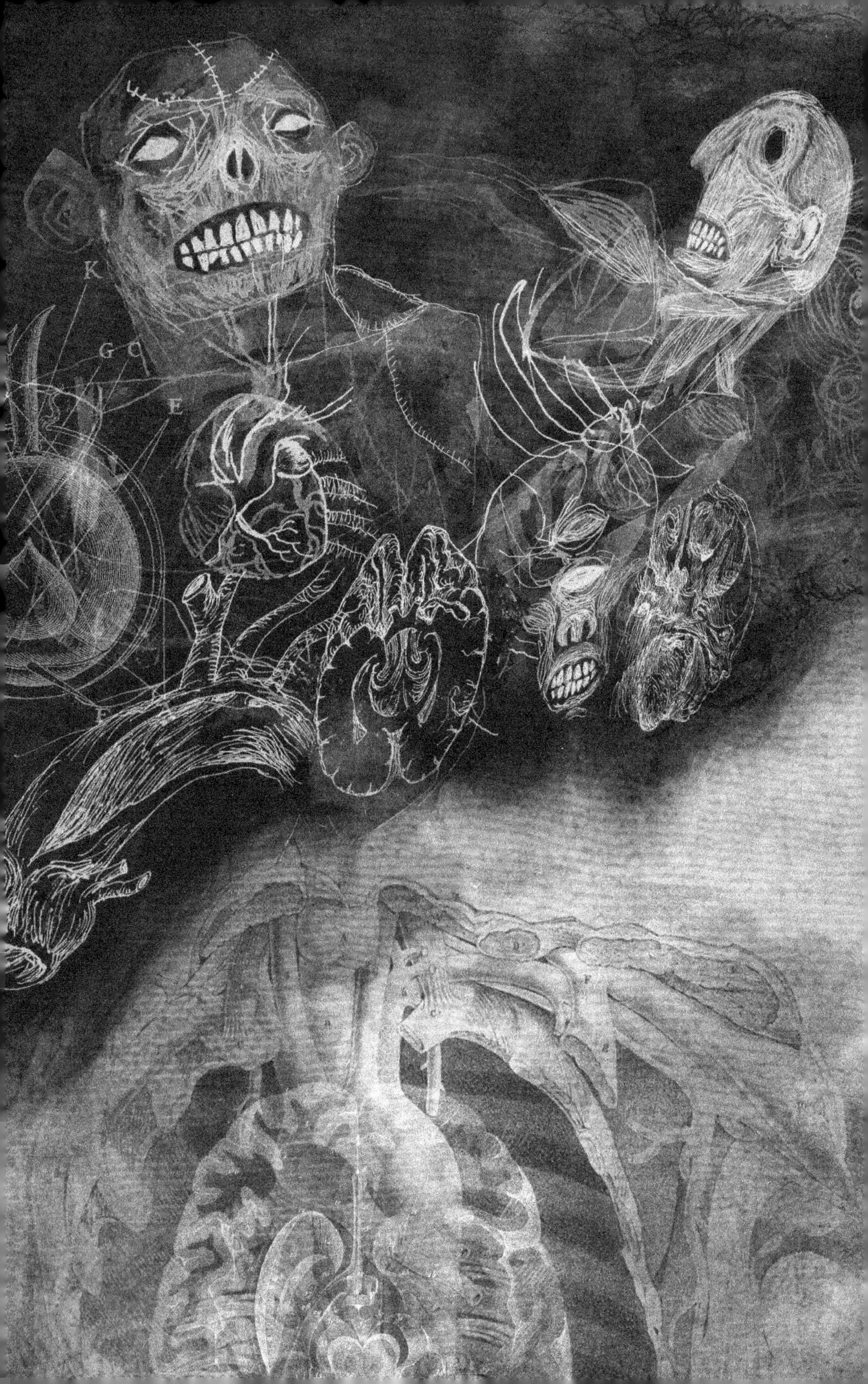
K
G C
E

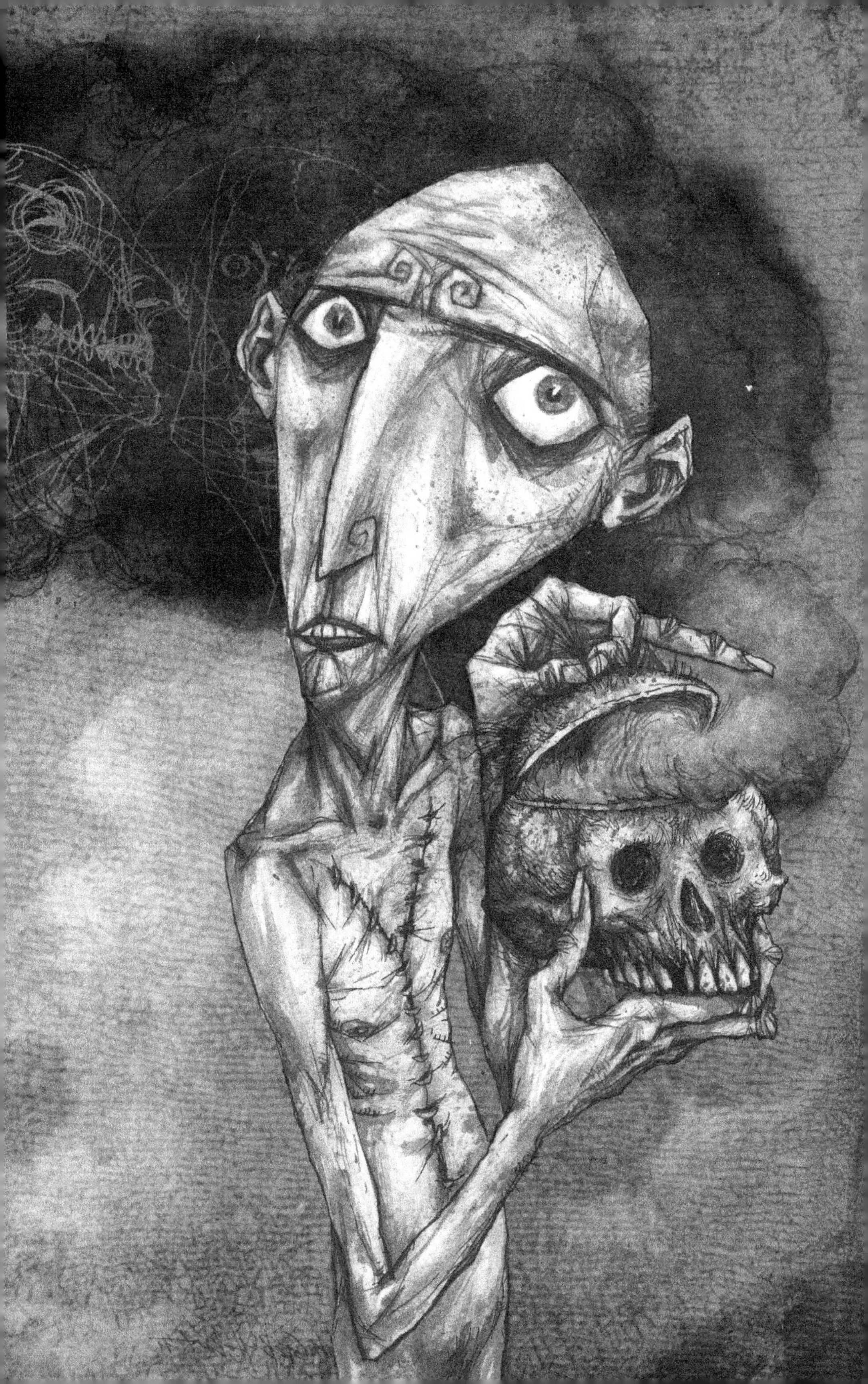

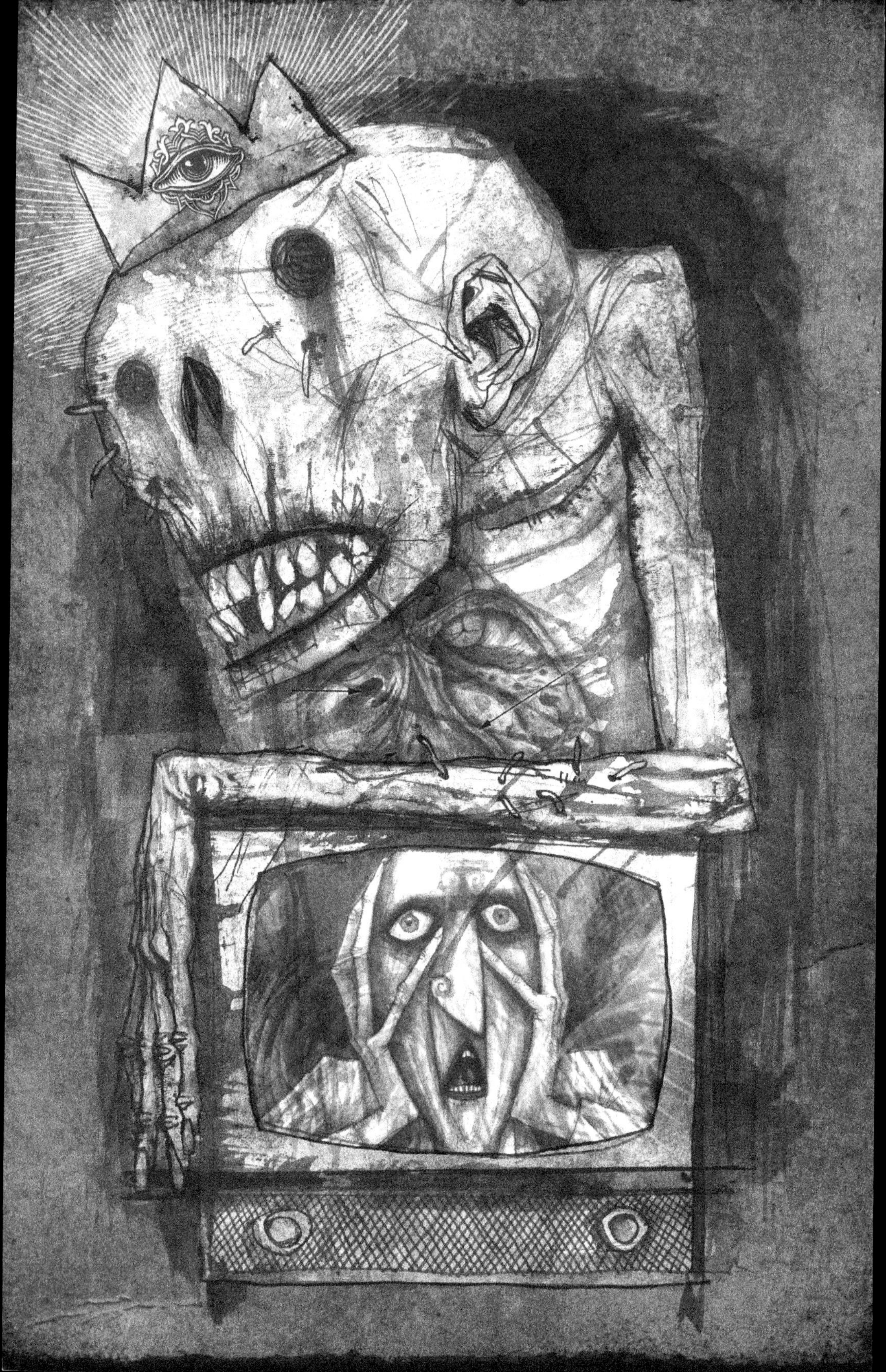

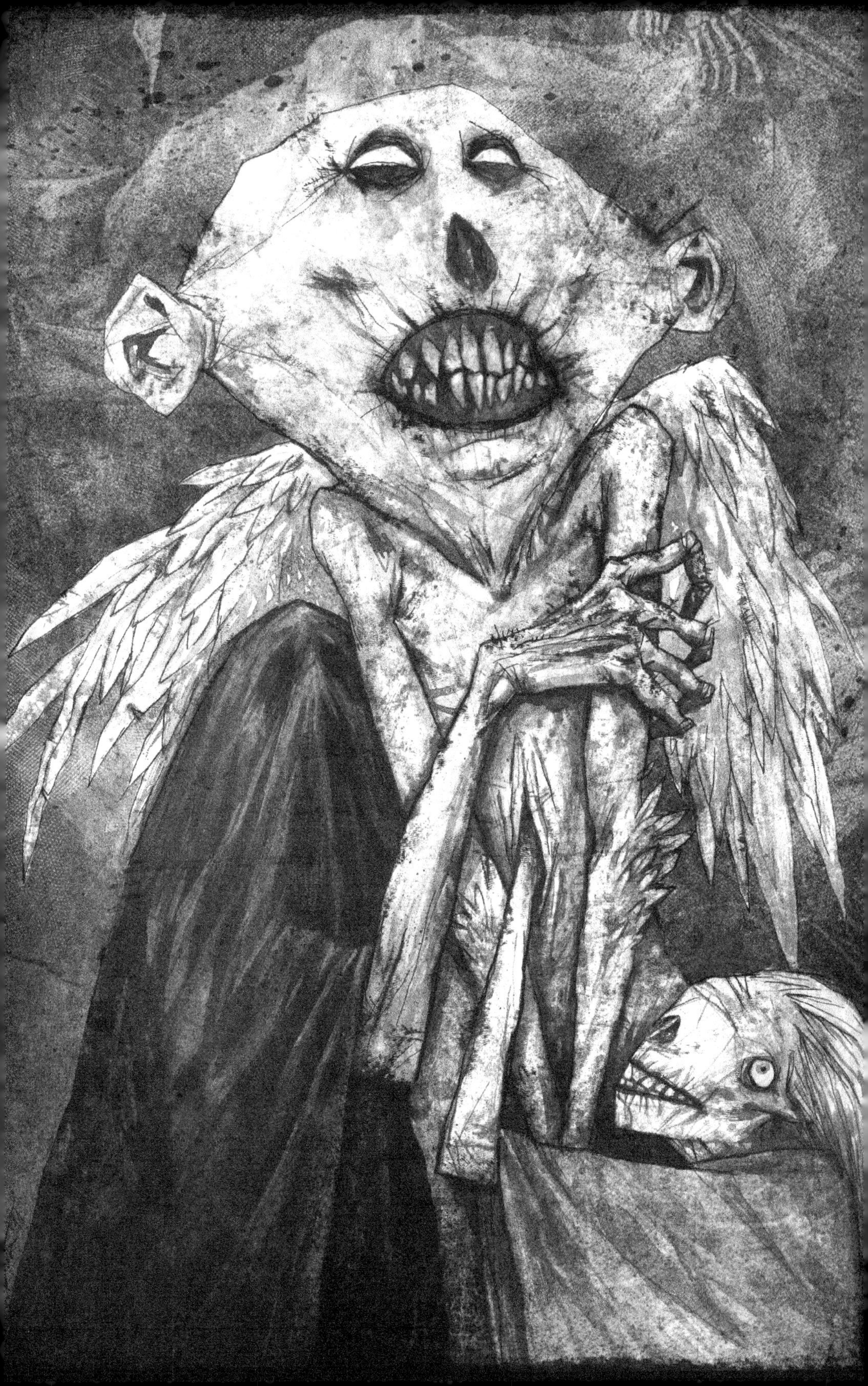

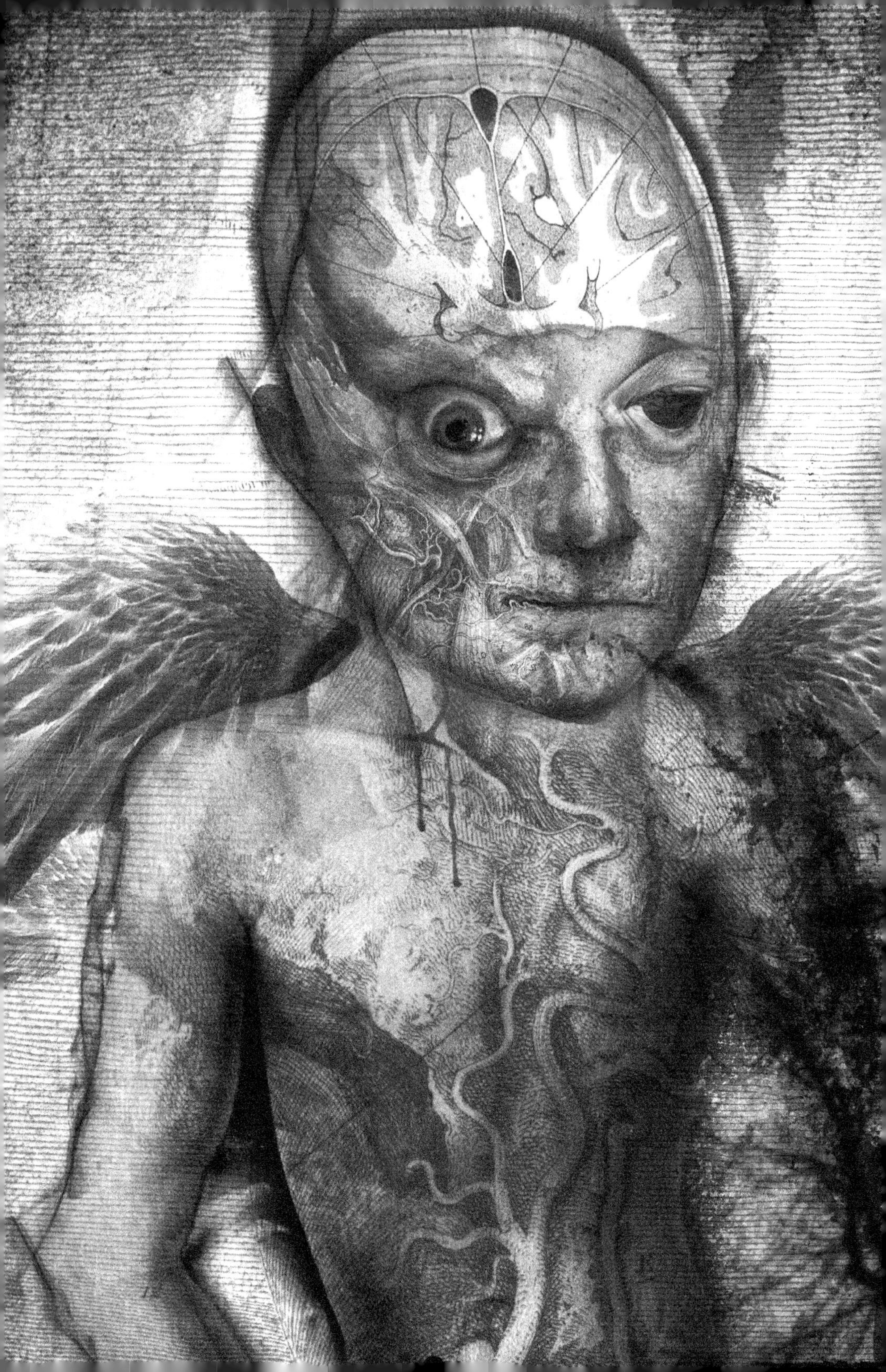

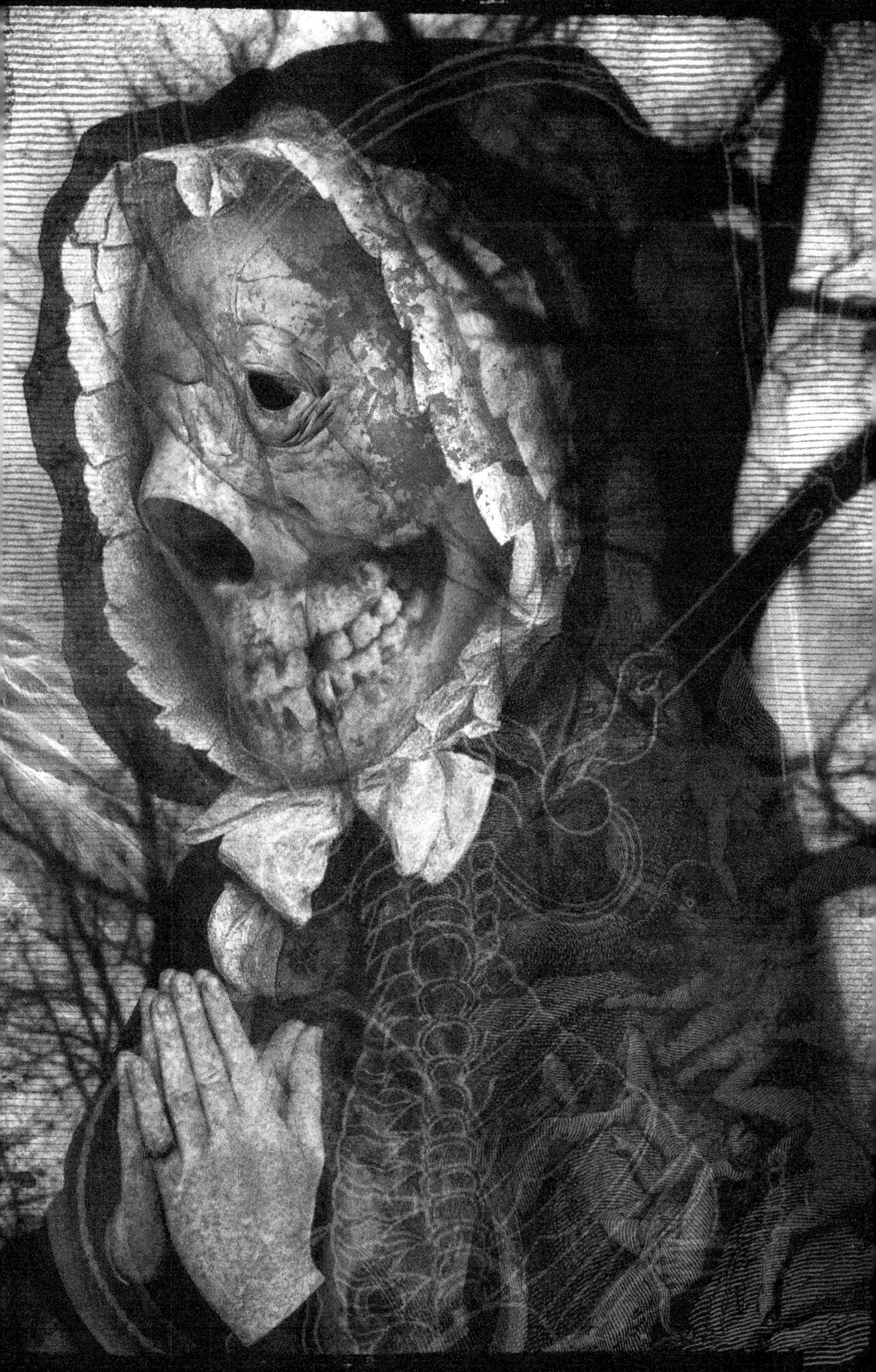

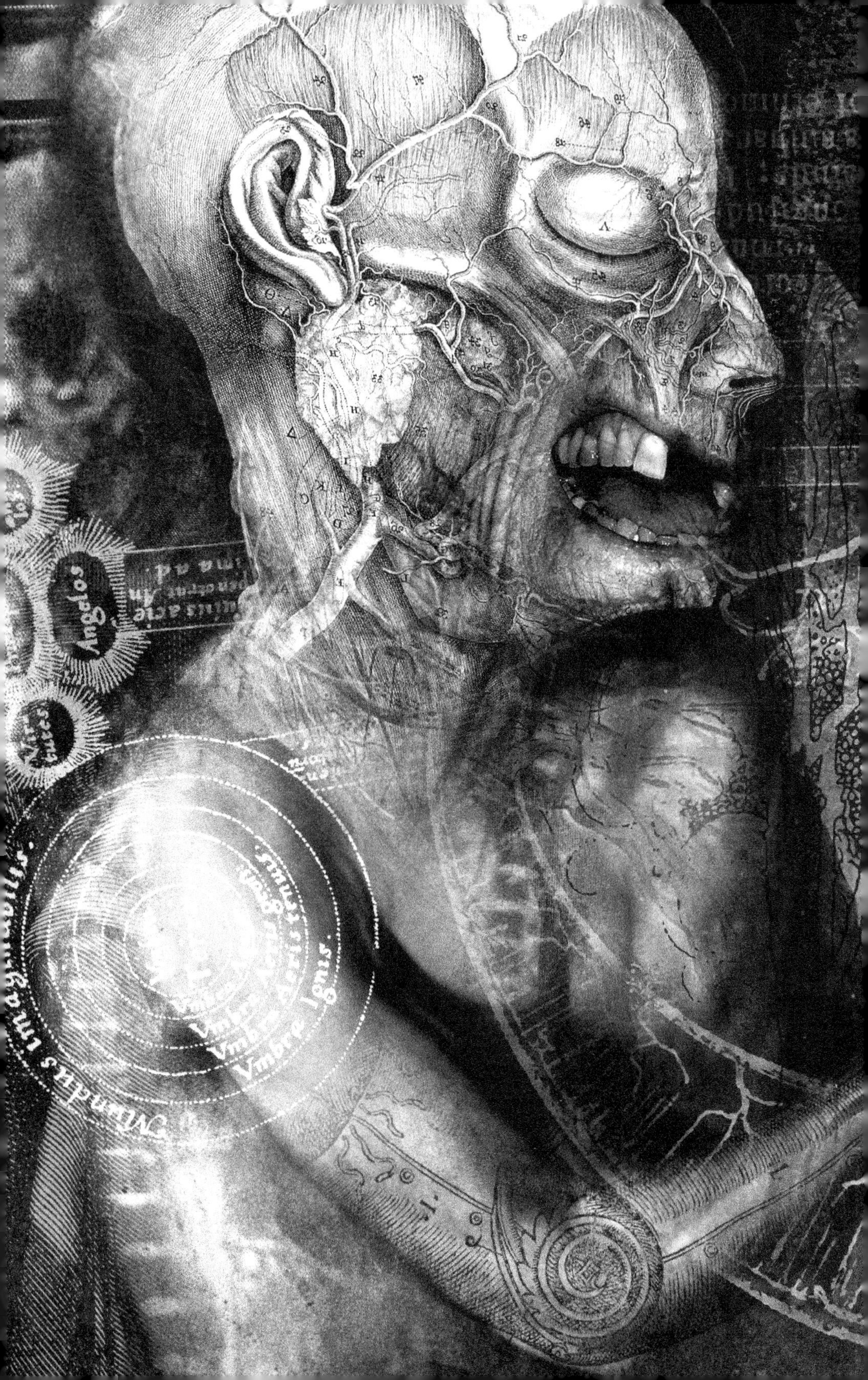

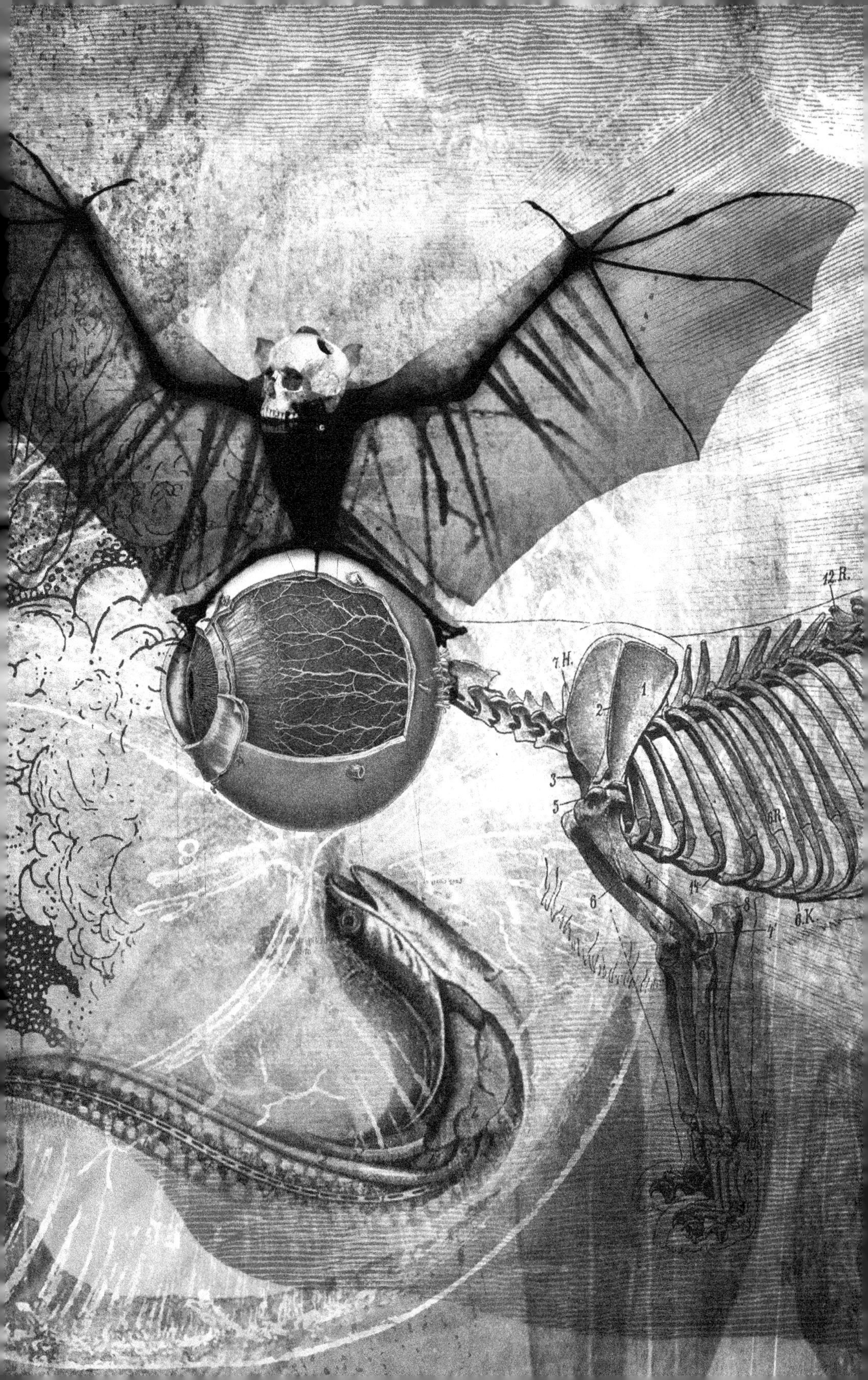

ZORAN PENEVSKI

158/A   (1967)

Zoran Penevski was born in Pancevo, Serbia. He studied physics and literature in Belgrade. He has published several novels (*Less Important Crimes, Trails of Absence, Sara and Forgotten Square, Copy-Editor*) comic books (*Corporate Pandemonium* with A. Zolotic), and also stories, articles, reviews, and essays on literature, comics, music, and illustration. With Ivica Stevanović, he created *Kindly Corpses* (the first Serbian graphic novel, in 2004; on Paul Gravett's list of *The Best Works in 2011: An International Perspective*); as well as *Lexicon of Art Legions* (2005) and *L' Anatomie du Ciel* (2006).

158/B   (1977)

Ivica Stevanovic is an illustrator of children's books and a graphic designer. With his unique style and original approach to illustration, his works are significant pieces of Serbian contemporary art. He is well-known for his books *The Lost Cases* (Orfelin / Komiko, 2014), *Serbian Mythology* (Orfelin, 2010-13), *Creepy Cases or Accidents* (self published, 2009), *Katil* (Everest media, 2008), *L' Anatomie du Ciel* (Les Humanoides Assosies, 2006), *Lexicon of Art Legions* (SKC Novi Sad, 2005), and *Kindly Corpses* (SKC Novi Sad, 2004). His latest illustrations appeared in *The Bestiary* (Centipede Press, 2016). He works at the Art Academy in Novi Sad as a professor of Applied Arts and Design.

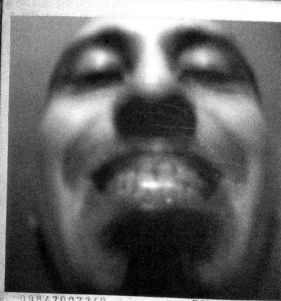

IVICA STEVANOVIĆ
https://www.behance.net/IvicaStevanovic

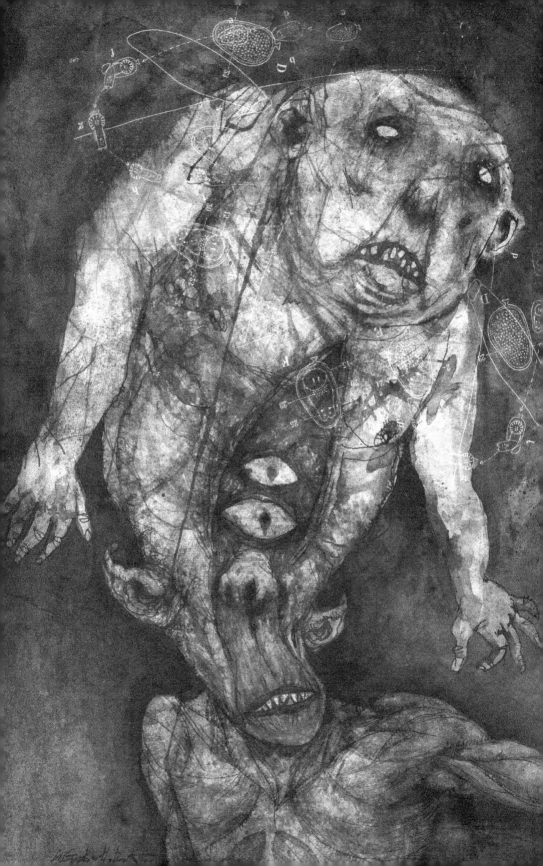

A Word about *Kindly Corpses*

Kindly Corpses is a graphic novel that deals with the notion of death as the subject of humanistic cognition. The story starts as the imaginary Ministry of Death prescribes the look of an acceptable corpse as a fuel for political immortality. Except as a political manipulation, this could be explained as a disease of the main protagonist, forensic Chris Ware, who is otherwise a renowned American illustrator and comic artist.

Kindly Corpses can be contemplated in more ways than this. It is a biopolitical thriller, philosophical science fiction, and manifest of nihilism. At its core, it is a "graphic conspiracy," which implies a dominance of picture over our reality. Ivica Stevanović developed a personal version of the text using a spectrum of techniques available to such an outstanding artist: the basic approach is watercolour, followed by drawings, collages, photographs, and an extraordinary use of multilayered digital illustration. The contrasting game of warm and cold palette remains, at all times, in the field of claustrophobic grotesque, surreal horror, and ironic stylization. Stevanović overlaps a disturbingly real communication with the medieval views of Hell, baroque blackouts, German expressionism, and contemporary comics.

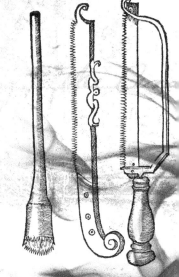

Kindly Corpses originated as an answer to our existence, because I felt that the term "kindly corpse" (something that owns only its own death, and only strives to be of service to the living, not unlike the "grateful corpse" from folk literature) describes a state of an individual at the beginning of the 21st century.

On the other hand, the power of books fascinates me. I believe in books that can change you, books that are incredibly dangerous, books that are on the edge. I believe that everybody who understands *Kindly Corpses* will start to think about themselves as new beings who want to revolt against death.

—Zoran Penevski, writer, comics critic, and editor

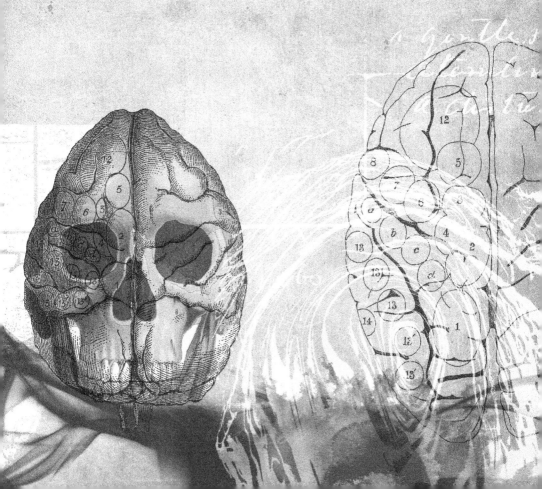

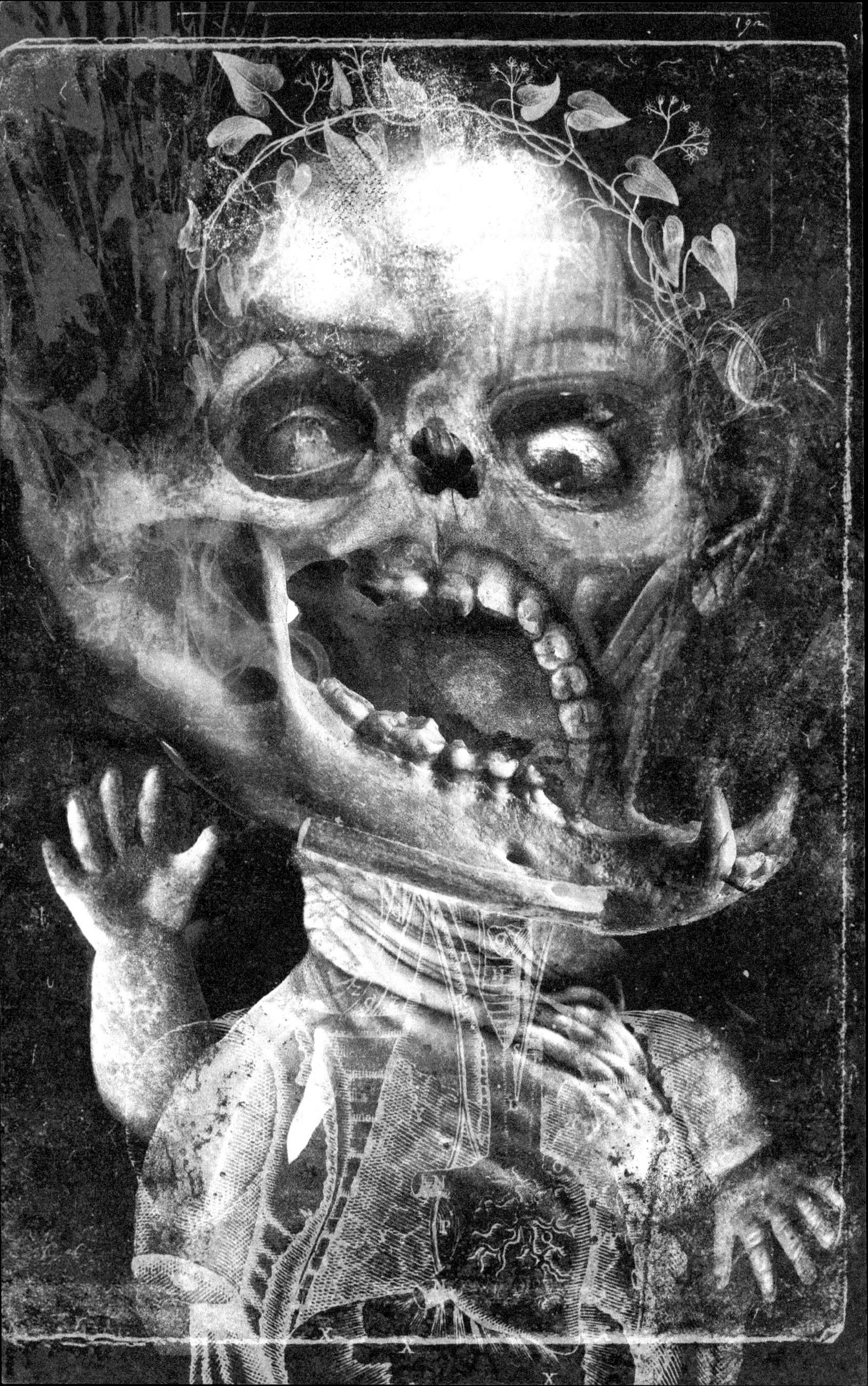

KINDLY CORPSES

GALLERY OF SKETCHES AND DRAWINGS

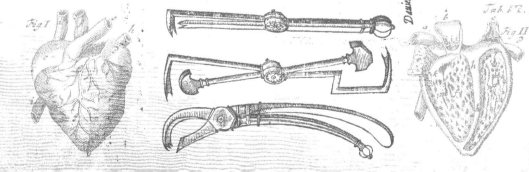

Tab. VI.

Fig. I.

Dennÿ

Fig. II.

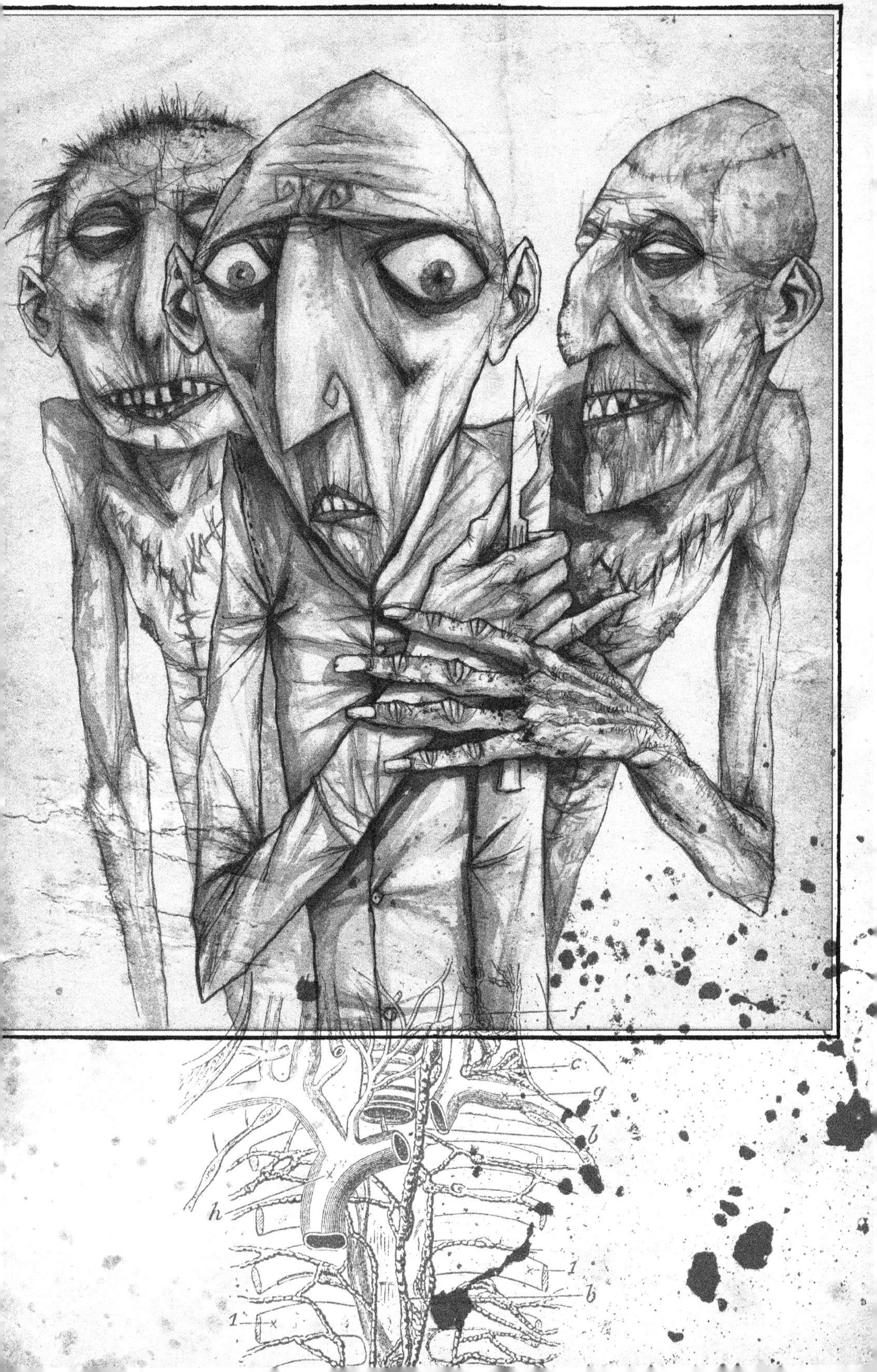
f
c
g
b
h
1
b
1

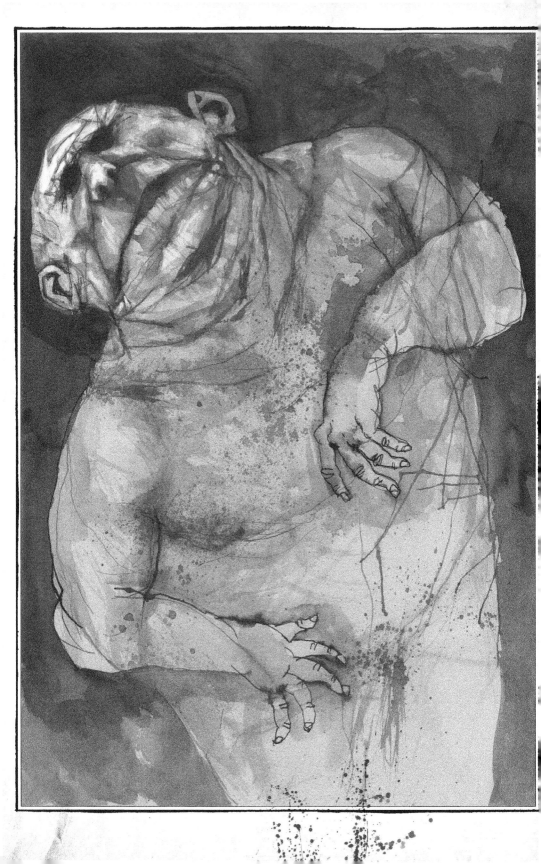

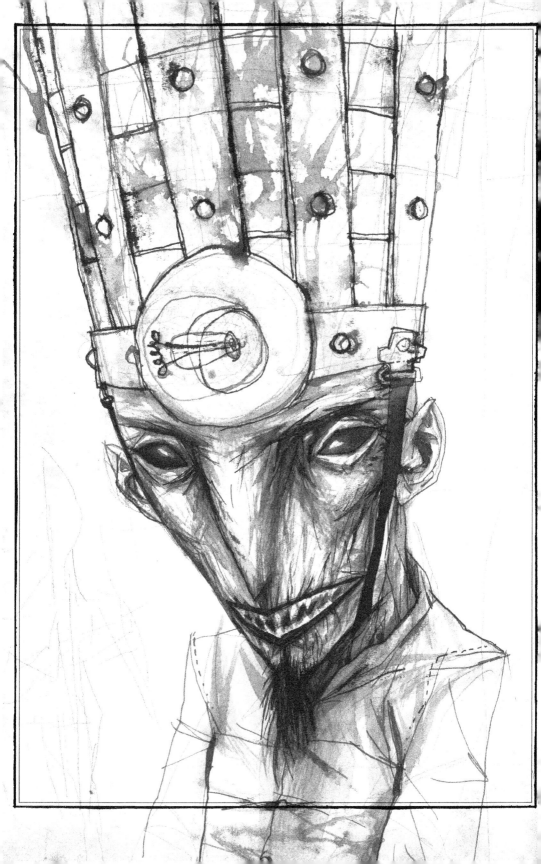

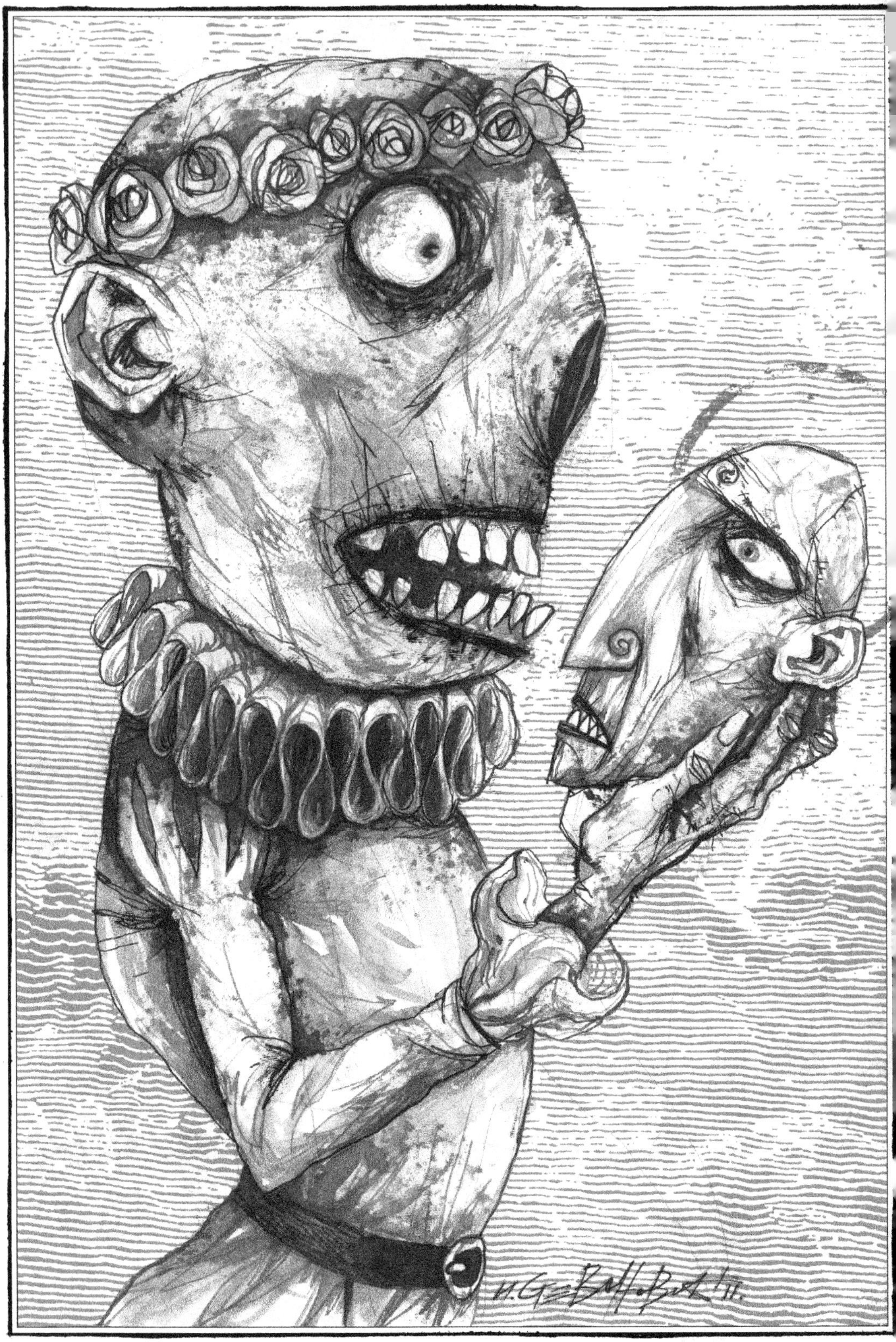

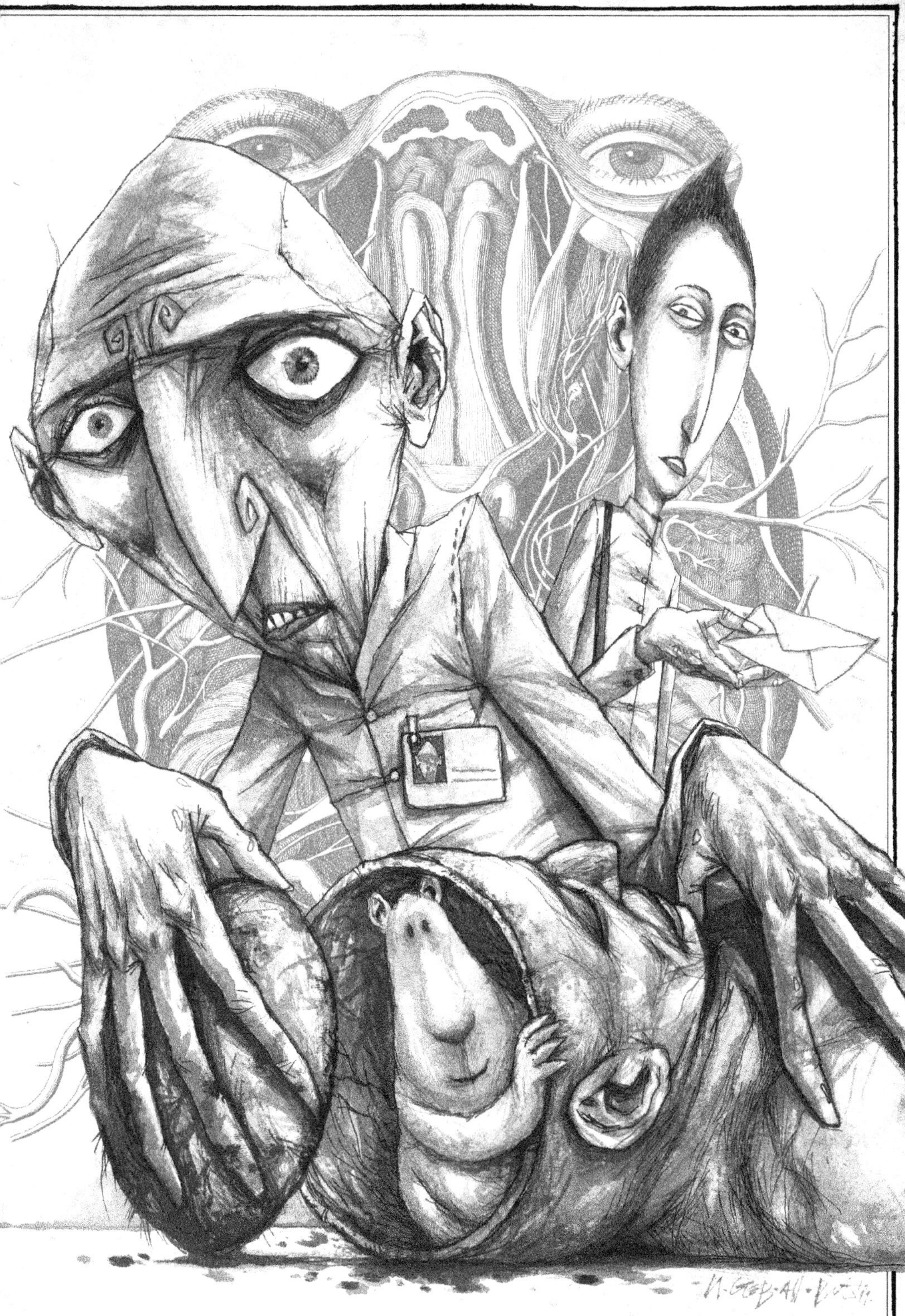

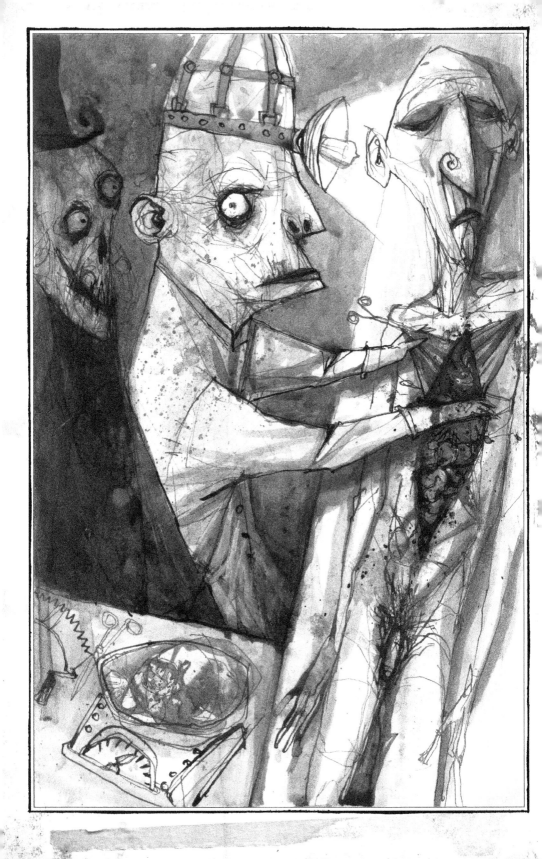

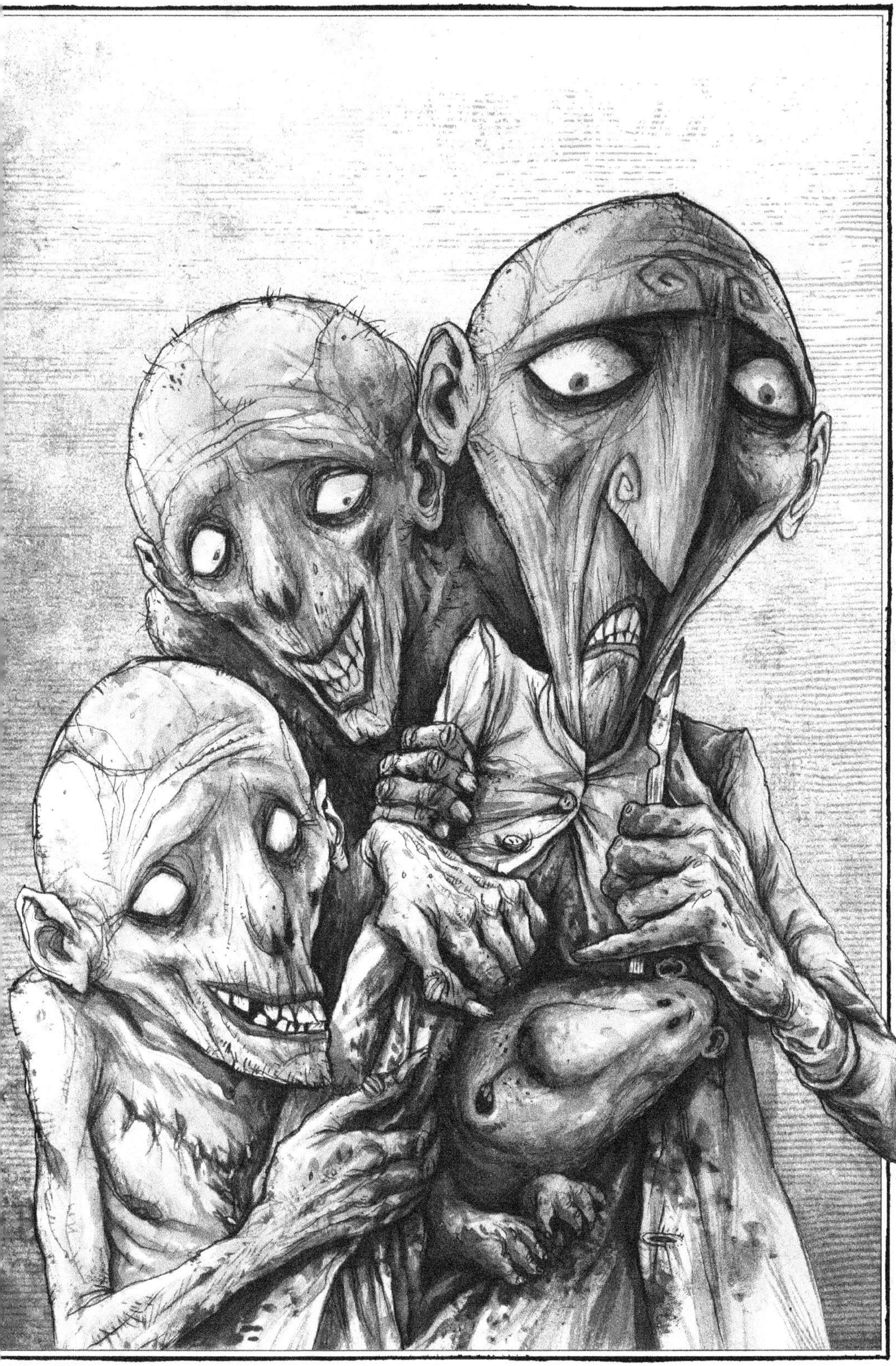

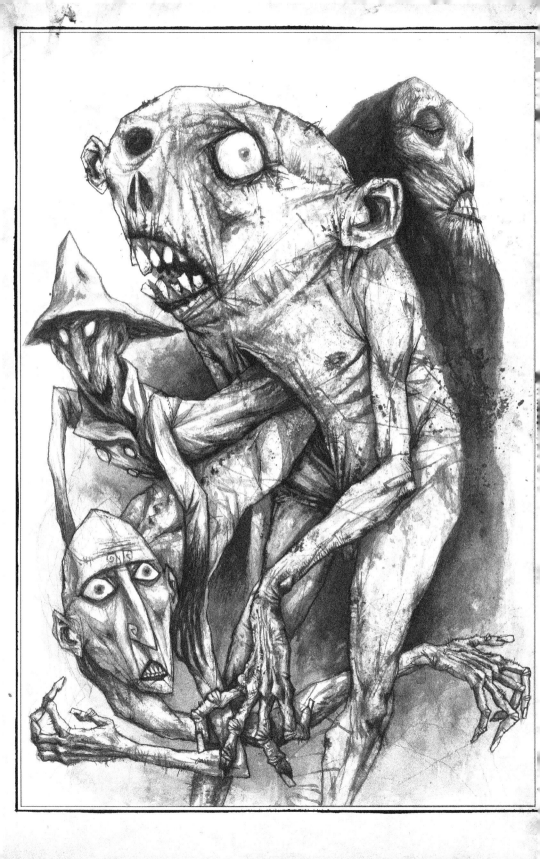

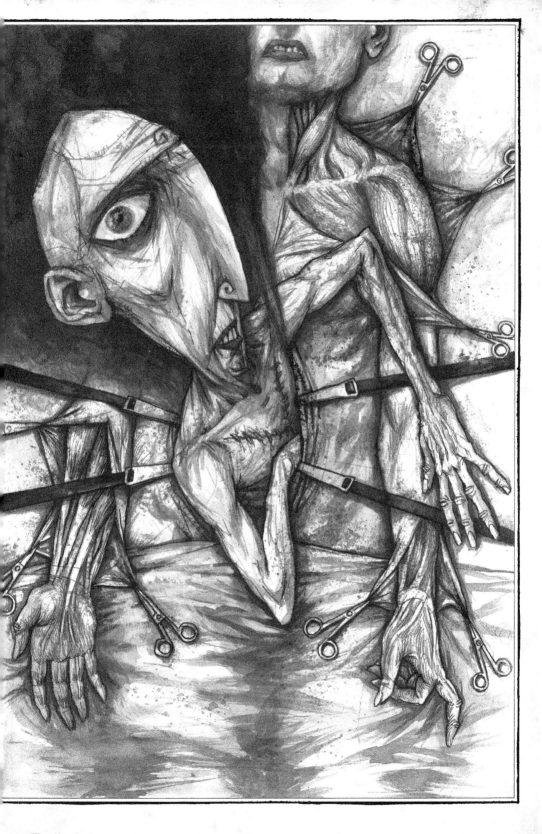

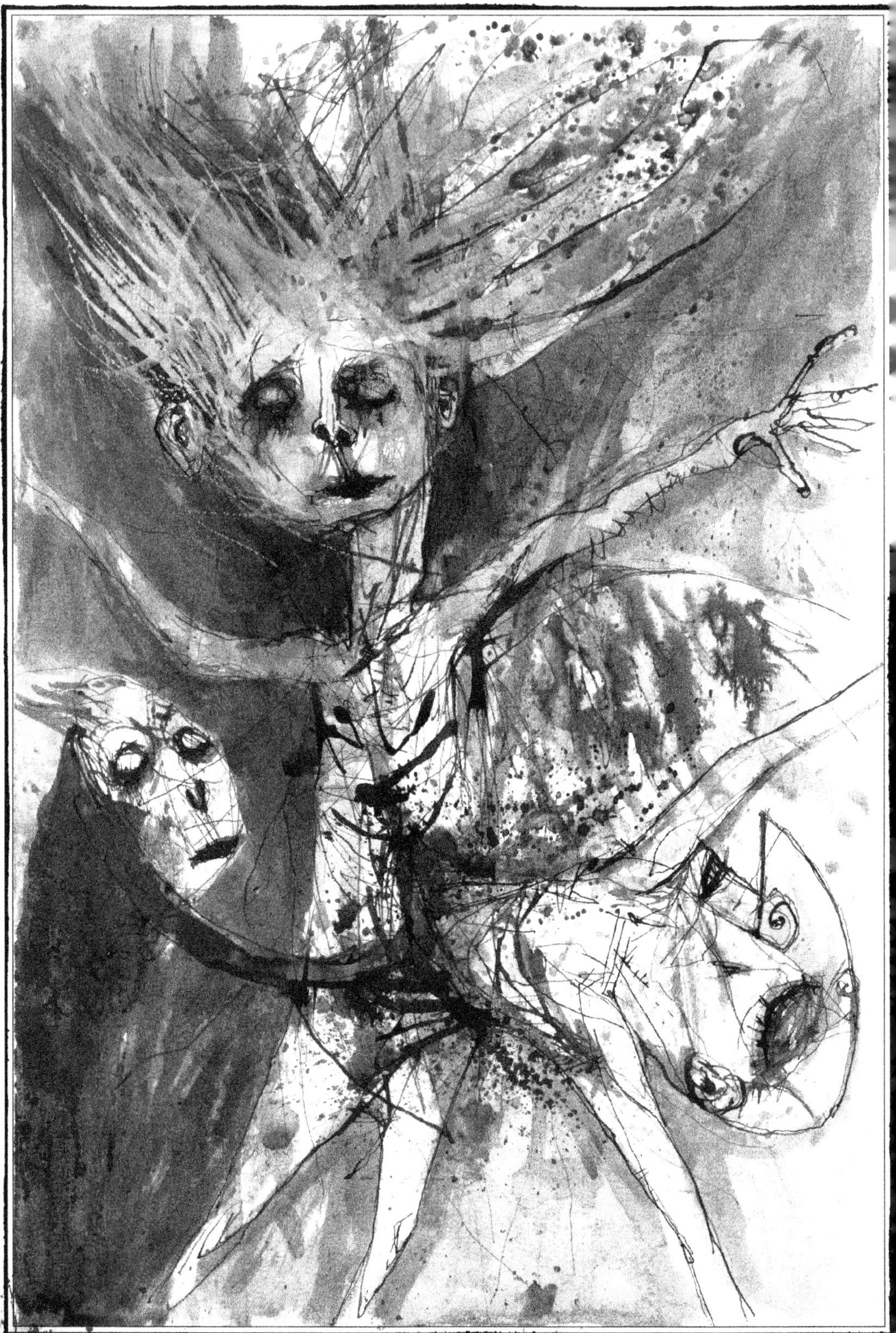

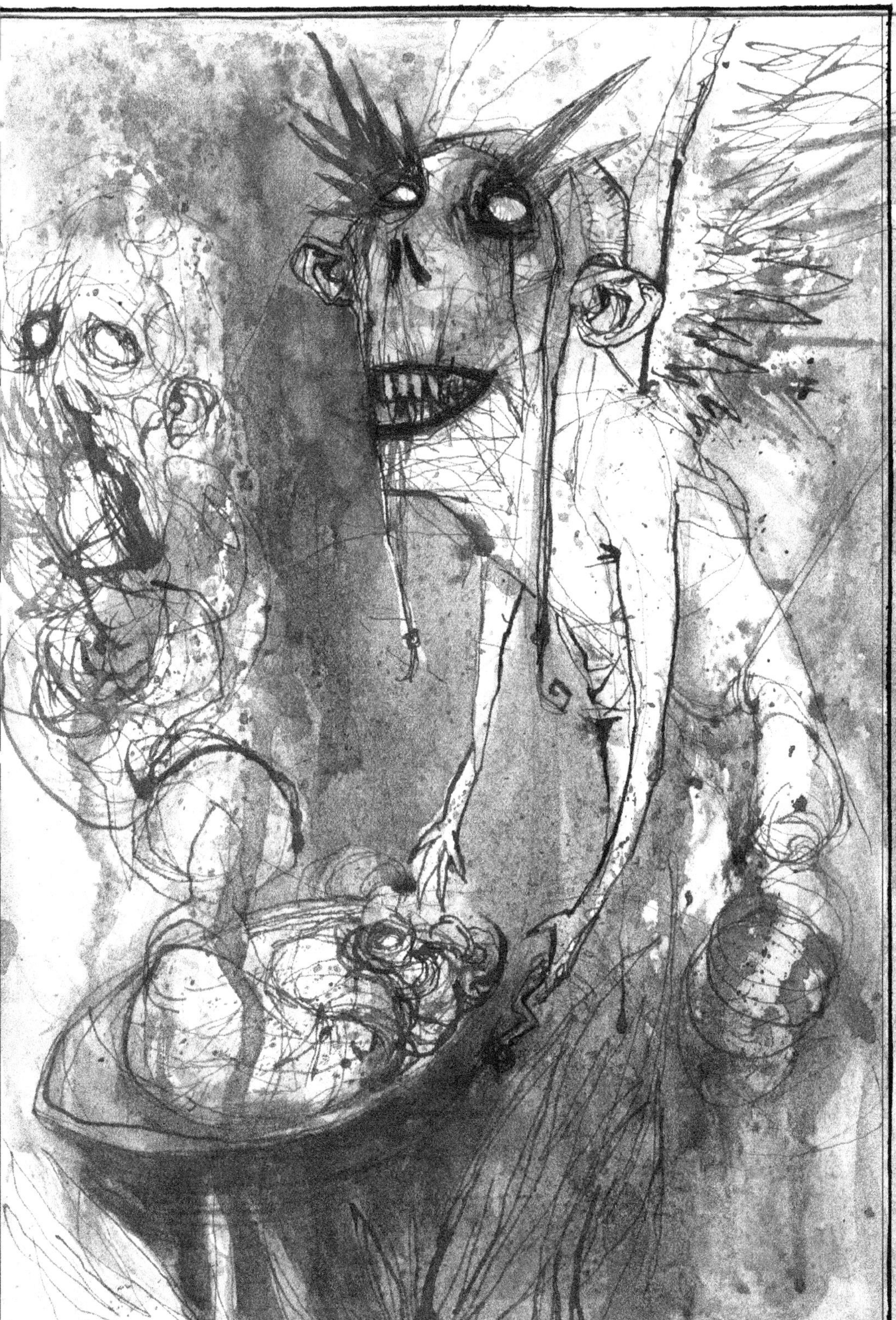

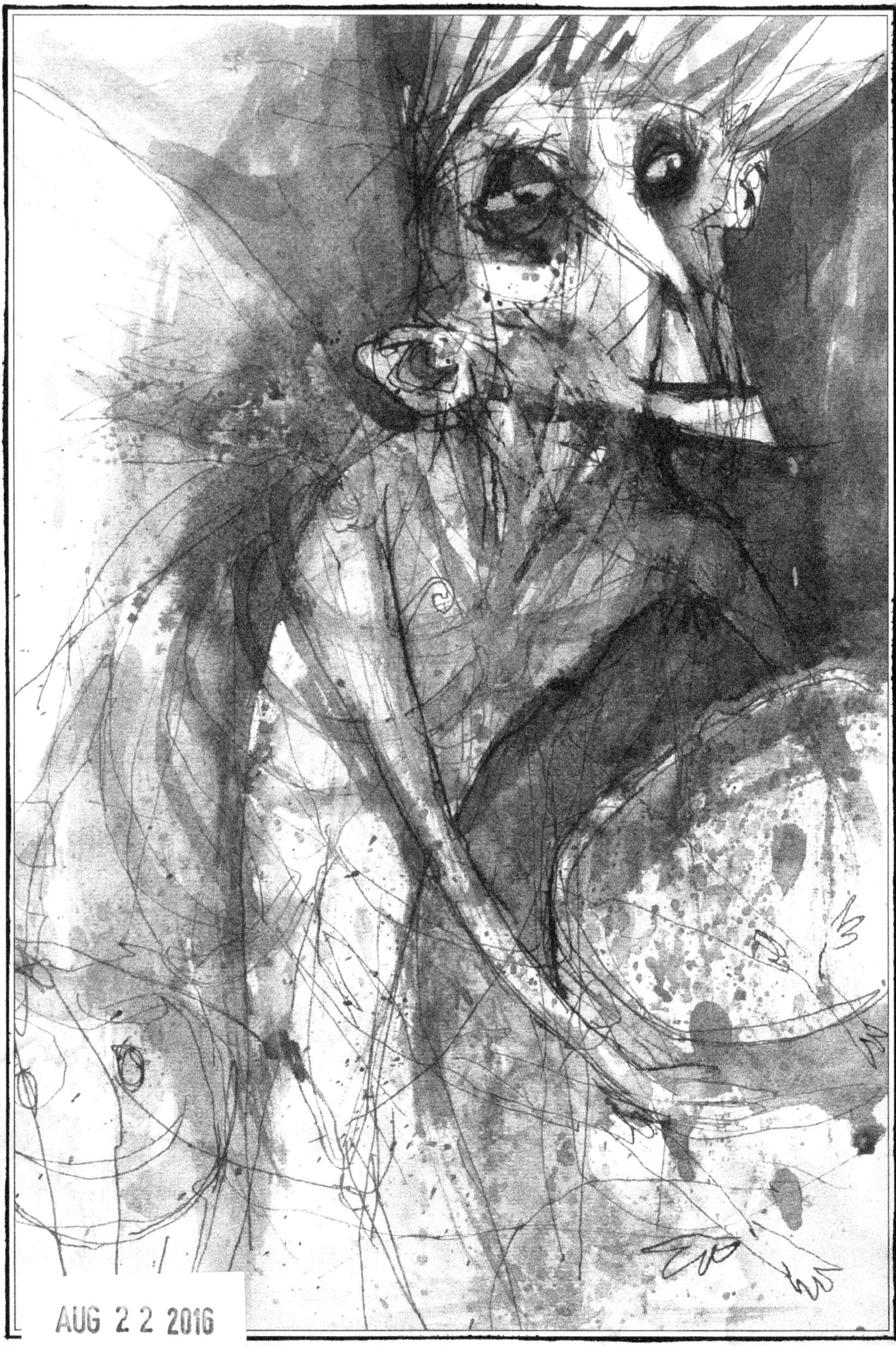